SEX EDUCATION
AIDS and Sexuality

S. P. Singh

AUTHORSPRESS

First Published 2001
by Authorspress

E-35/103, Jawahar Park (Shree Ganesh Complex),
Laxmi Nagar, Delhi-110 092
e-mail: authorspress@yahoo.com

Typeset in NewCenturySchlbk by Chitra Computers

Sex Education: AIDS and Sexuality
ISBN 81-7273-043-8

Printed in India at Tarun Offset, Delhi.

Preface

We are living in an age when concern about sex and sexual issues are at an all-time high. Sex, it has been said, may not be the most important thing in life, but there is nothing else quite like it. Sex can be a source of great happiness and fulfilment; it can also be an area of insecurity and worry in our daily lives. Misinformation, ignorance or embarrassment can blight what should be as natural as eating and sleeping.

There is no great mystery about sex, and no reason why we should not make the most of this aspect of our lives. We need, however, to contetxualise it by understanding the nature of sex, and by unburdening ourselves of the baggage of sexual myths, prejudices and inhibitions passed down to us by previous generations.

Over the last few years, as the impact of the HIV virus has become more widely felt in the world, there is an increasing consensus about the need for sex education for young people. Education about sex and AIDS does not encourage young people to have sex; rather it makes them realise the risks involved and enables them to make responsible decisions about delaying sex or protecting themselves.

This book belongs on the family bookshelf. It is not a 'sex guide' to be hidden away at the back of Dad's sock-and-underwear drawer for curious and naughty children to find. It is not a book that a mother would be worried to find in a teenage daughter or son's bedroom. Everyone in the family can use it openly. This guide is for adults in the family who want to understand their own problems and relationships more clearly or need to talk to their children about such matters. Older children and adolescents can use the book to explore questions on their own.

This book will create a space of helpful talk about a dynamic realm of family life.

S. P. Singh

Contents

Preface v

1. Sex and Relationships 1
2. Healthy Body 36
3. Family and Sexuality 82
4. AIDS and Sexuality 99
5. Sexual Counselling 121
6. The Middle Years 142
7. Contraceptive Methods 157
8. Safe Sex among Sex Workers 206
9. Fighting AIDS Together 219
10. Questions on HIV/AIDS/STD 230

Appendices 238

Glossary 248

Bibliography 260

Index 262

1
Sex and Relationships

Sex is the sensual and sensory manifestation of the attraction between two people, and it can be one of the greatest pleasures in life. Sex can also cause disappointment, frustration and unhappiness. The aim of this chapter is to look at the sexuality of women and men, as well as at some of the issues that arise from the expression of sexuality in our everyday lives. Before looking at the area of sexual pleasure, however, it is necessary to answer a number of fundamental questions. What exactly, is the human sex drive and how is it controlled? How does the human body work sexually and how can we be confident that we are sufficiently in tune with a partner's needs to give them sexual satisfaction? Does fantasy have a useful role to play in our sex lives and where does sexual variance fit in? We have always to keep in mind that successful relationships have to be worked at. Too many people are surprised when their partner claims to feel unloved or unappreciated. For despite all the intimate things that people do with each other when having sex, communication between a couple is often neither good nor easy.

It is not always easy to keep a relationship fresh and exciting, especially if a couple have lived together for many years, even if they have been very happy. They may find that changing their normal routine in order to spend more time together enhances their sexual feelings for each other. Above all, whatever their temporary dissatisfactions, a couple should never lose sight of the enormous benefits to be gained from a happy relationship that encompasses mutual love and respect, the enjoyment of each other's company and a fulfilling sex life.

SEXUAL DESIRE

Sexual desire is the subjective feeling that we want to have sexual pleasure, which most of us experience from time to time—ranging from many times a day to a few times a year. It is triggered by stimuli from outside the body and from inside the body. Just because we experience sexual desire does not mean that we will necessarily engage in overt sexual behaviour—if we did have sex every time we experienced sexual desire, our way of life would be very different! That we are experiencing sexual desire is often indicated by sexual daydreams and sexual fantasies, and by genital arousal—stiffening of the penis or clitoris and lubrication of the vagina. Sexual desire is created and controlled by the brain, but is believed not to be a single driving force: that is, sexual desire is not just a basic biological need like hunger. Instead, it is the result of a complex interaction between three different factors.

Unlike the other primary instinctive urges—such as hunger and thirst—a person's sex drive does not affect their ability to survive, although it obviously does affect the survival of the species. Some people seem to have a greater sex drive than others, but there is no reason to suppose that men necessarily have a higher sex drive than women. Sexual thoughts desire for sex may also be based on a desire for its consequences, such as a boost to self-esteem or a sense of femininity or masculinity, and by the need to be loved. Traditionally, it was believed that men had a greater interest in sex than women. Men were thought to be driven by their libido and easily aroused, while women were more interested in sex in terms of a relationship.

While sex drive in both men and women is controlled by the brain, it is triggered by hormones called androgens, the commonest of which is testosterone. This particular hormone is often referred to as the 'male sex hormone' because it is produced by a man's primary sex organ, the testes, and because it maintains his secondary sexual characteristics. Most of their testosterone is produced in the adrenal glands, located on top of the kidneys, but some is also made by the ovaries. Although levels of testosterone are higher in men than in women, this does not mean that men have a higher sex drive.

A 'suitable' level of testosterone, appropriate for each sex, is essential to ensure that a man or a woman has an adequate sex drive. Lower-than-normal levels will reduce the sex drive in men and women. This may occur, for example, following illness in men or as a consequence of the menopause in some women. Similarly, naturally raised levels of testosterone typically increase sex drive. For example, many women feel sexier around the midpoint of their menstrual cycle, about two weeks before their period is due, because their testosterone level temporarily increases when ovulation occurs.

Sex and age

Male sex drive is thought to reach a peak when men are in their late teens. Women on the other hand, apparently reach the peak of their sex drive in their late thirties. On the surface, these physiological differences would appear unfortunate: while a man's sex drive is waning, his female partner's is getting stronger. Libido—as indicated by time taken to get an erection, for example—may decrease in men, but it does not mean that their sexual desire is in steep decline as well.

Desire is much more complex than sex drive alone. And as a man gets older, his sexual urges often shift from being purely genitally focused to being more sensual and cerebral. As a result there does not have to be an imbalance in sexual interest between partners of the same age. And a beneficial spin-off of the changing nature of sexual desire is that a man's sexual endurance—ability to delay and control ejaculation—will increase with age, as will a woman's ability to achieve orgasm.

Sexual love is a powerful and very personal emotion. It is a state in which the happiness of a sexual partner becomes essential to that of his or her lover. Being in love can cause a number of noticeable physical symptoms, including loss of appetite, disturbed sleep, increased pulse rate and raised blood pressure. Only time will tell which direction a relationship will take. Love lasts, infatuation does not. And in the long term loving has more to do with companionship than with lust.

SEXUAL PLEASURE

Like all skills, having good sex needs to be worked at. It is not something that we instinctively know how to do well. Rather, it needs to be learned and—like most things in life—it usually improves with practice. Nor is it enough to simply understand how the body works, because there is no universal recipe for sexual pleasure and satisfaction. Everyone has his own individual preferences and his own unique physical likes and dislikes.

Finding out about each other's sexual needs is part and parcel of having a sexual relationship. An important part of this involves understanding and discovering how your own body is best stimulated and sharing those discoveries with your partner. Despite these personal differences in sexual likes and dislikes, the sexual response itself follows the same stages—arousal, leading on to orgasm and finally resolution—in every individual alike.

The first part of sexual pleasure is arousal, when each partner becomes sexually excited. Arousal can result from the sight or smell of a partner, through thoughts about sex, or through the direct physical stimulation of foreplay. Women usually become aroused more slowly than men during foreplay; men are aroused relatively quickly, often becoming excited initially by visual stimuli such as sexy clothing or the naked body. As arousal progresses, a plateau stage is reached, during which a high level of sexual tension is maintained.

The penis and vaginal lips become engorged with blood and darken in colour, and individuals tend to focus on sex and their partner, and ignore everything else that is going on around them. If sexual interest is maintained, and if sexual stimulation continues, a point is usually reached where sexual tension peaks and orgasm occurs.

During foreplay partners stimulate each other in as sensual a way as possible to the point where they both become fully aroused and are ready for intercourse and/or orgasm. Foreplay can involve just about anything that both lovers find enjoyable—kissing, caressing, stroking or licking any part of the body.

Erogenous zones are the parts of the body's surface that evoke sexually arousing sensations when stroked, kissed or touched. This description of erogenous areas is not intended to be prescriptive. In theory any part of the skin can be erogenous: no two people are exactly the same, and everyone likes to be touched in a different way. There are none the less certain areas that give most men and women supreme pleasure when these are touched, caressed and kissed. Men and women share some common erogenous zones; areas specific to each sex—which tend to be the most responsive sites—are described below.

In both men and women, areas that commonly aid arousal when stimulated include the face, lips, ear lobes, nape of the neck, arms, elbows, armpits, fingertips, buttocks, anus, backs of the knees, inside of the thighs, and feet. In fact, almost any part of the skin's surface can be erogenous, depending on the individual. In both sexes, however, there are specific areas where stimulation generally results in intense arousal. A woman's erogenous zones may include:

— the genitals, including the vaginal lips, just inside the vagina itself, and the clitoris—the most sensitive of all her erogenous areas, the sole function of which is sexual pleasure;
— the breasts and nipples. Many, but not all, women find their breasts very responsive, and a few may achieve orgasm simply by having their nipples sucked;
— in some women, the perineum, the area between the vagina and the anus.

A man's erogenous zones may include:

— the genitals, including the scrotum, the shaft of the penis and the glans of the penis, usually its most sensitive part;
— the perineum, the area between the base of his penis and the anus;
— in some men, the nipples.

As a woman becomes aroused through being sexually excited by her partner, various changes typically take place to her body.

— Her vagina becomes moist and lubricated, and the whole vulva may become moist.
— The inner part of her vagina expands.
— Her vaginal lips become thicker, separated and turned outwards.
— Her clitoris becomes larger and erect.
— Her breasts enlarge and the nipples may become erect.
— Her heart and breathing rates increase.
— Her skin may become flushed.

The clitoris plays a central role in a woman's sexual arousal. It can be stimulated by the fingers, the tongue or a vibrator, by penile thrusting, or by body pressure. When a woman is highly aroused, the tip or glans of the clitoris retracts under its hood and may no longer be seen or felt. Touching different parts of the clitoris produces different sensations: some women like the base of the clitoris to be touched; some prefer to be stimulated along the side; others get pleasure from the tip being touched. Some women like harder friction than others, although most dislike the clitoris being rubbed too hard and some find direct stimulation almost unbearable. The considerate lover will always try to find out what his partner prefers.

As a man becomes aroused, these changes typically take place to his body.

— His penis becomes erect.
— His testes begin to elevate.
— His scrotum thickens.
— His nipples may become erect.
— His heart and breathing rates increase. The penis, the most responsive of a man's erogenous zones, can be stimulated by fingers, mouth or tongue, or by the vagina during intercourse. Just as a women may show her partner what she likes, a man can show his partner how he likes his penis to be stimulated so that she is neither too gentle nor too rough.

Sexual intercourse

The fact that her vagina is lubricated may not necessarily mean that she is fully aroused and ready for intercourse, although he is ready: further foreplay—without becoming mechanical or pressurising her to hurry up!—may be required. During intercourse the man moves his penis inside the vagina or, if the woman is on top, she moves her vagina around his penis. The result is that his penis is stimulated, which may lead him to reach orgasm and ejaculate; the movement of intercourse also pulls on her labia and may move the clitoral hood over the clitoris, as well as stimulating the inside of the vagina and possibly the G-spot.

Although a woman may orgasm through intercourse, it is not a certainty, and she may need additional clitoral stimulation during intercourse if she wants to have an orgasm with her partner inside her. A couple can have intercourse in many different positions—lying down, sitting, standing, kneeling—and it is up to the individual couple to discover which positions give them the most pleasure. Even when couples have found a favourite position, it is still worth having sexual intercourse in different positions because they produce different degrees of penetration and different sensations for both partners.

Orgasm

Sex should not be 'orgasm-driven'; whether and how a couple achieve orgasms is a personal matter for them alone. Orgasm is an intensely pleasurable sexual feeling during which the body experiences muscular contractions followed by a loss of tension before falling into a relaxed state. Any description of orgasm has to be general because it is an intensely personal feeling. Although orgasm is perceived as happening in the genitals and spreading to the rest of the body, it is orchestrated by the limbic system and hypothalamus in the brain.

If a man is sexually aroused and his penis is stimulated by hand or mouth, or by the vaginal walls, he will usually reach a point of inevitability when he knows he is going to ejaculate. Within a couple of seconds, ejaculation takes place and this is normally, although not always, accompanied by orgasm. While the sensations appear to focus on his penis, he may also feel pleasure and a release of tensions in his pelvic area and over his entire body. During orgasm he may make a sound or cry out. When the contractions cease, the man relaxes and his penis soon loses its erection.

Once a woman reaches the plateau state of arousal, stimulation of her clitoris by fingers or mouth and/or vaginal stimulation during intercourse can result in orgasm. As a woman reaches orgasm, her vagina, pubic muscles, anal sphincter and uterus all contract rhythmically, her body may arch and she may be thrown into spasms. Many women feel a wave of pleasure passing from their genitals throughout their body. She may make some kind of grimace, or cry out or even scream, depending on how intense the occasion is for her.

Once the contractions of the pelvic muscles, uterus and vagina have ceased, she will soon begin to return to her normal state, although this process is usually much slower than in men. Unlike men, many women are capable of having several orgasms, one after the other. They remain at the plateau stage and can be stimulated to orgasm repeatedly. This is known as a multiple orgasm. Women tend to experience a wider range of types of orgasm than men do. This appears to depend on a number of factors, including whether the clitoris is stimulated directly, or indirectly by, for example, movements of the bodies during intercourse. While men almost always experience orgasm during sex, this may not be true for women.

The process of arousal and ejaculation appears to be fairly automatic, while the ability to have an orgasm appears to be, at least partially, learned in women. Some women rarely or never experience orgasm. Many of these women are believed to be potentially orgasmic, but to have never been in a suitable sexual situation. Some have been helped to experience orgasm by individual sensate focus exercises and through learning about their own sexual responsiveness through masturbation.

The body enters a phase of resolution: it relaxes, and heart and breathing rates return to normal. A man's penis becomes flaccid, and he may suddenly feel very sleepy. He enters a refractory period during which he cannot have a new erection: this may last for minutes in an adolescent to days in older men. In women, the period of resolution takes much longer. Her genitals can take up to 30 minutes to return to their pre-orgasmic state. Many women enjoy continued physical intimacy during this stage, and may have a sense of 'afterglow' following orgasm. Unlike men, women do not experience a refractory period.

Oral sex

Oral sex simply means mouth play on any part of the body, including the ear lobes, fingers, toes, nipples and so on. But in practice, oral sex usually refers to oral-genital contact. Using tongue and lips to lick, kiss and gently suck a woman's clitoris, vaginal lips and vagina is known as cunnilingus; licking, kissing and gently sucking a man's penis and scrotum, and moving his penis inside the mouth, is known as fellatio. While many people enjoy oral sex, some do not: both are quite normal. Oral sex, like other aspects of sex, is a skill to be learned. And the fastest way to find out whether it is being done properly is to ask a partner whether he/she is being stimulated, and how he/she would like to be stimulated. For example, while some women enjoy having their clitoris stimulated directly during oral sex, others find the sensation too intense. Some people—both men and women—are reluctant to try oral sex because they do not quite understand what is expected of them, or because they are inhibited by fears.

Perhaps the most common of these is the fear of smelling or tasting unpleasant to a partner, or of finding the smell or taste of a partner overpowering. However, provided the genitals are kept clean by daily bathing, they will not generally smell bad but will have only the normal healthy odour of sexual arousal, which should be both pleasant and exciting for a partner.

A woman may worry that she will choke on her partner's penis, but how much of it she takes into her mouth is up to her. She may also be reluctant to perform fellatio for fear that he may ejaculate in her mouth—

something that can perhaps be discussed in advance, and which he should avoid doing unless she agrees. No one should be afraid to talk about what they would like to do and what they prefer not to do. However, it is advisable not to perform oral sex if a partner has a cold sore or a sexually transmitted disease.

Anal sex

The anus and its surrounding region form an area that is just as erogenous, in many people, as the nipples or genitals. Touching or stroking the anal area—known as postillion-age—can be highly arousing, especially if done while stimulating the clitoris or penis or during vaginal intercourse. Lubrication of some form may be needed to make insertion painless. Some men derive great pleasure from having their partner insert a finger to stroke the prostate gland, as this can intensify feelings during his orgasm.

Fingers that have been in contact with the anus or rectum should be washed before touching the genitals to avoid the risk of vaginal or urinary infection. Some people stimulate the area around their partner's anus with their tongue, a form of stimulation known as rimming—a risky practice, as partners are putting themselves at risk of developing a gastrointestinal infection and, possibly, hepatitis. Anal intercourse involves a man inserting his penis, from behind, just into his partner's rectum. This is made easier if lubrication, such as K-Y Jelly, is used and if the partner can relax their anal sphincter, the ring of muscle that normally keeps the anus closed.

Men tend to enjoy giving anal intercourse more than women enjoy receiving it because the penis is gripped tightly by the anus, enhancing the pleasure of intercourse. Many women simply do not find anal intercourse arousing, and may experience pain on penetration. If a couple have anal intercourse, it is wiser to do so after rather than before oral sex or vaginal intercourse, to avoid infection of the mouth or vagina. Apart from questions of hygiene, the wall of the rectum is more likely to tear during intercourse than that of the vagina because it is much thinner. For this reason, unprotected anal sex is regarded as being a particularly unsafe form of sexual contact and couples who have anal intercourse are advised to always use a condom. In some countries and states, anal intercourse is illegal.

Sex between homosexual couples is essentially the same as sex between heterosexual couples, but without vaginal intercourse. Kissing and caressing are the usual preambles to sexual arousal. Many homosexuals use oral sex or mutual masturbation to arouse their partner and bring them to orgasm. Gay men may use anal intercourse to reach orgasm, although not all gay couples enjoy anal sex.

SEXUAL ATTRACTION

The sexual chemistry of physical attraction is not easily explained—one person's idea of attractiveness leaves another person cold; some people seem to prefer a particular physical type, while others are attracted by a certain kind of personality. But there is actually a lot more to it than that. If someone is widely perceived as being 'attractive', that does not necessarily mean that they are conventionally good-looking. Good looks do, however, tend to be particularly important to teenagers and young adults. This is because young people are often less secure in themselves than mature people, and the approval and envy of others is therefore very important to them. As they get older and more secure, they will probably place less importance on good looks in a partner. It is generally accepted that far more men than women consider good looks an important element of attractiveness. So it may come as something of a surprise to learn that in a survey conducted by the British magazine *Woman* men rated personal qualities more important than physical attributes as prerequisites for feeling attracted to a woman. 'Nice' breasts and bottom, together with shapely legs, came bottom of the poll, with only 30 per cent of men saying that these were important to them. It may be that the emphasis on physical attributes in men's public appreciation of women is more closely connected with impressing other men than with what they really feel about women. Women seem to place a strong emphasis on kindness—to themselves and others. Surveys reveal that they value a man who, more than being good-looking, is understanding, intelligent and monogamous, and has a good sense of humour.

Touching someone's arm, making eye contact, leaning towards someone—these are all elements of body language. It is a language we all use, and in fact cannot help doing so. Most of the time we are unconscious of the messages we are conveying through our body language, but we are constantly, albeit subconsciously, monitoring the messages conveyed to us by other people's posture and gestures. The environment we live in is bound to have a certain amount of influence on our body language.

For example, people who are used to living in the country seem to need more personal space and therefore tend not to stand close to other people, while people who live in towns and cities are usually more used to the close physical presence of others.

Generally, however, body language is understandable wherever you live. Even people who speak a different language and cannot communicate with each other verbally are often able to communicate through gestures and facial expressions. The most obvious clues about what two people think of each other are to be found in their posture and gestures. Body language is not simple, however.

A single gesture does not determine whether or not one person is attracted to another. Rather, the message conveyed is a complex interplay of posture and gesture signals that may say 'I find you attractive' but which are being constantly modified in response to the language shown by the other person. Interest in another person and openness to being approached are shown in various ways. These include leaning towards someone; standing in an open posture, with the arms loose or outstretched, as opposed to crossed in front of the body (a defensive pose); and exposing the wrists or turning the palms outwards, an extension of this open posture.

When two people who are attracted to each other are standing near each other, their feet will 'do the talking'. In a group of men and women who are talking to each other, for example, there will probably be nothing in what they are saying to indicate who is interested in whom; but a close look at their feet will soon reveal unspoken messages—those who like each other will unconsciously be pointing a foot in the other's direction.

According to psychologists, the best clue that people are close and get on well with each other—or would like their relationship to be even closer—is if they mirror each other's actions. These behaviour patterns can be observed between people who know each other well, such as close friends and family, as well as between potential sexual partners, even those who have only just met. Mirroring means unconsciously copying the other person's posture and gestures.

Thus if one person leans forward, the other does as well; if one person folds his arms, so does the other; and if one person crosses their legs, the chances are the other person will too. In general, people are unaware that they are doing this, but it is fascinating for an informed bystander to watch. This behaviour pattern not only says a lot about what people are feeling but can also be used deliberately to elicit a desired response.

For this reason, some salespeople use mirroring in order to help their clients feel at ease and increase their chances of making a sale. Deliberate mirroring may also encourage a potential sexual partner. Men and women also tend to fidget when they are attracted to one another. Experts call this 'displacement behaviour', and it plays a noticeable part in almost all early flirtatious exchanges between two people who are still sounding each other out.

Displacement grooming behaviour is common, too—looking in the mirror, patting the hair or adjusting clothing. These gestures all indicate that the person is seeking reassurance that they look their best because they are particularly keen to impress. There is an almost irresistible desire to touch those to whom we are attracted.

Two people who have up to this point shown each other only non-touching sex signals will probably follow these with tentative physical contact. It's important not to assume, however, that if anyone touches you it means they want to embark on a sexual relationship—it may not have even occurred to them! Some people naturally touch much more than others. Touch may be used in various non-sexual situations and it can be embarrassing if a person jumps to the wrong conclusion. For example, people often touch someone if they are:

— offering a piece of friendly advice.

— asking a favour.

— extending sympathy.

— expressing happiness.

Eye language between potential romantic partners is very important, although it is in some ways more subtle than the messages given out by posture and gesture.

Lovers are often happy just to gaze into each other's eyes longingly and lovingly for hours at a time, unlike people who are 'just good friends'. Staring into their loved one's eyes is a sure sign that a person is fascinated by what he sees, almost as if he was trying to see into her mind. More importantly, perhaps, it reveals whether someone is genuinely attracted to the other person or is merely playing some sort of flirtatious game. When someone is experiencing feelings of intense attraction, the pupils dilate with pleasure.

On the other hand, when someone is experiencing strong feelings of dislike, the pupils contract with distaste. However, our pupils also react in this way in response to changes in light—expanding in poor light and contracting when the light is bright—so it is only possible to gauge intense emotion in someone when the light is constant and not too bright.

People who are sexually attracted to one another tend to talk in a lower, more intimate tone of voice than usual, and to adopt a slightly hushed, confidential way of speaking, as if they were trying to exclude the rest of the world from the conversation.

Most people pair off with someone who comes from a similar background, profession or religion. Obviously this is likely to happen because it is easier to meet people who live close by, share the same interests, go to the same place of worship, belong to the same clubs, or work together.

The similarities that bring people together tend to keep them together, and having things in common seems to increase the chances that a relationship will last in the long term. Any great difference between a couple, be it in race, religion, class or education, may not seem to matter at first but, as marriage guidance counsellors have frequently observed, seems to matter more as people get older.

Certainly, a shared interest often appears to help partners to form a bond—although having separate interests can also invigorate and refresh a relationship. When looking for a relationship, it is unwise to have too rigid a view of an ideal partner, especially their physical attributes. If, for example, a man is only willing to consider women who are tall, with blue eyes and long blonde hair, he is considerably reducing his chances of ever finding a partner, when he might have turned out to be very happy with a brunette. And even if by some chance he does manage to find his ideal partner, inflexibility may continue to be a problem in a long-term relationship: people change, and partners will not stay just as they were when the relationship began.

Sex before marriage

Whether or not it is advisable for people to have sex before marriage is a question that is tied in with their moral and religious outlook. If they feel comfortable about it, having sex before marriage can be a good idea in that it may help them to establish that they are at least sexually compatible before tying the knot.

Conventional wisdom 'pigeonholes' most people as being heterosexual (having a sexual preference for members of the opposite sex) or homosexual (preferring same-sex relationships) or bisexual (enjoying both hetero- and homosexual relationships). In fact, humanity cannot be divided easily into distinct groups on the basis of sexuality. It is more realistic to see each of us at some point on a continuum of sexual preference ranging from completely heterosexual at one end to totally homosexual at the other. Homosexuality, however, is a more subtle and complex concept. Rather than simply describing same-sex attraction, homosexuality encompasses the attitudes, affections, friendships, standards and social expectations of people whose predominant or sole sexual preference is for members of the same sex. Identifying someone as being homosexual, however, does not define a person's identity, personality, skills or attributes: it is simply an aspect of their whole life experience. The word 'gay' is commonly used to describe homosexuals of both sexes, but is more commonly applied to homosexual men.

Homosexual women usually prefer to use the term 'lesbian' to describe themselves. Many people have homosexual feelings—or even experiences—at some time in their adolescent or early adult life. These experiences do not mean, however, that they will necessarily be gay or lesbian as adults. If a man reaching adulthood has no interest in heterosexual activity, the chances are that he will be gay. It is estimated that about one per cent of men are exclusively homosexual throughout their lives.

American and British social surveys have found that approximately 0.6 per cent of women have a sexual preference for members of their own sex alone. None the less, many adult heterosexuals fantasize about homosexual behaviour and may even have occasional homosexual experiences: this does not make them homosexual, anymore than gays or lesbians who enjoy occasional heterosexual sex are heterosexual.

A person's sexual orientation may, however, change during the course of his adult life. Homosexuals, especially gay men, are commonly exposed to discrimination and prejudice, despite a more open attitude to homosexuality in most Western societies nowadays. It is important for gays and lesbians not to feel guilty about their sexual orientation, but to feel positive and free about this central aspect of their lives.

Bisexuality

Some men and women are bisexual—they are attracted to and can enjoy sex with members of both sexes. Bisexual behaviour can vary considerably. Some people may have sexual relationships with men and women at the same time, while others spend part of their life in same-sex relationships and part in relationships with the opposite sex. Some people are bisexual as young adults, while 'opting' for either homosexual or heterosexual relationships as they get older. Occasional bisexual behaviour, however, does not define someone as being bisexual.

SEXUAL FANTASY AND VARIANCE

Fantasies may be private or shared between partners. And if someone's fantasy world is not exciting enough for them, they may prefer to buy some 'real', in the sense of tangible, sex aids. Other types of sexual variance that don't appeal to everyone but nevertheless have a role to play in many people's sex lives include fetishism, sadomasochism and transvestism.

Many people are able to enrich their sex lives simply by using their imagination. A rich fantasy life is one of the greatest aphrodisiacs at our disposal. People are notoriously coy about their fantasies and reluctant to reveal them to their friends—and even their lovers. Yet sharing their fantasies with their lover and exploring them together can add an exciting new perspective to a couple's sex life. The most common time for people to use fantasy is while they masturbate, while the second most common time is during foreplay. Fantasy can also play an important part in intercourse, helping many people, especially women, to reach orgasm.

Sex aids have been around for at least 2,500 years. Some, such as alleged aphrodisiac tablets and potions, are fairly useless and not worth paying good money for. Others, such as erotic lingerie, are a bit of harmless fun and may help to spice things up a little. However, sex aids such as vibrators and ribbed condoms do actually help some people, particularly women, to reach orgasm.

A vibrator, an electrically powered device that is used to give sexual pleasure, is one of the most popular sex aids. It is mostly used by women to give themselves sexual pleasure during masturbation, although it can also be used by couples as part of foreplay. Vibrators can be mains or battery-powered. The battery-operated ones are usually noisier. Some types have interchangeable heads and some offer a choice of speeds. There are also special double vibrators that are intended to be used in both vagina and anus, while others have a special attachment for the clitoris. If the vibrator is to be used in the anus, it is important to check that the design is suitable for this purpose, as otherwise it can disappear into the rectum and require medical intervention to remove it. Another popular aid is a penis ring, which fits closely around the base of the penis, supporting it, and helping to sustain an erection.

Variant sexual behaviour is a term used by sexologists to describe sexual behaviour that is not engaged in by everyone but nevertheless provides sexual pleasure for a minority of people. It is a purely descriptive term, not implying right or wrong, or any abnormality.

Fetishism is a sexual habit in which a particular object or a specific part of the body (other than the sexual organs) gives the fetishist sexual pleasure. Common fetishes include rubber, leather, fur and feet. Whether or not this is a problem depends largely on how dominant such feelings become.

For example, there is a big difference between someone whose enjoyment of sex is enhanced if their partner wears fur, black leather or a plastic mac while having sex and someone who only enjoys sex when their partner is wearing such garments. It is often possible for a couple to incorporate the fetishes of one partner into their sex lives. But if a person becomes totally reliant on their fetishes in order to enjoy sexual activity, this is likely to become a problem, and they may need to see a marital and sexual counsellor or therapist.

Some people enjoy playing sadomasochistic games during sex. Such games may include spanking, caning, whipping or bondage. Although these games can be fun, care must be taken not to take them too far. Both partners should enter into them willingly, neither should be drunk, the object should never be to hurt anyone, and either partner should be able to call a halt to the game whenever they want to, perhaps by a special 'stop' signal agreed beforehand.

Transvestism is the practice of dressing in clothes of the opposite sex as a means of achieving sexual excitement. It is most usually practised by men. This is probably more common than many people realise, but because it is nearly always done in secret, there are no accurate figures of the men involved. A transvestite can spend years leading a double life—male one day, female the next, with two distinct personalities. Support groups also enable transvestites to meet other people who have the same needs and interests as themselves. Most transvestites are heterosexual, and many of them marry and have children. Many wives are able to accept their partner's need to dress in women's clothes and will not only tolerate it but may actually encourage it, perhaps by buying them clothes. A homosexual transvestite is less likely to try to dress like a real woman and more likely to want to attire himself like a drag queen.

Transsexuality

A transsexual will often take his or her conviction to what he believes is its natural conclusion, and have a sex reassignment operation. Most doctors are understandably reluctant to refer transsexuals for drastic and irreversible surgery until they are absolutely sure that this is the right decision for him or her and that they will be able to cope with their new role in life.

A therapist or counsellor should be able to help someone prepare for the operation, and hormonal treatment may be prescribed to help ease the passage to being a member of the opposite sex. In the sex reassignment operation for male transsexuals, the testes and penis are removed and a vagina is constructed from the skin of the penis and scrotum.

The operation for women generally involves breast removal and the construction of a penis from other tissues. Some transsexuals find that it is difficult to come to terms with their 'new self', and may be disappointed by their reduced sexual capabilities.

Good communication between partners is believed to be as essential to good sex as any particular ability to stimulate a partner or any physical attribute. Few of us would go into a restaurant and expect the waiter to know, without being told, what we want to eat. Yet many people are reluctant to convey to their partner precisely what their sexual desires actually are. And they end up with sexual cheese sandwich instead of the orgasmic banquet of their dreams! However, a lack of communication is not surprising. Partners—both men and women—may think they know what their partner wants, or may simply feel deeply embarrassed by talking about sex, however long they have been in the relationship.

Most people cannot be expected to know instinctively what their partner enjoys—even if they know sometimes, they will not always get it right—and need to rely on communication, often verbal, to convey their feelings about what arouses them and what sexual positions they prefer. Lovers should be prepared to ask each other questions, to make requests, and to suggest different ways of making love. Never discussing sex may result in sex lives that seem boring or routine.

Verbal communication is not the only, and not always the most appropriate, way of communicating sexual needs. It is possible, for example, to communicate by moving your partner's hand to a part of your body where the sensation is more exciting, or by making appreciative sounds when what they are doing feels good, or by shifting your position as and when the situation demands. People should pay particular attention to what their partner does to them in the course of sex. It is usually valid to assume that if someone makes a particular sexual move, particularly if he or she does it repeatedly, this is something they particularly enjoy. Non-verbal clues may therefore be a valuable way of communicating sexual preferences. So if one partner sucks his lover's nipples, or fondles his genitals, or stimulates his anus, the chances are usually high that reciprocation would be appreciated.

Some people find it easiest to talk about sex when they are in bed, while others feel less threatened when they are both relaxed and on neutral ground, such as over a meal or a drink. This may well be true of people who are not in the habit of talking about sex, even if they are involved in a long-standing relationship. It is essential, too, to respect each other's feelings and never say anything accusatory or angry, or make cruel personal remarks. Negative comments or views about your partner's sexual behaviour are both inappropriate and self-defeating.

Sexual relationships may be one-sided, with one partner taking the lead and dictating the pace and direction of the relationship, and the other unquestioningly following that lead. Learning to be more assertive can often be a good way of making a relationship more equal. Being assertive is not the same thing as being aggressive, but rather means making decisions and saying yes or no firmly in response to another person's actions or wishes.

A person should learn to be just as assertive in his sexual relationships as in other areas of his daily life. Men often see themselves as the dominant partner in a sexual relationship, and it is often men who take the lead in making love. There is no better way, however, for a woman to show her sexual enjoyment than by occasionally taking the lead and making the first move. Her partner may be surprised by this change in the pattern of their relationship, and his initial reaction may even be one of alarm, but not only will this variation take the pressure off him but he may well get a great deal of pleasure from it. Nothing kills pleasure in sex more effectively than the feeling that it has become predictable. So if the same person always initiates sex and dictates the pace, it is often an excellent idea to change the usual pattern.

SEXUAL DIFFICULTIES

Sex is not always as straightforward as it might be. It is rare, in fact, for a couple in a long-term relationship never to experience any kind of problem with their sex life. There are both physical things that can go wrong with people's sexual organs and psychological problems that can compromise a sexual relationship. Both can damage the relationship, calling into question as they do the most intimate aspect of a couple's partnership. If these difficulties are transitory, a couple can usually weather them provided their relationship is reasonably strong. This is another reason why it is so important for a couple to communicate openly and honestly throughout their relationship. If it is not discussed, a minor problem can be exaggerated, and a serious one cannot hope to be solved.

One of the most common sexual problems is lack of desire. Among the many reasons why a person may feel a lack of desire are:

— stress
— tiredness
— feelings of tension or anxiety
— a disturbing sexual encounter in childhood
— feelings of guilt associated with sex

These are widely used by many sex therapists as a way of combating one or other partner's inability to respond sexually. Sensate focus exercises are particularly beneficial when they are conducted under the guidance of an experienced therapist. But if lack of desire is the result of sexual trauma, ingrained socio-cultural attitudes, or a mental disorder, treatment will be more complicated and, perhaps, less likely to succeed. Of course, if lack of desire is caused by a couple disliking each other, there is probably no solution.

The exercises are intended to focus a couple's minds on the sensations produced by exploring each other's bodies. Each partner follows a series of progressive exercises in which he or she touches, strokes, fondles, massages, kisses and generally gets to know and appreciate every part of his/her partner's body. The exercises always stop short of intercourse.

Partners should take in turns to be the active or the passive partner, also alternating their roles so that the person who was the first to give pleasure at one session becomes the first to receive it at the next. The active partner should lubricate her hands with body lotion or oil. The passive partner should lie down, face downwards, and the active partner can either kneel beside him or sit astride him. The woman should now gently stroke and massage the man's entire body, working from head to toe. She can do anything she likes at this stage, using either her hands or mouth. If she does anything that he does not like, he can show this by pushing her hand away. This part of the exercise should continue for at least 10 minutes.

The partners should now change places. It's the woman's turn now to relax and simply enjoy the feelings evoked by her partner's caresses. She should allow herself to let go as much as possible and to feel each touch as fully as she can. This stage should last for at least 10 minutes. The partners should now change places again, and change position so that the man is lying on his back while she massages his body and face.

She should not touch his genitals. Do this for at least 10 minutes. The partners should now change places again, so that she is lying on her back while her partner strokes her face and body. He should not touch her breasts or genitals. Continue for at least 10 minutes. When first stage has been practised for a minimum of two weeks, the couple can progress to second stage i.e. is pleasure in receiving. This stage should be practised at least three times a week for at least two weeks.

The exercises are the same but the passive partner should give his partner positive feedback on what he finds particularly pleasurable. He can do this either by telling her or by guiding her hand. He should let her know not only where he likes to be touched but also how firm or how gentle he likes that touch to be. She may also kiss him wherever she wishes (but not on his genitals) and he should let her know what he finds most pleasurable. There is still a ban on intercourse and on touching the genitals.

At the end of second stage, the couple should talk to each other about what they liked best. If they feel happy with first and second stage after practising them for at least a month or so, they are ready to move on to third stage that involves taking it in turns to arouse each other by touching the genitals.

Once again, they should not have intercourse and they should not bring each other to orgasm. This stage should be practised at least three times a week for at least two weeks. By the end of third stage, a couple should be ready to move on to full intercourse. The exercises should have done much to improve what they now know not only about their own sexuality but also about each other's.

A period of temporary sexual abstinence can be useful for recharging the batteries when the edge has gone out of a sexual relationship—and can actually do a lot to heighten sexual enjoyment when a couple returns to having sexual relations. If a couple's sex life has lost its edge, it is often best to abstain from sex for a while. Partners should try behaving like new lovers and learn to be friends again, enjoying each other's company in ways other than sex. By taking the focus off a sexual relationship, the problem may resolve itself.

Most people are, to a greater or lesser extent, inhibited. Inhibitions are generally the result of childhood influences that have instilled feelings of anxiety or guilt about sex. Unfortunately, inhibitions about sex can permanently damage a person's sex life. They interfere with their natural sexual response and prevent a person from enjoying sex, or even from becoming aroused in the first place. We therefore should try to 'unlearn' our sexual inhibitions as quickly as possible. We can do this by:

— learning to like our bodies, preferably through masturbation;

— realising how many inhibitions come from the way we were brought up;

— giving ourselves permission both to receive and to enjoy pleasure;

— allowing ourselves to fantasize.

A woman should not find intercourse painful. There are several reasons, however, why penetration may cause persistent pain, all of which—apart from insufficient vaginal lubrication—should be investigated by a doctor. Among the possible causes of painful intercourse are:

— insufficient vaginal lubrication

- a vaginal or pelvic infection
- recent childbirth
- involuntary tightening of the vaginal muscles
- endometriosis.

Vaginismus causes the muscles around the entrance to close so tightly that intercourse becomes impossible. Many women who experience this problem, although sexually responsive in other ways, have a deep fear of intercourse. The more a couple attempts intercourse, the more painful it becomes and the tighter the vaginal muscles squeeze. This reluctance to have sex may be because the woman:

- has been brought up to believe that sex even with her husband is wrong;
- is scared of becoming pregnant;
- had an earlier unhappy experience of sex; or
- has been sexually molested or raped.

Fortunately, vaginismus can be treated in almost all cases. Treatment involves muscle relaxation; pelvic floor exercises (learning to control the muscles that are in spasm); using fingers or a vaginal dilator to insert into the vagina; and counselling to help the woman, and her partner, overcome the feelings that caused the problem in the first place.

A form of sexual dysfunction experienced by some men is the inability to achieve an erection, or to sustain an erection once it has been achieved. This may happen only occasionally, in which case it is unlikely to be a serious problem, or it may happen on a longer-term basis and require professional help.

Problems of erection (which used, misleadingly, to be called impotence) can be caused by overindulgence in alcohol or by extreme fatigue. This can happen to any man from time to time, and there are few men who have never experienced this problem. Most occasional erection problems have a psychological cause. Men suffering from problems with erection should ask themselves:

- Do I feel guilty about sex?
- Am I bored with my relationship?

— Am I no longer attracted to my partner?
— Do I feel anxious?
— Do I feel guilty about any aspect of my relationship?
— Am I worried about my sexual 'performance'?

The chances are that he is trying to have sex with the wrong person, at the wrong time, or in some other respect under the wrong conditions. The self-help measures below are designed to help ensure that erection failure occurs as rarely as possible. He should:

— have sex only when he really feels like it;
— avoid casual encounters—at least until he has regained his sexual confidence;
— try not to become overanxious, and make light of the situation as much as possible; and
— remember that he is a human being, not a machine, and can't expect everything to work like clockwork every time he has sex,

If the problem of lack of erection persists or if the man has never had an erection, he should see a doctor to have tests for medical causes such as diabetes, hormone problems and diseases of the nerves or blood vessels. Certain drugs, especially ones given to treat high blood pressure, can sometimes cause loss of erection.

If the problem is a long-term one, masturbating is one way of reassuring yourself that you can indeed achieve an erection, and that even if your erection subsides it can usually be brought back by gentle stimulation. Take this programme slowly, one step at a time. Within a few weeks or months your confidence should return. Do this exercise when you are feeling completely relaxed.

— Stimulate your penis with your hand. Use whatever fantasy most turns you on. If you have trouble achieving an erection in this way, try again every day until you get an erection.
— Once you have an erection, stop stimulating yourself and let it subside completely.
— Once your penis is soft, start to stimulate it again, using

fantasies as before, until it is fully erect. If you find this difficult, using a lubricant may help. Then let it subside again.

— Now stimulate your penis for a third time and, this time, continue until you ejaculate.

— Do this exercise several times, until you feel quite confident that you are in charge of your erections and can control them at will.

— Having regained your confidence, you should be ready for the next stage, which you need to do with a partner. Now follow a programme of sensate focus exercises, while avoiding full sexual intercourse.

— When you have done these exercises several times a week for three or four weeks, you are ready to progress to the next stage, full sexual intercourse. It is probably best to start with one of the woman-on-top positions. If all goes well, you can then progress to one of the man-on-top positions.

If erectile dysfunction has a medical, rather than a psychological, cause—as it does in many elderly men, and in some younger men with specific medical problems—the condition can often be successfully treated. Medical treatments currently in use include the following.

— A vacuum device may be placed over the penis. This produces a partial vacuum that draws blood into the penis, creating an erection which is maintained by putting a ring around the base of the penis. However, not all users are happy with this device as the erection is not very firm.

— Easy-to-use injection systems involve a man injecting a drug directly into the spongy part of his penis, which increases the volume of blood flowing into it and produces a firm erection. The erection will then last for an hour or so. While some men find this perfectly satisfactory, others may find self-injection unacceptable. A few users experience priapism, where the penis stays erect for a prolonged period. Priapism requires urgent medical attention to prevent damage to the blood vessels inside the penis.

— Penile implants are surgically inserted hydraulic devices. The implant consists of two hollow cylinders inside the penis which are connected to a fluid reservoir in the abdomen and a pump, often in the scrotum. By pumping fluid in the cylinders, the man achieves an erection; by opening a valve, fluid drains out of the cylinders and the erection subsides. While not suitable for all men with erectile difficulties, especially if they have reduced penile sensitivity or sex drive, penile implants have enhanced the sex lives of many men.

Premature ejaculation—meaning that a man ejaculates sooner than he wants to—is not only a problem experienced by many men but may also be a cause of marital conflict. It is very common in young men in the early years of their sex life who are still learning how to control their ejaculation. There are no hard and fast rules as to exactly when premature ejaculation may happen.

A man may ejaculate before the penis becomes erect, it may be at the moment of penetration, or it may be immediately afterwards. There are many possible causes for premature ejaculation. These may be psychological (such as problems in a relationship), although in the vast majority of cases premature ejaculation is simply caused by a lack of sexual sensory awareness. Exercises that deal with this sensory deficit can usually cure premature ejaculation. Although rare, there can also be physical reasons, including:

— an infection of the genitals.

— an injury to the spinal column.

— a disease of the nervous system, such as multiple sclerosis.

First of all, the woman needs to make it clear that she loves her partner, is sympathetic to his problem, and will do everything she can to help. When they make love, he should give her a signal that he is about to come and she should lie still, not making any movements, including vaginal ones. In the rare cases where a patient suffering from premature ejaculation does not respond to behavioural treatment, he will almost always respond to medication prescribed by a doctor.

Squeeze technique is a technique that a couple can use to treat premature ejaculation. When the woman uses this method, it will inhibit her partner's urge to ejaculate. To apply this method, follow these steps.

— Stimulate your partner's penis until he is about to ejaculate.

— Squeeze his penis by holding it just below the glans. Grip it firmly, with your thumb on the frenulum—the part of the underside of the penis where the head and shaft meet—and your first finger opposite the thumb and the other fingers around the shaft. Apply firm pressure for 15-20 seconds without moving your fingers—even the lightest movement may arouse him, which is not what is required at this stage.

— Release your grip. This should have stopped him ejaculating for now (but if he does ejaculate, put it down to inexperience and try again another time). Repeat the stimulation/squeeze procedure several times before going on to have intercourse.

— Repeat the process each time you have sex.

— As his control improves, start having intercourse without using the squeeze technique, but get him to withdraw when he is about to ejaculate, and repeat the squeezing process.

— Finally move on to sex without squeezing. With his new-found confidence, he should gain greater control over his ejaculation.

Retarded ejaculation may be caused by a number of factors, psychological or physical. Physical causes can include spinal injuries, hormonal imbalances, the effect of certain drugs, including antidepressants and drugs for high blood pressure and consumption of too much alcohol. Psychological causes can include a belief that sex is 'dirty', fear of losing control, fear of the partner becoming pregnant, anxiety about sex, or the feeling that the woman is hostile.

The man's partner is encouraged to masturbate him to orgasm, so that he ejaculates in an unthreatening environment. From this they progress to a combination of masturbation and intercourse, until he reaches orgasm inside her. Although it is never easy to maintain a long-term relationship with a partner, some couples become even closer and more 'in love' after a number of years together. But it would be wrong to assume that, that particular couple is unusual or just lucky. Like many other couples, these two people may have fallen deeply in love earlier in their lives, convinced that they were right for each other and would live happily ever after. However, they will then almost certainly have found that living out their romantic dream requires a great deal of understanding and hard work. They will also have discovered that there is no magic formula and that maintaining a successful relationship depends on keeping in touch with each other's feelings, being able to adapt to changes, both in themselves and in their circumstances, and on continuing to respect each other and enjoy each other's company. Inevitably, any couple will find that the excitement of living together wears off in time and that eventually they will have to confront any underlying problems in their relationship.

Changing lifestyles can also mean that partners move in different directions or at a different pace; sometimes one or both partners become so bored with the pattern of their lives that they may think about having an affair. But whatever their dissatisfactions, a couple should never lose sight of the enormous benefits that are to be gained from a long-term relationship, including mutual love and respect, the enjoyment of each other's company, and the time to develop an increasingly fulfilling sex life.

Adapting to change

People's work patterns may get busier, a new job may mean moving home, a worsening financial situation may drive them into taking on more work, redundancy or retirement may force them into a completely different way of life, or a child may put varying demands on them as he or she goes through adolescence or decides to leave home. Ideally, both partners in a relationship will change at roughly the same pace, with the result that their relationship will absorb—and be strengthened by—those changes.

What is usually more difficult for a couple to deal with is when one partner moves at a different pace and direction from the other. This can lead to a situation in which a couple, despite having been together for years, suddenly feel as if they no longer know each other. Most of us will have heard statements like: 'He's not the same man I married', 'I don't understand her any longer', or 'We don't have anything in common anymore'. Remarks like these usually mean that the couple are going through difficulties in their relationship.

The most misleading aspect of these statements is the implication that the relationship has only recently altered or that the partner at fault has suddenly become a different person. Perhaps if they'd been more tuned in to their partner and if communication between them had been better, it wouldn't have come as such a shock. More importantly, they might have been able to adjust to the new situation. Most people are prepared to spend a lot of time on all sorts of things: work, shopping, watching television, reading a book, attending sports events. But how much time do we devote to our close relationships?

If the honest answer is 'not a lot', then it would obviously be a good idea for a couple to move their relationship up their list of priorities and not wait until there's a problem before spending more time on it. They should remember to sometimes make a fuss of each other; to go out to dinner and treat it like a first date, or to cook a special meal at home with all the trimmings—wine, flowers, soft lights and music. Sexual relationships, too, deserve to be treated as a special part of a couple's life together. Sex is one of life's greatest pleasures and shouldn't just be something a couple do on automatic pilot or for 10 minutes last thing at night.

A rewarding sexual relationship requires both time and concentration. Whispering endearments or calling each other by a pet name isn't silly. It can make someone feel loved and special, as well as creating a private bond between two people. It is also important that both partners sometimes make an effort to look their best; and equally important that the other person is appreciative.

A positive effort deserves a positive reaction. Everyday affectionate gestures are never a waste of time. They help maintain a positive attitude to a relationship and create a strong foundation for the inevitable highs and lows of living together.

Good sex doesn't necessarily always remain good; bad sex, equally, can get better. But whatever the state of a couple's sex life, this part of their life together will always need both time and consideration. It is normal for the nature of our sex lives together to change as a relationship matures. Sex might get more satisfying, or it might get less exciting; one partner might want sex more often than the other, or a couple's sexual preferences might not be as much in tune as they were earlier in the relationship. Changes in people's sex lives are usually brought on by the other things happening to them. It is virtually impossible to keep sex exciting for both partners unless they are prepared to talk about their sexual relationship.

There are surprisingly few couples who actually manage to set aside time to do this, however long they have been together, yet it makes no sense to restrict themselves to guesswork. There is no place for embarrassment here. It is important for a couple to be as frank and open as they can with each other—and that includes being honest with themselves. They should tell each other which part of their body they like to be touched, and how and what they like and, of course, don't like. They need to talk about what pleases them most about each other's bodies, what position gives them the most pleasure, what time of day they find sex most exciting—about anything, in fact, that makes sex good (or bad) for them.

SEX AND ILLNESS

People need to be healthy, in both body and mind. When anything goes wrong with our bodies, our sex lives may suffer, although in what way and how much depends on the exact nature of the illness. Sex may be a major concern for anyone who is seriously unwell, or recovering from illness. Ill-health may also cause someone to feel less attractive and therefore less confident, and severe disability or surgery may give rise to a major change in their body image. Solutions to these problems are never easy. Above all, they will need the help of an understanding and sympathetic partner. Some of the most common illnesses that can affect a person's sex life are described below.

Arthritis is the inflammation of a joint, characterised by swelling, stiffness and pain, which can be severe. It may affect the joints of the hands, knees or hips and, although mild arthritis generally has little noticeable effect on a person's sex life, severe arthritis can cause serious problems, at least initially. Any deformity of the limbs can cause someone to lose confidence in their attractiveness, while severe pain can cause loss of interest in sex.

In addition, arthritis in the hips can make it difficult to find a comfortable position for intercourse, and arthritic hands can make it difficult both to caress a partner and to masturbate. Arthritis may also cause a decrease in vaginal lubrication. However, anti-inflammatory drugs and painkillers taken before sex may help relieve pain. A hot bath before sex will help mobilise the joints.

The sufferer also needs to find a suitable position in which sex is comfortable. Physiotherapy and exercise may help alleviate pain and enhance sex.

Diabetes mellitus is a disorder caused by insufficient production of the hormone insulin by the pancreas. Insulin helps to control levels of glucose in the blood. In a diabetic, glucose levels can be controlled by diet and/or insulin injections. For older men, the side-effects of diabetes may lead to erectile problems, although sex drive and ability to ejaculate remain unimpaired.

Careful control of diabetes makes sexual problems a lot less likely, but on rare occasions some drugs used to treat diabetes may cause erectile problems, and this should be checked with a doctor. Diabetes in women can result in a dry, itchy vulva, difficulty in achieving orgasm and an increase in vaginal infections, especially thrush. However, the problems can generally be eased by medication.

Some male epileptics may have trouble maintaining an erection, while some female epileptics may find it difficult to become aroused, and epileptics of either sex may lose interest in sex. Some of these problems may stem from a decrease in self-confidence, and if this is restored through counselling, sexual function may soon return to normal.

Sexual problems are common, with men reporting difficulty in achieving an erection and ejaculatory disturbances, and women reporting loss of vaginal lubrication and difficulty in achieving an orgasm. One common feature in Multiple sclerosis (MS) is that symptoms often come and go, with periods of exacerbation followed by periods of remission.

Sexual difficulties may follow a similar pattern. It is important that patients continue sexual activity if they want, even if they are not always able to reach orgasm. Patients who still have an interest in sex should experiment to see which positions suit them best.

How much effect a stroke has on a patient's sexuality will depend on how much disability remains afterwards and on how permanent this disability is. Some patients may lose interest in sex for a time, while others may remain interested in sex but experience difficulties because they are paralysed in one or more limbs.

There is no reason why a stroke victim should not continue to have sex if he so wishes, and stroke patients should be reassured that sex is most unlikely to induce another stroke.

A colostomy is an operation in which part of the colon is brought through an opening in the abdomen and formed into an artificial outlet so that body wastes can be removed to a special bag attached to the skin. There is no need for a colostomy to affect sex. Any problems tend to be ones of attitudes and emotions rather than physical difficulties.

Loss of a limb can have a major effect on a person's sex life, not least because it may have reduced their self-esteem and confidence and made them worry that no one will ever find them attractive again.

Hysterectomy is the removal of the womb, usually performed because of gynaecological problems. There is no medical evidence to support the view that removal of the womb has any effect on sex, but some women do report that sex afterwards is different. For some this may be because their orgasms feel less intense, while for others sex may be better because there are no longer any worries about the possibility of pregnancy and because symptoms such as pain or heavy bleeding are relieved. A woman should wait for six weeks after the operation before resuming sexual intercourse, to allow time for the wound to heal.

The removal of a woman's breast (Mastectomy) has strong sexual associations and a woman may feel she has lost an essential part of her femininity. A couple who have enjoyed a strong relationship before the operation can usually come to terms with the change and resume normal sexual activity.

The removal of a man's prostate gland (Prostatectomy) when it has become abnormally large may in a few cases cause impotence. More often, it can cause retrograde ejaculation, whereby the semen is ejaculated into the bladder rather than out through the penis—but this should not cause any sexual problems. Although the operation can have a major effect on a couple's sex life, this is often largely psychological, and the couple should have fewer concerns if everything is explained to them carefully beforehand so that they know what to expect. There is no reason why, in most cases, a man's sex life should not continue as normal after a prostatectomy.

A person's sex life is one the first casualties of depression and lack of interest in sex may in fact be one of the first symptoms of the condition. Depression has an effect on many other areas of a depressed person's life as well as sex and can wreak havoc with a couple's overall relationship.

Those who suffer from physical disabilities often say that other people don't regard them as sexual beings and assume that they never make love. Some people say that other parts of their body have become more sensitive than they were before their disability, to compensate for any loss of sensation in the conventionally 'sexy' places.

2

Healthy Body

Life is vastly easier in the industrialised world than it was 150 years ago. Most people live longer, eat more and work less. Many live in private homes and drive to work alone in their own cars. Office workers communicate instantaneously across continents through telephone, fax, e-mail and internet. Industries crank out new goods faster than people can buy them in ever-bigger shopping malls. But the advantages of modern life are not available to everyone, nor do they come without a price: new kinds of health problems, many caused by our own bad habits or by the dirty air and water left behind by industries; the loss of parkland as highways devour open space; declining literacy as television beats teachers in the competition for children's attention; cadres of unemployed and homeless people overlooked by the free market system; and sprawling, desolate suburbs where neighbours are strangers and fear of crime isolates people behind locked doors.

Added to these is the disinvestment in services and physical infrastructure over the past 15 years, which has hit urban dwellers—especially poor urban dwellers—the hardest. The cuts in government spending for social programmes are all the more stark when viewed in the context of a world with a widening gap between rich and poor. The fraying of social safety nets, most severe in the United States, has increased the percentage of children under six living in poverty from 20 per cent of US children in 1980 to 24 per cent in 1995. Without addressing these fundamental inequalities, programmes developed to mend worsening urban conditions will be unable to secure long-lasting solutions. Even when government agencies and private organizations have the economic means and political will to address these ills, the typical approach is fragmented and specialised: a programme is created to fix a problem. A clinic is opened to treat disease, ignoring the fact that good health is much more than the absence of illness. Schools are upgraded, but the curriculum ignores lessons learned on the streets and in the media, which set the patterns for children's beliefs and perceptions.

There is a better way. It is rooted in the simple but revolutionary idea that health is less about medical care than about equitable access to such basic prerequisites of health as food, shelter, transportation, clean air and water, education, physical safety and meaningful jobs paying sufficient wages. This way of thinking expands on the idea that no person or family is an island; everyone's life is bound up in the whole community.

The body's natural defences, including its immune system, are in action constantly to withstand the battalions of bacteria and viruses that attempt to invade the body. Many of these infectious diseases can be transmitted from one person to another; some of them, known as sexually transmitted diseases, are transferred by sexual contact.

Modern medicine has developed many weapons to combat the infectious and non-infectious diseases that can affect the body. What is important is for men and women to be aware of when their body is not functioning as it should, so that they can report any symptoms to their doctor as soon as possible. The doctor, in turn, will look for signs that will, along with the patient's description of the symptoms, enable him or her to make a diagnosis, in order to suggest a cure.

EXERCISE

People who are fit, look healthier and more sexually attractive. They are less likely to be stressed and therefore more likely to have a strong sex drive. And they are likely to be happier and so be able to enjoy sex more. A fit body is generally one that is fed with a balanced diet rich in fresh foods, vitamins and minerals, and low in animal fats; that is exercised at least two or three times a week; that is not abused by drugs or excessive amounts of alcohol; that does not have cigarette smoke inhaled into its lungs; and that is emotionally healthy and not stressed.

A balanced diet contains around 55 per cent carbohydrate (from foods such as potatoes, bread and pasta); less than 30 per cent fat, with less than 10 per cent being animal fats; and around 15 per cent protein (from foods such as meat, fish, beans or eggs). If the diet is balanced and contains a range of fresh foods, it should also provide all the vitamins and minerals required.

Diets in the developed world are too high in animal fats and too low in fresh fruit and vegetables. This imbalance leads to high rates of obesity, heart disease and high blood pressure, as well as other conditions including some cancers. Health authorities in these countries are advising people to consume less fat and more carbohydrates, fresh vegetables and fruit.

A person can ensure that his or her heart is working more efficiently: a fit heart pumps 25 per cent more blood with each beat than an unfit heart does while a person is at rest. Regular exercise is the most reliable way to keep fit on a day-to-day basis, and as an insurance policy for future health in the years ahead. Ideally, exercise should be aerobic. It should make a person sweat and become somewhat breathless; it should last at least 20 minutes per session; and take place at least three or four times a week. Anaerobic exercise, such as weightlifting, increases strength by increasing muscle bulk but does not itself promote cardio-fitness. Exercise should aim to improve three elements of fitness: strength, flexibility and stamina. Regular aerobic exercise has increases cardiovascular fitness, making a person more active and lively and decreasing the risk of their developing heart disease, strokes or high blood pressure. Combined with a balanced diet that contains the right amount of calories (energy), exercise helps prevent obesity which, apart from making the body look less attractive, increases the risk of developing high blood pressure, heart disease and diabetes.

First, exercise causes the release of endorphins into the bloodstream. These are naturally occurring opiates that induce a feeling of relaxation and well-being. Secondly, feeling both tired and relaxed after exercise helps a person sleep well and regular deep sleep is essential for stress reduction. Thirdly, having a healthy, well-toned body also makes a person feel better about themselves and boosts their self-esteem and often makes them feel and look more sexually attractive. It normally boosts the immune system so that people who are fit are probably less likely to develop infectious diseases such as colds, or non-infectious diseases such as cancers. Fitness also aids recovery if illness does strike. But it cannot guarantee protection against disease—fitness is not the same as health.

Exercises tones and strengthens muscles, improving body shape and enabling muscles to work more efficiently. This, in combination with avoiding obesity, can improve posture and decrease the occurrence of backache. It also strengthens bones and increases joint mobility, reducing the problem of stiff and painful joints in old age.

PERSONAL HYGIENE

One of our first sensations would probably be the smell of unwashed bodies. Nowadays, there is a much greater awareness of cleanliness and personal hygiene and a vast range of products are available to wash, perfume and deodorise the human body. Cleanliness is certainly an important factor in many sexual relationships. Most people would find sharing a bed with a dirty, smelly body something of a turn-off. The reason that unwashed people develop an unpleasant body odour is because of the sweat produced by the apocrine glands of the armpits and around the genitals and anus.

The sweat is odourless when first produced, but after it has been 'processed' by bacteria living on the skin, it takes on an unpleasant, musky smell. Daily bathing or showering is not only refreshing but removes sweat and dirt from the body and minimises the chances of developing armpit and other smells. Many people find that underarm anti-perspirants and deodorants help reduce the risk of body smells developing during the day. Of course, it is also important to keep the genitals clean.

Genital hygiene is particularly important for men who are not circumcised. If the penis is left unwashed for a few days, the secretions of the sebaceous glands under the foreskin produce a white material called smegma. It is important during washing to pull back the foreskin and wash the glans thoroughly. Accumulation of smegma can cause balanitis—inflammation of the glans because of the development of fungal or bacterial conditions under the unwashed foreskin.

The vulva—the external female genitals—also produces secretions that generate a particular odour, but provided that it is washed regularly that smell will not become unpleasant. It is best to wash the vulva from front to back, to avoid transferring any bacteria from the anus into the vagina or the urethra and to reduce the risk of developing any infections. A healthy vulva smells slightly musky, a smell that may become more noticeable during sexual arousal and that may act as an attractant for a sexual partner.

The use of vaginal deodorants and fragranced pantyliners has become more prevalent, but these only serve, in a clean person, to mask natural, pleasing scents produced by the body. In addition, some of the chemicals contained in the products may cause irritation leading to vaginitis and increase sensitivity to spermicides and lubricants used for condoms.

Feeling happy, relaxed and confident about oneself plays an important part in having and maintaining a successful relationship and in experiencing a good sex life. Yet the pace of modern life causes many people to feel anxious and not enjoy life to the full. One word serves to encapsulate all these worries and fears, and that is 'stress'.

Stress

Stress is now recognised as a major health issue that reduces our quality of life, makes us more prone to disease and, if prolonged, shortens our lifespan. It also makes us feel less sexual. Fortunately, stress can be managed and even avoided. The most common signs and symptoms of stress include breathlessness, nausea, loss of appetite, insomnia, tiredness, feeling tearful, constipation or diarrhoea, headaches, dizziness, backache and trembling. Stress also reduces the effectiveness of the immune system, so that people who are stressed are more likely to become ill. Stress affects a person's sexuality, too. Both men and women who are stressed may lose interest in sex altogether, thereby putting a strain on their relationships. Men who are stressed are more likely to lose an erection, or not have an erection at all.

Women who suffer long-term stress may develop irregular periods or may stop having periods altogether. Worrying about sexual problems can make them worse and lead to more stress and a risk of more serious illness. To break this vicious circle it is important to talk to your partner about difficulties and/or to seek outside help. In the long term, stress can lead to more serious conditions such as anxiety disorders, or a 'nervous breakdown', where a person is unable to cope on a day-to-day basis because of their state of emotional health. To manage stress effectively, first of all identify the factors that are probably causing stress and talk them over with a partner or with colleagues at work in order to eliminate them or reduce their impact and set realistic goals on a daily basis to avoid getting behind and letting work mount up. Try to avoid pressure by not taking on too many commitments. Taking regular breaks during working hours and during the break concentrate on something else other than work can also help to reduce the stress. Exercise on a regular basis and should learn to relax completely and forget problems. This may involve regular exercise or other kinds of relaxation, for example, reading or meditation. Take regular short holidays away from home in order to experience a complete change of scene. Avoid too many lifestyle changes at once and adopt a more positive attitude to life, focusing on the present and not worrying too much about the future. Avoid using alcohol, or other drugs, for relaxation. They simply put off decision making and interrupt sleep patterns, making stress even worse in the long term. If necessary, seek medical help to break the vicious circle of stress.

MALE HEALTH

Major disorders of the male reproductive system mainly concern two organs—the testes and the prostate gland—and tend to occur in two particular phases of the lifespan. Cancer of the testis, although rare, is most common in younger men. Enlargement of the prostate gland and cancer of the prostate are more prevalent among older men. As with cancer of the breast or the cervix, the sooner testicular and prostate cancer are detected, and the quicker they are treated, the greater chances cure.

Cancer of the testis is the most common form of cancer in young men between the ages of 15 and 35. If detected early—usually by self-examination of the testes—there is a very good chance of a complete cure. The risk of developing testicular cancer is much higher in men who have an undescended testicle—one that is still located in the abdomen during adolescence or adulthood. Testicular cancer also appears to occur more frequently in Caucasoids (men of European or Indian ancestry) than it does among other ethnic groups. Testicular cancer usually appears first as a hard, painless swelling on the side of the testicle. This can usually be detected by self-examination if a man feels his testes on a regular basis and is therefore familiar with their normal state. In later stages of the disease, there may be pain. If a man goes to his doctor with a lump in the testis, the doctor will first ensure that it is not due to any other disorder of the testis. If cancer is confirmed, a surgeon will remove the affected testis under general anaesthetic—orchiclectomy—at the same time examining the other testis to make sure it is healthy.

Radiotherapy and anticancer drugs may also be used. Some surgeons insert a testicular prosthesis—a firm but flexible ball—into the scrotum to restore its normal appearance. If the cancer has been detected early, there is a survival rate of almost 100 per cent over a five-year period. The first symptoms of testicular cancer are most likely to be discovered by men themselves. And if discovered early, testicular cancer can be completely cured in the vast majority of cases.

These two statements underpin the importance of carrying out regular self-examination of the testes from puberty onwards. Each testis should be examined in turn, using the fingers of both hands, to feel for any changes in size, shape or texture. The best time to do this is after a bath or shower, when the scrotum is soft and relaxed. By gently rolling each testis between thumb and fingers, the entire surface can be felt for any hard lumps or bumps. If present, these commonly occur on the side or front of the testis. These bumps should not be confused with the epididymis, a rubbery band that runs down the back of the testis, and the vas deferens, the tube that carries sperm away from the testis: these are perfectly normal parts of the body.

The size and shape of a walnut, the prostate is located at the base of the bladder, surrounding the urethra, the tube which carries urine from the bladder to the outside of the body through the penis. The prostate may become swollen and inflamed by bacterial infection, a condition known as prostatitis. But the major disorders affecting this gland are enlarged prostate and cancer of the prostate.

Enlargement of the prostate gland, also known as benign prostate hypertrophy (BPH), is common in men aged 50 years or over. It is not the same as cancer of the prostate. As the prostate gets bigger it presses on the urethra and interrupts the flow of urine, producing its main symptoms: a frequent need to urinate, especially annoying at night; difficulty in starting to urinate; and a weak urinary stream, sometimes just a few drops at a time.

An enlarged prostate is detected by rectal examination. If it causes urinary problems, an enlarged prostate gland requires treatment, most commonly by surgery to remove all or part of the prostate. Newer treatments include introducing a narrow balloon-like device into the penis and inflating it to widen the urethra where it passes through the prostate; using lasers to remove excess prostate tissue; and using drugs which shrink the prostate.

Symptoms of prostate cancer are similar to those experienced by someone with an enlarged prostate and should be investigated by a rectal examination. In addition, a sample of blood can be screened for prostate-specific antigen (PSA), high levels of which may indicate the presence of prostate cancer. If the prostate feels hard when examined, or the PSA screening is positive, the doctor will perform a biopsy to confirm whether or not there are cancerous cells present and may also do a blood test to seek further confirmation. Since prostate cancer can spread to the bones, the doctor may also perform a bone scan.

Routine examinations of the prostate and PSA screening are important for older men. Prostate cancer is treated by surgery to remove all or part of the prostate gland, or by radiotherapy to destroy the cancer. If the cancer spreads to other parts of the body, drugs may be given to inhibit the release of testosterone from the testes; female hormones may be given; or, in some cases, the tests may be removed, in order to shrink the tumour. A healthy prostate is smooth and rubbery; an enlarged prostate is, obviously, larger than would be expected; and a cancerous prostate feels hard and knobbly.

Prostate surgery usually takes one of two forms. Transurethral resectoscopy (TUR) involves putting a type of endoscope (viewing tube) called a resectoscope into the urethra, through the tip of the penis, then using a heated wire on the end of the resectoscope to cut away part of the prostate and washing out the pieces through the resectoscope. As a result of prostate surgery is retrograde ejaculation, which means that semen shoots backwards into the bladder during ejaculation instead of coming out through the penis.

Hydrocele is a painless swelling of the scrotum that is common in middle-aged and older men, produced by fluid accumulating in the space around the testis. Sometimes this is caused by an injury, although other causes include inflammation or infection. Orchitis—inflammation of a testis, causing swelling, pain and fever—is normally treated with painkillers and bed rest for several days until the swelling has gone down; antibiotics may be prescribed if an infection is suspected. Orchitis also occurs in around one in four men who develop mumps after puberty.

In Epididymal cyst, a fluid-filled 'bag' may sometimes form inside the scrotum. These are generally harmless, although if a man detects an unusual growth when examining his testes, he should report it to his doctor to check that it is not a tumour.

The following are the disorders of penis:

a) *Balanitis*: It may be caused by an infection, such as thrush; poor hygiene through failing to wash the penis, especially under the foreskin in uncircumcised men; irritation from spermicides, particularly those used in condoms; rubbing against clothes; excessive washing or use of antiseptics; or having a tight foreskin. Treatment involves washing the penis regularly and, if prescribed, taking a course of antibiotics.

b) *Blood in the semen* is a rare condition caused by the rupture of tiny blood vessels in the urethra during an erection. It should heal rapidly, but if it recurs the man should consult his doctor.

c) *Tight foreskin*, however, if it continues to be tight into adulthood, a condition known as phimosis may make erection painful and sexual activities impossible. It may also cause balanitis because the glans cannot be washed.

d) *Priapism*: Erection is produced when blood accumulates in the spongy tissues of the penis; when excess blood drains from these tissues the penis softens. In the case of priapism this natural drainage does not occur, and the condition must be treated immediately to ensure that the penis is not damaged permanently. Priapism is usually found as a side-effect of drugs given to men with erectile problems; or in men who have sickle-cell disease, an inherited disorder of red blood cells.

e) *Cancer of the penis* is the most prevalent among uncircumcised men whose standards of genital hygiene are poor. Initial symptoms include a wart-like lump on the foreskin or glans or a painful sore on the glans. A man who has these symptoms should consult his doctor immediately, although these symptoms are more likely to be caused by a sexually transmitted disease.

SEXUAL INFECTIONS

A disease is an abnormality in the way the body functions. It can be non-infectious (such as the cancers) or infectious (such as the common cold) and caused by microorganisms, such as bacteria and viruses. The term 'sexual infections' in is used to describe some common infectious diseases that affect the organs of the male and female reproductive systems and sometimes the female urinary system.

Some of these are not usually passed on by sexual contact and are described under non-sexually transmitted diseases. Unfortunately, many people feel unnecessarily confused and ashamed if they develop a sexual infection and may be too embarrassed to consult a doctor. The description of sexual infections that follows is not intended to be a guide to self-diagnosis. If you or your sexual partner show signs or symptoms of a sexual infection or irritation, you should consult your doctor or visit a hospital genito-urinary medicine (GUM) clinic as soon as possible to obtain an accurate diagnosis.

Doctors and nurses who treat sexual diseases are used to seeing people who have—or turn out not to have—these infections. They will not be embarrassed, patronising or judgmental. Their job is to treat a patient with a sexual infection in the same way that an orthopaedic surgeon would treat someone with a broken leg. Ignoring a sexual infection or irritation will not make it go away. Nor will it do any good to blame a partner for passing on a disease that may not even be present. It may well be the case that the infection has not been passed on sexually or that it is non-infectious.

NON-SEXUALLY TRANSMITTED DISEASES

The non-sexually transmitted diseases are sexual infections that are not generally transmitted by sexual contact and that mainly affect women (usually in the urinary tract). So what causes them? On the skin and inside certain body openings, such as the mouth, vagina, rectum and anus, a community of micro-organisms including bacteria and fungi live quite harmlessly, keeping each other in check and stopping any one type of micro-organism from taking over.

The community of bacteria and fungi on or in the body is often described as a 'flora'. But sometimes things go wrong. Bacteria that are harmless in the rectum, for example, might be accidentally transferred to the vagina, where they cause infection. Alternatively, the vaginal flora might be disrupted so that one micro-organism grows out of control and causes an infection. Non-sexually transmitted diseases can occur in women of all ages, who may or may not be sexually active. Vaginal and urinary infections cause discomfort to many women.

Acute urethral syndrome is a condition that affects the urethra in women. Common symptoms include a frequent urge to urinate, a feeling of discomfort in the lower part of the stomach and pain around the vulva. It may be caused by infection of the urethra by bacteria from the large intestine, in which case it can be treated with antibiotics and by drinking plenty of water. Alternatively it may, in women who have gone through the menopause, be caused by an inflammation of the vulva which can be treated with hormonal creams. However, in a large proportion of women the cause is unknown.

Bacterial vaginosis (BV) is an infection of the vagina that occurs in sexually active women. Its main symptoms are the presence of a greyish-white, often frothy vaginal discharge that has a fishy odour and sometimes mild irritation and burning in the vagina and vulva.

Bacterial vaginosis is caused by a disturbance in the vaginal flora: naturally protective bacteria decrease in number, while others undergo a 'population explosion' that produces the symptoms of vaginosis. This bacterial imbalance is believed to be caused by sexual activity, but is not sexually transmitted.

Cystitis is caused by bacterial infection. It is common in women of all ages and can be irritating and annoying, especially if it lasts for long periods. The main symptoms are a frequent urge to urinate, although only releasing a small amount of urine each time; and a burning or stinging feeling during urination. The bladder and urethra are normally free of any micro-organisms. The bacteria that cause cystitis are unwanted invaders either from the vagina or from the rectum via the anus.

Cystitis is much more common in women than men because the female urethra is much shorter than the male's, so bacteria do not have far to travel to the bladder. Movement of bacteria into the urethra may be assisted by sexual intercourse. Cystitis can often disappear of its own accord. If symptoms persist beyond 48 hours, or if they are severe—especially if the urine is foul-smelling or tinged with blood, or if a woman has a chill or fever—she should consult her doctor. If bacterial cystitis has been confirmed—by taking a urine sample—a doctor will prescribe antibiotics to remove the infective bacteria.

Women who are sexually active and prone to cystitis may find it helpful to urinate before and after intercourse to flush out any bacteria. Some women find that using the diaphragm as a contraceptive method makes them prone to cystitis.

Thrush is an infection of the vagina. Like cystitis, it can occur in women of all ages, sexually active or not. Symptoms typically include a thick, white vaginal discharge, rather like cottage cheese, which has a yeasty smell; vaginal irritation and itching; and, possibly, a burning feeling in the vagina if a woman has sexual intercourse.

Thrush is caused by a yeast-like fungus, called *Candida albicans,* found in the vagina, vulva, rectum and mouth, and on the skin. But sometimes the vaginal flora is disrupted and the fungus grows uncontrollably to produce thrush symptoms. Usually this happens because the vaginal environment is altered—for example, by taking antibiotics to control a bacterial infection which also kill vaginal bacteria; by using certain types of combined oral contraceptive pill; or by becoming pregnant. Treatment involves the use of an antifungal drug. For women, this usually takes the form of a pessary or cream to be inserted into the vagina, and possibly as a cream to be applied on the vulva. Doctors may also prescribe a cream for a male partner to apply to his penis to prevent possible reinfection.

A natural remedy that may help to treat thrush is the use of natural yoghurt containing live bacteria, *Lactobacillus acidophilus.* Some yoghurt should be applied inside the vagina and left for at least two hours. During infection it may be preferable to refrain from intercourse—this may be painful in any case—or to use a condom. Thrush can grow in the mouth, so oral sex should also be avoided until treatment is completed.

Vaginitis is a general term which describes the uncomfortable, irritating and sometimes painful condition caused by inflammation of the vagina, which may also produce an abnormal and excessive vaginal discharge. It may be caused by thrush or by a sexually transmitted disease called trichomoniasis, both conditions that require medical treatment.

Vaginitis can be a non-infectious disease, resulting from an allergy to a spermicide, irritation by soaps or bath oils, or the use of vaginal deodorants. In all these cases, alleviation of symptoms can be achieved by avoiding using particular products.

Practical ways for women to reduce the risk of vaginal and urinary infections are as follows. When using toilet paper, wipe from front to back, so that intestinal bacteria are nor carried from the anus to the vagina or urethra.

— Urinate when you need; do not hold back.
— Avoid 'feminine hygiene' products that may irritate the vagina.
— Avoid unprotected sexual intercourse.
— Wear underwear made from cotton, rather than nylon or other synthetics which make the vulva warmer and moister than normal, so providing a perfect environment for micro-organisms to infect the vagina or urethra.
— Avoid douching—flushing out the vagina with water or deodorant solutions. Douching may upset healthy bacteria normally found in the vagina by destroying

beneficial bacteria, thus allowing potentially harmful bacteria to thrive and cause infection.

SEXUALLY TRANSMITTED DISEASES

Sexually transmitted diseases (STDs) are passed from one person to another by sexual contact. Specifically, an STD may be passed on to someone if they are exposed to infected body fluids (such as semen or vaginal fluid, and sometimes blood) during vaginal intercourse, anal intercourse and sometimes during oral sex. There has often been an assumption that infection with an STD implies that a person is promiscuous and deserves to get an infection because of their immoral behaviour.

However, the STDs are diseases like any others. They simply happen to be passed on by sexual activity. Some STDs are more infectious than others, although anyone—regardless of sex, class, age, ethnic background or wealth—may develop an STD if he or she has sexual contact with an affected partner and is not protected by the use of, for example, a condom. Like many other diseases, an STD requires medical treatment. Left untreated, they may cause further complications. Unfortunately, some they can be present, especially in women, without causing symptoms. This is why it is important for people with STD symptoms to let their partners know, so that they can get treatment as well. If a man or woman thinks they may have an STD, they should visit a GUM (genito-urinary medicine) clinic (formerly known as STD or special clinics). These are normally found at hospitals. They will also help the patient psychologically and enable their partner (contact) or partners to be traced if necessary, tested and treated. To reduce the risk of contracting STDs—apart from complete abstinence—it is advisable always to practise safer sex by using a condom. Considered first in this section is HIV, a virus which can be transmitted sexually, and which eventually causes AIDs. The rest of the section deals with common STDs.

HIV and AIDS

HIV (human immunodeficiency virus) is a virus that was

first identified in 1981. HIV, recognised as the causative agent in 1983, is commonly passed on by sexual intercourse through body fluids such as blood, semen and vaginal secretions. HIV can be passed on by injecting equipment (needles and unsterilised syringes) shared by drug users, infected blood in transfusions, from infected mothers to newborn babies and (less commonly) by blood contact through open cuts. At present HIV appears to be incurable and, over time, causes the body's natural defence system to stop functioning so that the carrier becomes prey to one or more opportunistic diseases which eventually cause death (although new therapies are allowing people with HIV to live much longer).

The most encouraging aspect is that people can considerably reduce the risk of contracting HIV and developing AIDS by altering their sexual behaviour and practising 'safer sex'. AIDS in Europe and North America appeared to be confined mainly to homosexual and bisexual men and intravenous drug users. But the number of men and women who have contracted HIV through heterosexual sex has increased in Europe and North America, and AIDS has become a major cause of death among young people in their twenties and thirties.

In Africa, however, HIV has, from the very start, spread mainly through the heterosexual population, probably because the predominant HIV sub-type in this part of the world is 'better' at infecting the cells that line the vagina. By the end of 1994, the WHO (World Health Organisation) estimated that worldwide approximately 4.5 million people had developed AIDS. With no cure in sight at present, it has become clear that people need to be aware that they are at risk of developing an HIV infection if they have unprotected sex.

The chances of contracting HIV through unprotected anal intercourse—where delicate tissues are more likely to tear—are much higher than through vaginal intercourse. The risk is also greater if other STDs that cause breaks in the skin, such as herpes, are already present. To understand how HIV infects the body, and how AIDS develops, it helps to understand, in simple terms, the workings of the body's immune system. Those that penetrate the first line of defences—such as the skin—are then detected and destroyed by the immune system. This system consists of billions of cells that enable us to fight off infections. Some, called macrophages, roam through the bloodstream and tissues in search of invading micro-organisms and eat them. Macrophages also 'inform' other cells of the immune system that there are invaders inside the body. First on the scene are the helper T-cells which alert the entire immune system to launch an all-out attack on the specific invader.

The cells that HIV selects for invasion are the helper T-cells, key elements in the immune response. HIV viruses take over the genetic material of these cells and replicate themselves, destroying the helper T-cells in the process. Although the body produces antibodies to combat the growing HIV menace, the immune system is gradually worn down over the years as the number of key helper T-cells decreases. Eventually, one or more of these diseases completely overwhelms the body, leading to the death of the AIDS sufferer. Since the disease was only identified relatively recently, long-term studies have not yet been able to identify which of the people who are HIV-positive will not develop AIDS. However, men and women who are infected with HIV, and who do develop AIDS, typically progress through four noticeable stages.

a) *Initial acute infection*: These symptoms can include general body aches, sore throat, fever, chills, widespread rash, oral and genital ulceration and swollen lymph glands. However, it is very important to realise that these are non-specific symptoms which could indicate other mild viral infections apart from HIV.

b) *Asymptomatic HIV infection*: During the asymptomatic (without symptoms) phase, which lasts on average up to 10 years or longer, a person looks and feels completely healthy, although the virus is actively replicating inside the body. But he or she may suffer from lymphadenopathy: swelling of the lymph nodes (or glands)—centres for fighting infections—found in the neck, armpits and groin. During this phase a person is infective and may pass on the virus to other people without realising that he or she is infected. Some people—known as non-progressors—have remained symptom-free for many years, and only time will tell if they will ever develop AIDS. If they do not, it may be the result of their particular lifestyle, the type of HIV they were infected with, or the potency of their individual immune system.

c) *Symptomatic HIV infection*: These include the fungal infection thrush (candidiasis) in the mouth—in healthy women thrush is a common infection of the vagina. Other common symptoms are skin complaints, weight loss, bouts of tiredness, diarrhoea and sweating. Men or women may pass on the infection unknowingly at this stage, unaware that they are infected.

d) *Advanced symptoms of AIDS*: As the symptoms of AIDS develop, there is a fixed set of symptoms and diseases that characterise the syndrome. Some are worsening of the symptoms experienced during symptomatic HIV infection: fevers and night sweats, and progressive weight loss. Opportunistic infections, such as *Pneumocystis carinii pneumonia* (PCP), extensive herpes, tuberculosis or encephalitis, which eventually prove fatal, are also AIDS-defining. HIV may infect brain cells too, causing dementia. Once a person has AIDS—with one or more of these specific conditions and HIV—it will probably prove fatal at some time in the next four years.

If someone is worried that they may have been infected with HIV, there are a number of people to talk to. A helpline such as that run by the Terrence Higgins Trust or the National AIDs Helpline might be the first stop. At a GUM clinic or at an HIV/AIDS advice centre, there should be a counsellor or doctor with whom to talk through the issues, to discuss the possible advantages and disadvantages of testing, and to enable someone to come to an informed decision as to whether or not to take a test to see if they have an HIV infection. If a person does decide to be tested, a blood sample is taken and sent to a laboratory for testing.

The blood test identifies the presence or absence of antibodies against HIV. If the test is negative it means that the person is probably not infected with HIV, although antibodies can take some time to appear in the blood (more than six weeks) and a further, later blood test may be suggested. If the test is positive, it will be repeated with a more sensitive test to check its correctness before the patient is informed of the result. If it is still positive it means that the person is infected with HIV—they are HIV-positive. Once the test result comes through, a doctor or counsellor at the clinic will inform a patient in person whether the test was positive or negative.

Many people react with shock and despair when they discover they are HIV-positive. Usually clinic staff will refer them to suitable counsellors and self-help groups. If an individual has told his or her trustworthy friends or relatives, they can be of great help in providing support, and helping to plan for the future, although unfortunately some people have a more hostile reaction. People with HIV can lead normal working and social lives and may well appear healthy for a number of years.

Since the late 1980s, the drug AZT has been used to slow the progression of HIV infection, although recent research has shown that its benefits may be limited when used alone. However, many centres use AZT as part of a cocktail of drugs (combination therapy) employed to inhibit the development of the HIV infection. Patients also receive antibiotics to prevent AIDS-related infections. People with symptomatic HIV or with full-blown AIDS are given specific treatment according to the condition, although there comes a time when the infections are no longer treatable. Following are the common sexually transmitted diseases:

— *Chlamydia*: Chlamydial infections occur in both men and women and are transmitted mainly by vaginal intercourse, or less commonly by anal intercourse or oral sex. *C. trachomatis* is the main infective agent in mucopurulent cervicitis (MPC) in women and non-gonococcal urethritis (NGU) in men. A high proportion of women with chlamydia do not have MPC or any of its symptoms.

— *Mucopurulent cervicitis (MPC)*: The main symptom of MPC is a discharge from the cervix, although many women do not notice that it is any different from a normal vaginal discharge. If MPC is diagnosed (by seeing a red cervix and pus discharge), it can be treated with antibiotics. Untreated, *C. trachomatis* and other micro-organisms that cause MPC can spread to other parts of the reproductive system and may cause pelvic inflammatory disease.

— *Non-gonococcal urethritis (NGU)*: Over 50 per cent of cases of NGU are caused by *Chlamydia trachomatis*. Symptoms of NGU include a clear or pus-like discharge from the penis, and pain or a burning feeling when urinating. Some men, however, have very mild symptoms or none at all. NGU is usually treated by antibiotics, although the type of treatment depends on what type of agent has caused the disease. Female partners should also be treated, as transmission of NGU may cause MPC or PID, and the couple should refrain from sexual contact until both of them are cured. Untreated, NGU can cause painful inflammation of the epididymis (part of the testis) or a urethral stricture, a narrowing of the urethra.

— *Genital herpes*: Once a person has become infected by herpes simplex, the virus stays inside the body for life, although it may remain inactive for much or all of that time, and some infected people never show any symptoms at all. Genital herpes is highly infectious. However, it appears that the virus may sometimes be passed on by someone who is infected but shows no outwards signs of infection. Oral sex may sometimes cause infection if the person performing the act has cold sores, as may the use of infected sex toys, such as vibrators. Some three to six days after infection, a person who develops symptoms of herpes first feels irritation or burning in the genitals before small, clear blisters appear on the penis or vulva. After this first occurrence of herpes, one-third of sufferers have no further flare-ups, another third have a few further episodes, and the remaining third have frequent attacks—more than three times a year. Recurrences may be triggered by sunbathing, stress or sometimes sexual intercourse.

A tingling feeling in the genitals is often an early warning sign that an attack is about to start. Subsequent attacks may be less painful than the first because the body starts to build up resistance, but men and women who experience repeated occurrences of genital herpes commonly find the condition distressing and painful. There is no 'cure' for genital herpes because the virus cannot be eliminated. If a sexual partner has been diagnosed as having genital herpes, condoms should always be used to prevent infection of the other partner.

However, the antiviral drug acyclovir is very effective in reducing the pain and duration of the first attack. In patients with frequent, long-term attacks, the use of acyclovir will reduce or abolish the attacks while the drug is taken. Genital herpes passed from a mother to her newborn child can cause severe illness and possibly death. For this reason, mothers who suffer an attack when they are about to give birth may be delivered by caesarean section and acyclovir given to the infant.

Along with antiviral drugs, there are several self-help strategies that may help alleviate the effects of an attack of genital herpes.

— Avoid sexual contact during an attack and until two or three days after blisters have healed completely.
— Wear loose-fitting cotton underwear.
— Take aspirin or ibuprofen to reduce pain.
— Wash the genitals regularly during an infection and pat them dry with a towel—this should be washed afterwards.
— Wash hands carefully after touching the affected area, in order to avoid spreading the infection to other parts of the body.
— After swimming, do not sit around wearing damp swimwear.
— *Genital warts*. Genital warts, however, appear on the genitals or around the anus and must be treated medically. Soft and generally painless, genital warts

range in form from individual small, flat bumps to pink or greyish-white growths that resemble tiny cauliflowers and can form an extensive covering. Genital warts are caused by certain types of the human papilloma virus (HPV) that can be transmitted by sexual contact. Over 60 per cent of partners of individuals who have genital warts will develop the disease.

However, it may take weeks, months or even years before signs and symptoms appear, and even before they do, the virus can be passed on to a new partner. Sufferers may experience embarrassment about their warts, and possibly discomfort. They should, however, seek treatment as soon as possible. In addition, women should seek diagnosis if their partner has genital warts because, even if they themselves show no signs of infection, the warts may be concealed inside the vagina or on the cervix.

Various types of treatment are available, including application of podophyllin, a caustic chemical which erodes the warts (not to be used for pregnant women); liquid nitrogen, which is used to freeze the warts; or laser treatment to burn away the warts. However, no treatment can remove the virus from the body; it remains inactive within body tissues, but it may reactivate and genital warts may recur.

— *Gonorrhoea*: Gonorrhoea is one of the commonest STDs worldwide, although it is becoming uncommon in most Western countries. It is a highly infectious disease caused by the bacterium *Neisseria gonorrhoea,* which affects more men than women and is more prevalent among teenagers and young adults, especially those with numerous sexual partners. It is usually passed on by anal, vaginal or oral sex. Symptoms of gonorrhoea, when they occur, appear within two days to two weeks of getting the infection.

Male symptoms include a burning feeling on urination, followed by a milky discharge from the penis, which becomes thicker. However, some 10 per cent of men and 50 per cent of women show no initial symptoms. Untreated, gonorrhoea may spread to the prostate gland or the epididymis of the testis, causing inflammation and, possibly in the latter case, permanent sterility, although this is now rare. Women infected with gonorrhoea may also feel burning when urinating, although the most usual symptoms are vaginal discharge, dyspareunia and pelvic pain.

The problem is that, left untreated, the bacteria that cause gonorrhoea can travel through the reproductive system and cause PID, which can have serious consequences, including infertility. For this reason it is vital that, should a man discover he has gonorrhoea, he must tell his female partner or partners that they may have the infection, because it may remain hidden inside their body and cause further damage. Once diagnosed by taking a smear of discharge for microscopic examination, gonorrhoea is treated with a course of antibiotics. Women may also be given antibiotics that eliminate any chlamydia infection. Around a quarter of people with gonorrhoea also have chlamydia.

— *Hepatitis B*: Hepatitis is an inflammation of the liver caused by a number of different viruses. Hepatitis B is a form of the disease caused by the hepatitis B virus (HBV). A person infected with hepatitis may show no symptoms, but if symptoms do develop they usually include a flu-like illness, fever, loss of appetite, nausea, possibly jaundice (a yellowing of the skin and eyes) and a feeling of tenderness in the upper abdomen. One of the major routes of transmission of hepatitis B is through sexual activity, including oral sex and kissing. It can also be transmitted via blood, shared needles, unsterile tattooing and earpiercing, as well as from a mother to her newborn infant via her milk.

The reason for this is that the HBV can be found in most of the bodily fluids of an infected person, including semen, saliva and vaginal secretions, and it is highly infectious. The HBV can also be passed on from mother to foetus. Hepatitis B was once more common among male homosexuals, although it appears that heterosexual intercourse is now the main route for the sexual transmission of HBV, with having many partners the main risk factor. There is no specific treatment for hepatitis B, although rest, a good diet and avoiding alcohol should aid recovery. Vaccination against hepatitis B is available, but at present it is targeted at those most at risk, such as doctors, nurses, people with multiple sexual partners such as prostitutes, and intravenous drug users. The HBV persists and the person becomes a carrier, able to pass on the disease but not showing any symptoms. Carriers may also risk developing other liver diseases, such as cancer, which may lead to death.

— *Pelvic Inflammatory Disease (PID)*: Pelvic inflammatory disease (PID) is an inflammation of the female reproductive organs, especially the ovaries, fallopian tubes and uterus, and is a common cause of lower abdominal pain in women. PID is often caused by a sexually transmitted disease that has not been treated, often because it has shown no symptoms. Women with PID may have pain in the abdominal or pelvic regions, especially during or just after sex. However, many women with PID show no symptoms. Once diagnosed, PID is treated immediately with antibiotics; specific antibiotics can be prescribed once the micro-organism(s) causing the infection have been identified. Present and past sexual partners should also be treated to prevent further cases of infection. Left untreated, PID can cause infertility, or increase the risk of ectopic pregnancy—a pregnancy occurring inside the fallopian tube which has to be terminated to avoid harming the mother.

— *Pubic lice*: Another species of these tiny insects lives on and among the pubic hair of adults, feeding on blood and causing irritation and itching. These pubic lice are also known as crab lice or crabs because they have 'claws' which they use to grip the shafts of pubic hair in order to avoid being dislodged. Pubic lice are usually transmitted by sexual contact—they simply move from one person's pubic hair to his or her partner's—although they may also be spread by infected sheets or towels.

Infection can be confirmed by inspecting the pubic hair. If the pinhead-sized lice cannot be seen, their white eggs—called nits—may be visible, attached to the pubic hairs. Normal bathing or showering will not remove lice or their eggs. A special shampoo that contains insecticide is needed to do this. Bedding and towels should be washed in very hot water to prevent reinfection.

Syphilis is now less common because of effective treatment, although it is still a serious illness. In recent times, localised outbreaks of the disease have occurred among some groups of drug users who have turned to prostitution on a large scale to finance their habit. Primary and secondary syphilis are highly infectious and can be transmitted by most forms of sexual contact with an infected person including oral sex and kissing. Syphilis can also be transmitted across the placenta from mother to foetus, although this is now less common because of routine testing for syphilis during pregnancy. Syphilis is caused by the bacterium *Treponema pallidum,* which remains in the body indefinitely if not treated, causing a disease that follows three distinct stages.

The symptom of primary syphilis, which appears between 10 and 90 days after infection, is a painless ulcer that appears at the site of exposure—either on the genitals or around the anus or mouth—and heals within 6-10 weeks. In the following weeks, secondary syphilis develops. Its symptoms can include skin rashes, headache, sore throat, enlarged lymph nodes, mild fever, hair loss and flattened, wartlike growths that occur on moist areas around the genitals and anus. These symptoms disappear within a few weeks or months, and a person moves into the latent, symptomless phase of the disease. Some years after infection, some untreated people develop the tertiary, and most destructive, stage of the disease. Its effects include damage to the brain and nervous system, and to the cardiovascular (blood) system, which may cause mental disorders or even death. Progression to the latent and tertiary phases is unusual, however. If syphilis is diagnosed—by a blood test—in its primary, secondary or latent stages, the disease can be treated effectively with the antibiotic penicillin.

Symptoms of trichomoniasis include painful irritation of the vulva and vagina; an excessive, yellow, frothy discharge, with a foul smell; and possibly pain on urination. Some women show no symptoms, and T vaginalis may live inside the vagina for sometime without causing infection and then suddenly flare up and produce trichomoniasis symptoms. Although the disease is sexually transmitted, men rarely show symptoms. So a man may unwittingly pass on the disease, picked up months or years previously, to a new female partner, and she might erroneously think he has been unfaithful. Some men, however, develop NGU as a result of infection. Once diagnosed, trichomoniasis is treated with antibiotics.

GUM clinics

GUM (genito-urinary medicine) clinics, also sometimes known as special clinics, provide expert advice, diagnosis and treatment for suspected sexually transmitted diseases. Typically, they do not require referral of a patient from another doctor; the patient simply turns up at the clinic. Attitudes towards STDs and their treatment have been transformed in recent years.

Today, with far less stigma attached to them, a more enlightened attitude is taken towards STDs, and this is reflected in the workings of GUM clinics. The welcoming, relaxed atmosphere found in the majority of GUM clinics puts most people at their ease. Health advisers and psychologists are available to help patients deal with the psychological aspects of sexual infections such as the HIV virus and genital herpes. After an initial examination by a doctor who specialises in STDs, the patient is given a full set of tests to screen for a number of different STDs. This is because, even when a patient only appears to have symptoms of one particular STD, that STD may be accompanied by others even though the symptoms of any other STDs may not be clear.

Testing may involve taking a sample from inside the vagina or from the cervix, or just inside the male urethra—the tube that runs inside the penis. Or it may require a urine sample or a blood test. This often takes the form of antibiotics, but again, it depends on the particular disease. A doctor will also ask about an individual's sexual history to ascertain whether he or she is at risk of further infections, or whether they have a sexual partner or partners who will also need treatment to prevent the disease spreading further.

DRUGS, ADDICTION AND SEX

There are hundreds of different drugs available to us. We take some—including alcohol, cigarettes, caffeine (in coffee and tea), cannabis and other 'soft' drugs—to help us relax or to relieve stress; these all have some sort of physiological effect. We take other drugs—including tranquillisers, sleeping pills and numerous other prescribed drugs—to help relieve pain, or to cure or relieve the symptoms of an illness or disease. Unknown to many people, a number of prescription drugs may affect their sex lives (for instance, by reducing their desire for sex, reducing a woman's vaginal lubrication, or making it difficult for a man to obtain an erection) especially if the drugs are taken over a prolonged period. If a man or woman feels that a prescribed drug may be affecting their sexuality, they should consult their doctor to find out whether there is any alternative type of medication available.

Unfortunately, there is so much ignorance (and fear) surrounding the question of drugs and how they can affect different individuals or groups of people that many people are unaware—or alternatively exaggerate—how a drug can affect their health. Although it is impossible to generalise about either drugs or drug users, there are some helpful guidelines that can be followed in regard to the most common drugs and their effect on our sexual health.

Physiologically, alcohol is a depressant of the central nervous system, the body's control and coordination centre. Initially the effect is one of relaxation, but as the amount of alcohol in the blood increases, a person typically becomes more uninhibited and starts to lose motor (movement) control, until, if they get very drunk, they suffer memory loss and blackouts and may even finally fall into a coma. What physiological effects does alcohol consumption have on sex? As the gatekeeper in Shakespeare's *Macbeth* explained so clearly, alcohol 'provoketh the desire but taketh away the performance': it is believed to be a sexual stimulant but in fact has the opposite effect.

Drinking may make people believe that they 'feel' more sexual and are more ready to take part in sexual acts, but it makes them physiologically less sexual. In men, alcohol suppresses erections and causes retarded (late) ejaculation; when copious amounts of alcohol have been consumed, there may be—despite the desire—no erection at all. Many women apparently feel sexier the more they drink, despite the fact that physiologically the opposite seems to be occurring: alcohol reduces blood flow to the vagina and vulva, delays orgasms, makes the orgasm less intense, and interferes with vaginal lubrication. Chronic alcohol use and alcohol addiction can cause all types of sexual problems. In addition, chronic drinkers of both sexes may find that they wake up with a partner they do not remember going to bed with; forget to use any form of contraception; pick up a sexually transmitted disease through promiscuity; or show violent behaviour towards husbands, wives or partners.

FEMALE HEALTH

Women are probably more aware of the workings of their repreoductive organs than men are of theirs because of the monthly sequence of events that occurs during the fertile years and which culminates in menstruation. Sometimes, the internal mechanism controlling the menstrual cycle can go wrong and a woman suffers menstrual problems. Other parts of her reproductive system, such as the ovaries or breasts, may also be affected by disorders. Fortunately, women today have a greater chance than ever before of successful treatment of reproductive system disorders. But they should be aware of the signs and symptoms that could give them early warning of possible disorders of their reproductive organs, so that they can seek medical advice as soon as possible.

Menstruation

Menstruation is a normal, healthy event that happens about once a month for many years of a woman's life. It marks the end of one menstrual cycle and the beginning of the next.

Each menstrual cycle includes the release of an egg from an ovary and the preparation of the uterus to receive a fertilised egg. This is menstruation, or the period, which normally lasts about five days, but may last as little as two days or longer than a week. More than any other biological function, menstruation has been and may still be, misunderstood and surrounded by superstition. In certain cultures women are still regarded as 'unclean' during their periods. And even in the 'sophisticated' developed world, the belief still persists among many men that any changes in a woman's behaviour before or during menstruation only confirm that women are the 'irrational' and 'weaker' sex.

Tampton is a tight roll of cotton or rayon which is inserted into the vagina, where it expands to fit naturally and absorbs the mestrual flow. Tampons are available in a range of absorbencies to suit different menstrual flows. The advantage of tampons is that they are inconspicuous, and they can be worn during swimming and other forms of exercise. However, they may cause leakage if the flow is particularly heavy, in which case some women may prefer to use a pad as well. Tampons should not be left in the vagina for more than six hours for reasons of hygiene, and also because of the increased risk of toxic shock syndrome. Some women prefer to use sanitary pads for overnight protection, rather than leaving a tampon in place for that length of time.

Sanitary towels are soft cotton pads absorbent on one side and waterproof on the other. They are worn inside the panties so that the absorbent part absorbs blood as it leaves the vagina. Modern pads are increasingly slimline and absorbent, with a 'press-on' panel to attach them firmly to the panties. Pads should be changed regularly for reasons of hygiene and to avoid the risk of odours.

Many women have years of menstrual cycles and periods which cause few if any problems. But the complexity of the internal mechanism that controls menstruation does cause problems for some women. These may be very mild or they may be so painful and disruptive that they upset a woman's life for at least part of each month. Although some women may well conform to the 'ideal' 28-day menstrual cycle, with a period that lasts five days and presents no problems, most do not.

Some suffer from emotional and physical symptoms before their periods start, or pains and cramps during their periods; others have very heavy periods, or irregular periods, or miss periods altogether. All or most of these conditions are treatable either by medications which modify the hormonal mechanism that controls the menstrual cycle; or by self-help techniques, such as a better diet and more exercise. A woman of any age who is concerned in any way about menstrual problems should consult her doctor. Many women notice certain physical and emotional changes which indicate that another menstrual cycle is reaching completion. Collectively, the symptoms that women may experience are known as premenstrual syndrome or PMS (previously known as premenstrual tension or PMT). They are probably related to fluctuations in the levels of the hormones oestrogen and progesterone, and possibly levels of prostaglandins, in the latter part of the menstrual cycle, which have an effect on the brain.

A woman may experience one or more of these symptoms such as depression and irritability, mood swings, headache, tiredness, dizziness or disturbances of vision, nausea, breast tenderness, fluid retention (feeling bloated), resulting in a temporary increase in weight, a feeling of clumsiness, a low tolerance to alcohol, a craving for sugary foods, back pain and breathlessness.

Symptoms of PMS often first appear when a woman is in her twenties or thirties. There is no cure as such, but the following precautions may provide relief from the symptoms. Each woman is different, however, and a method that works well for one individual may not be at all effective for another:

— taking regular exercise;
— changing to a healthier diet, with more fibre;
— eating less salt, to reduce fluid retention;
— reducing caffeine and alcohol intake, since both can aggravate PMS symptoms;

— taking evening primrose oil (which contains an essential fatty acid, gamma-linolenic acid);
— taking vitamin B6 and vitamin E;
— aromatherapy involving adding oils of lemon grass or lavender to bath water;
— the pill is prescribed by doctors for some PMS sufferers because it stops the normal menstrual cycle;
— taking diuretic drugs (on prescription) to relieve fluid retention;
— yoga and/or meditation; and
— the Alexander technique.

Most women, at some time in their lives, experience menstrual pain or cramps in the lower abdomen and sometimes lower back, just before or in the first couple of days of their period. There are two forms of dysmenorrhoea: primary and secondary. Most women who experience menstrual pain are suffering from primary dysmenorrhoea. Typically this starts some two or three years after a girl's first period and is most frequent in the 17-25 age group. By their late twenties, or after having children, many women who previously suffered from painful periods no longer experience any menstrual pain.

Secondary dysmenorrhoea are period pains that begin during adult life and are the result of some other disorder such as pelvic inflammatory disease, endometriosis or fibroids. Conditions like these need to be diagnosed and treated by a doctor. The pains are believed to be caused by prostaglandins, substances that, among other effects, cause contraction of the muscles in the wall of the uterus, most notably during childbirth. Excessive secretion of prostaglandins results in a tightening of these muscles, which squeezes their blood vessels, temporarily cuts off their supply of blood and oxygen, and results in cramping pains.

In dealing with cramps, it is worth trying different remedies to see which is effective:

— aspirin, ibuprofen or other antiprostaglandin painkillers;
— exercises that increase blood flow to the pelvis and uterus;

— back massage;
— resting with a hot water bottle on the lower abdomen;
— taking evening primrose oil;
— masturbating to orgasm—which also increases blood flow to the uterus;
— in more severe cases, a doctor may prescribe an oral contraceptive, which relieves symptoms by suppressing ovulation.

Menorrhagia can have various causes. In some women, an imbalance of the hormones oestrogen and progesterone produces a thicker-than-normal endometrium (lining of the uterus), thus increasing the menstrual flow during a period. In others, uterine disorders such as fibroids or polyps may cause excessive bleeding. An investigation of the uterus called a dilation and curettage (D&C) may be used to determine the cause of menorrhagia. If there are no uterine problems and the heavy bleeding does not cause anaemia (or if it causes anaemia mild enough to be counteracted by regular iron supplements), the condition may be left untreated. In cases that require treatment, there are several possibilities. For younger women, especially those who wish to have children in future, hormones may be used to control bleeding. In cases of severe and persistent menorrhagia in older women, a hysterectomy may be considered. Menorrhagia may also occur in some women who use the IUD (Intrauterine device) for contraception. If the bleeding is not much heavier than usual, this should cause no problems, but if it is severe, a woman may wish to consider an alternative form of contraception.

Women who do not experience the 'normal' pattern of menstruation are said to be suffering from irregular periods. This can take one of three forms i.e., a woman may experience considerable differences in the amount of blood she loses from one period to the next; a woman may find that the duration of bleeding varies greatly from one period to the next, so that, for example, one period lasts for one day, and another period for 10 days; and a woman may notice that the time between one period and the next is very variable, sometimes lasting for months and at other times for weeks. Irregular periods can have various causes. They are common and natural, in teenage girls whose periods have just started and in older women who are approaching the menopause. If a woman is not ovulating regularly because of hormonal problems, this may cause her periods to be both late and heavy and she should consult her doctor. Other causes of irregular periods include stress, frequent travel across time zones, and sometimes disorders of the uterus.

The most common cause of vaginal bleeding is during a period, when the lining of the uterus is shed though the vagina. But if vaginal bleeding is irregular, it may be caused by a disorder that requires medical attention. Tiny spots of blood appearing in the panties or on toilet paper between periods—known as spotting—can be the result of using an IUD as a contraceptive, or taking certain types of contraceptive pills. Normally it is harmless, but a woman may want to discuss this with her doctor. Bleeding after intercourse may be a sign of erosion of the cervix, or another condition affecting the neck of the uterus, which should be referred immediately to a doctor. If a woman has passed her menopause has not had a period for six months and she has vaginal bleeding, she should see her doctor as it might indicate a cancer of the uterus or cervix. However, the bleeding may be due simply to the vagina itself becoming dry and losing a little blood, a condition that may be helped by using a hormonal cream. If a woman has spotting during pregnancy she should see her doctor, especially in the later stages, when it may indicate a problem.

If a woman's periods have never started, or they are interrupted for more than three months, she is suffering from amenorrhoea, or absence of periods. There are two types of amenorrhoea: primary and secondary.

Primary amenorrhoea occurs in young women who have never had a period. This may be because late menarche (the onset of menstruation) runs in the family, in which case it is a matter of waiting. It may result from a girl being underweight if, for example, she undertakes intensive training in dance or has an eating disorder such as anorexia nervosa or alternatively it may be caused by a hormonal problem. If a girl has not started her periods by the age of 16, her parents should seek medical help.

The commonest causes of secondary amenorrhoea are pregnancy—which should be eliminated as a cause before treatment for any other conditions is implemented—and breastfeeding. Periods may also cease if a woman is stressed or depressed; if she takes the type of frequent exercise that results in excessive weight loss; if she suffers from anorexia nervosa and has too little body fat; if she has a hormonal imbalance; or if she has been using certain types of drugs over long periods. Obviously, treatment of amenorrhoea depends on its particular cause. In the case of pregnancy and breastfeeding, periods should start when these cease. The causes of stress and depression or the need to exercise excessively may be alleviated through counselling or self-help groups.

Breast health

Common breast disorders include breast pain and tenderness, usually just before a period, which normally requires no treatment; and breast lumps, which as many as half of all women experience at some time during their life. In a minority of cases, a lump may be cancerous, requiring treatment by surgery. The sooner it is discovered, the greater the chance of a successful cure. This is why it is recommended that women over 20 examine their breasts monthly and report significant changes to their doctor. For a quarter of breast pain sufferers, the pain is severe enough to affect their lives. It may stop them from sleeping; inhibit their normal relationship with a partner because they cannot bear their breasts being touched; prevent them from enjoying sports; or make them worry all the time that people will bump into them accidentally and cause them pain.

There are several ways in which a woman can alleviate breast pain or tenderness: wear a supportive, properly fitting bra; wear a bra at night to support the breasts when asleep; take a mild painkiller, such as aspirin or ibuprofen;

take evening primrose oil; take vitamin B6. Most women find that breast pain is cyclical, occurring in the week or so before their period. Cyclical breast pain is probably caused by hormonal fluctuations that are taking place at this point in the menstrual cycle. These cause the breasts to retain excess fluid, making them feel full and sore. Some women find that breast pain happens at any time during the month. However, neither form of breast pain is likely to be caused by any serious disorder. Tenderness may also occur during early pregnancy and during breastfeeding. And while some contraceptive pills make breast pain worse, it has been found that some low-dose contraceptive pills reduce breast tenderness. There is always the worry that breast pain means breast cancer. In fact, breast cancer is normally painless and not connected with breast tenderness.

Every woman should regularly examine her breasts for any changes or irregularities. This way she becomes so familiar with their usual texture that she can rapidly identify anything abnormal. Her doctor, on the other hand, may detect only relatively large breast lumps. The best time for women to examine their breasts is two or three days after their period finishes, when the breasts are usually at their least tender. Most women who examine their breasts do so by following this sequence:

— visual inspection in front of a mirror to took for any changes in breast size or shape; also, visual inspection with the arms raised to took for dimpling of breast tissue;

— manual inspection of all of both breasts while lying down.

Some women feel their breasts in the bath or shower, because lubrication by soap enables the fingers to slide easily over the breasts.

When a woman is carrying out breast self-examination she should look out for any of the following changes or irregularities that might indicate a breast disorder:

— any lumps or bumps in the breast or armpit—remembering that in many women, soft, sore lumps appear and disappear just before their period every month, and also that 80-90 per cent of unusual lumps are subsequently found to be benign and not cancerous;

— any changes in the shape of the breasts, especially bulges on the surface;
— the appearance of 'orange peel' skin;
— any swelling in the upper arm or armpit;
— any discharge or bleeding from a nipple;
— inversion (turning inwards) of a nipple, if it normally projects outwards;
— any dimpling or other changes to the areola, the darker area of skin around the nipple.

If a woman does notice something unusual, or is concerned with anything to do with breast health, she should get in touch with her doctor immediately. He or she may recommend further investigation using mammography or a biopsy. Mammography is a simple diagnostic technique used to check a woman's breast health. It involves exposing the breasts to low doses of X-rays in order to produce a mammogram, an X-ray photograph, of the breast's tissues. This technique can detect breast tumours as small as 0.5cm (1/5in) across—the size of a small pea—which are too small to be felt during self-examination. If a tumour is cancerous, the cancer is much less likely to have spread to other parts of the body.

Mammography is carried out using a special X-ray machine. A radiographer positions the patient so that her breast is placed on the machine and gently 'sandwiched' between an upper plastic cover and the lower X-ray plate, which contains the film. This may feel a bit uncomfortable, but it does not take very long and flattening the breast produces a better image. If a breast contains a tumour, it will show up on the mammogram in about 85 per cent of cases. The doctor will carry out a biopsy to determine whether the turnout is malignant (cancerous) or not. If the turnout is smaller than 0.5cm in diameter, it will probably not show up on the mammogram.

The United States' breast screening by mammography is recommended from the age of 40: every one to two years for

40 to 49-year-olds, and every year for the over-50s. In the UK, it is felt that regular mammography screening for younger women does not significantly reduce the death rate from breast cancer and regular screening by mammography is recommended only for women over 50. However, younger women whose immediate female relatives have had breast cancer and who are therefore at greater risk, are recommended to have regular mammography even before they reach 40. Most breast lumps are benign (not cancerous) and are caused by one of the following three common conditions.

Fibroadenosis is an increase in the glandular and fibrous tissue of the breast, possibly due to fluctuating hormone levels. It results in breast tenderness, pain, swelling and, occasionally, cysts.

Cysts are fluid-filled lumps which may result from the blockage of a milk duct. Usually they are drained by needle aspiration, and the fluid is tested to check that no cancerous cells are present if the cysts remain. Fibroadenomas are benign breast tumours, most common in women under 30. They are firm, round, painless lumps usually 1-5cm in diameter and can be moved under the skin.

A biopsy is a diagnostic test which involves removing a small sample of tissue from the suspect area and examining it for cancerous cells. If a turnout is found to be malignant, the doctor can discuss the best course of action with her or his patient.

Breast cancer is the commonest type of cancer among women, affecting around one in 20 women in Western Europe, North America and Australia. It is rare in women under 30, and more common in women over 50. This age distribution should not mean that younger women can feel complacent and not examine their breasts regularly. Women who are believed to be at a higher risk of developing breast cancer include:

— women with close female relatives who developed breast cancer;
— women who have never had children, or had their first child in their thirties or forties;

— women whose periods began early and/or whose menopause was late;
— women whose diet is high in animal fats. Studies have indicated that there is a direct relationship between the low incidence of breast cancer in Japan, Thailand and the Philippines and the low levels of animal fats found in the diets of these countries.

Breast cancer usually starts as a single lump in the breast, most commonly in the upper, outer part of the breast (closest to the armpit). Other signs and symptoms include swelling and dimpling of the breast and discharge from the nipple. If a lump is found to be cancerous, further tests—blood tests, X-rays and bone scans—are carried out to see if the cancer has spread, in order to determine what kind of treatment would be best. The initial treatment for breast cancer is the removal of part or all of the breast. In the past, the entire breast was removed as a matter of routine; today, less extensive and less disfiguring surgery is often just as effective.

The type of surgery depends on the type of cancer, whether it has spread to other parts of the body, and the age of the woman. Following surgery, she may also receive radiotherapy and/or chemotherapy to destroy any cancer that may remain. Surgeons generally remove as little of the breast as possible. If the turnout is discovered in its early stages, most surgeons will perform a lumpectomy. This involves removing the turnout and its surrounding tissues, and some of the underarm lymph glands, to leave a small scar and depression in the breast.

Partial mastectomy procedure removes the segment of breast tissue containing the tumour, leaving a visible scar and the breast smaller than before.

In simple mastectomy, the whole breast is removed but the lymph glands and underlying chest muscles are left in place. The breast may be reconstructed later by a procedure known as mammoplasty.

Subcutaneous mastectomy involves removing the inner tissue of the breast but leaving the skin and nipple intact. A silicone implant is then inserted under the skin so as to give the impression of a complete breast. Like a simple mastectomy, it leaves a scar across the chest. Some women may opt for breast reconstruction at the same time as, or after, the operation, in which case the breast is 'rebuilt' and a silicone implant is inserted under the skin.

Women who have major breast surgery may find it difficult to come to terms with the fact that they have lost all or most of one of their breasts. However, the better the counselling they receive before and after the operation and the more they are kept informed, the less likely women are to experience feelings of depression or despair. Where a whole breast has been removed, some women choose to use an external prosthesis which slips inside the bra. Alternatively, some women opt for breast reconstruction. Many women may also worry that their cancer might return. They may be helped by counselling or by self-help groups. Some doctors also recommend amendments to diet and other lifestyle changes.

Breast surgery need not necessarily mean that a woman loses her breast shape, even though part of the breast has been removed. The surgeon uses skin and fat from a site near the removed breast to rebuild the breast, inserting the implant to give it shape.

Many women are offered an artificial breast or prosthesis that fits into their bra and balances the remaining breast. It can give a woman confidence after her operation, because there is no external sign that she has had a mastectomy; and, by balancing the other breast it prevents shoulder and back pain produced by compensating for less weight on one side of the body.

Disorders of the ovaries

The ovaries are the primary female sex organs. The location of the ovaries deep in the abdominal cavity means that any ovarian disorders tend to be 'silent' initially, without obvious initial signs or symptoms. The main conditions affecting the ovaries are ovarian cysts and less commonly, cancer. Ovarian cysts are common and are abnormal swellings of the ovary. Inside a woman's ovary each month, an egg develops within its bag-like follicle. In the middle of the menstrual cycle, the follicle bursts and the egg starts on its journey towards the uterus. Sometimes a follicle falls to rupture and this is the most common cause of cysts. The vast majority of cysts are benign rather than malignant.

However, some enlarge and become solid and may cause disturbances in the menstrual cycle, unfamiliar pains and discomfort in the abdomen (which may also become swollen), and possibly pain during intercourse. If a woman has any of these symptoms, she should see her doctor. Cysts are usually discovered by pelvic examination, when the doctor feels the area around the ovaries and uterus, and confirmed by ultrasound or laparoscopy (examination through a viewing tube). Polycystic Ovarian Syndrome (PCOS) is caused by an imbalance in the hormones released by the pituitary gland that causes the development of eggs inside the ovary. This results in a thickening in the outer layer of the ovary and the formation of tiny cysts around its outside. Women with PCOS may not know anything is wrong until they try to get pregnant. PCOS can be treated with drugs which restore the normal hormonal balance, although the specific treatment depends on whether or not a woman wants to become pregnant.

Ovarian cancer

Cancer of the ovary is comparatively rare, but it kills more women than cancers of the uterus and cervix combined, mainly because it is difficult to detect in its early stages. However, if it is diagnosed early the outlook is optimistic. Women are more likely to develop ovarian cancer after the menopause. It also appears that the risk is increased if a woman has never had children; if there is a history of ovarian cancer in her close family; if she has a history of cancer of the breast or uterus, or of the rectum; and if she is overweight. Breast-feeding and taking the Pill appear to lower the risk. Ovarian cancer can develop in one or both ovaries. Typically, there are few signs or symptoms initially.

When the cancer is more widespread, a woman may suffer from stomach upsets, abdominal pain and flatulence and may have abnormal bleeding from the vagina or abdominal swelling. These symptoms may, of course, be due to another condition, so a woman needs to visit her doctor for an assessment. If a pelvic examination reveals a swelling, a laparoscopy (using a viewing instrument to look inside the abdomen), or laparotomy (opening up the abdomen) can be used to make a diagnosis. If confirmed, ovarian cancer in its early stages can be treated by oophorectomy; or by the removal of the ovaries, fallopian tubes and uterus, if at a later stage.

Oophorectomy is the surgical removal of one or both of the ovaries, usually because of ovarian cancer, but sometimes because of a large ovarian cyst and also sometimes as part of hysterectomy. For younger women, especially if they want to have children, the prospect of having both ovaries removed can be particularly upsetting because it means that menopause comes early. Where possible, surgeons attempt to perform a partial oophorectomy in women of this age group so that normal ovarian function is maintained.

However, if both ovaries have to be removed, younger women will experience a premature menopause. They can be given hormone replacement therapy to mimic the effects of hormones released by the ovary and thereby minimise the symptoms of menopause, but of course this will not restore their ability to have children.

Disorders of the uterus (womb) are among the commonest reasons for women to consult their doctor. Apart from menstrual disorders, other conditions that affect the uterus include growths that may be benign or cancerous. In the past, hysterectomy (removal of the uterus) was commonly used as a cure for many uterine complaints, but today a wider range of less drastic treatments are used where hysterectomy is not deemed necessary.

The most common type of tumour found inside the human body, fibroids vary from pea to tennis ball-sized, although in some cases they can become as big as a grapefruit. Small fibroids produce no symptoms, but as they grow they sometimes cause heavy periods. If fibroids are large they may distort the uterus; they can cause back pain, abdominal discomfort and frequent urination; and they may, in some women, cause infertility. Fibroids are diagnosed by pelvic examination and ultrasound scanning. Small fibroids require no treatment, but larger ones can be removed so that they do not cause infertility. Where fibroids are large and numerous, a hysterectomy may be required.

Medical therapy that suppresses oestrogen production may also be used as an alternative means of treating fibroids. These are small, benign growths from the wall of the uterus that protrude into its inner cavity. Most common among women in their late thirties or forties, polyps can result in cramps and irregular periods. If they cause problems they are usually investigated and removed by dilation and curettage.

During a menstrual period, the endometrium passes out of a woman's body through her vagina. But in some cases it seems that fragments of the endometrium pass in the 'wrong' direction along the fallopian tubes and into the pelvic cavity, causing the condition known as endometriosis. The small fragments of endometrium form cysts. Each month, during the menstrual cycle, these cysts respond to changes in hormone levels by increasing in size and bleeding, as if they were still inside the uterus. But blood cannot escape from the cysts, and they slowly enlarge, causing inflammation and pain. Endometriosis occurs most commonly in women aged between 25 and 40, and in women who are childless. Between 30 and 40 per cent of women with endometriosis experience infertility.

The commonest symptoms of endometriosis are heavy and extremely painful periods, back pain, diarrhoea and blood in the faeces. If cysts are located behind the uterus, sexual intercourse may be painful. How endometriosis is treated depends on how severe it is and the age of the patient. Hormonal treatment may be used to suppress normal menstruation so that the cysts shrink away. If a woman becomes pregnant, that may have the same effect. In more severe cases, the cysts may be removed surgically.

Prolapse happens when the ligaments and pelvic muscles holding the uterus in place are stretched by childbirth, or become weakened after menopause. Women often first notice the condition because they experience the sensation of something falling out of the vagina. If symptoms become annoying and the cervix has not descended too far into the vagina, a rubber device can be fitted around the cervix to support the uterus.

In some cases an operation may be carried out to repair stretched tissues. If the prolapse is severe and the uterus is protruding from the vagina, a hysterectomy may be considered. The risk of prolapse can be diminished by activities such as pelvic floor exercises to strengthen the muscles that support the uterus; avoiding obesity and stopping smoking, because a chronic cough can aggravate the situation.

Two parts of the cancer can occur in uterus: the endometrium or the cervix. However, the term 'cancer of the uterus, usually refers to endometrial cancer. Endometrial cancer is most common in women who have been through menopause. The risk of developing the cancer appears to be greater in women who are overweight, have high blood pressure, have never had children and have experienced a delayed menopause. The commonest symptom of endometrial cancer in women whose periods have stopped is irregular vaginal bleeding, and any woman who experiences this after menopause should consult her doctor as soon as possible. In younger women, it may be indicated by heavy periods, bleeding between periods or bleeding after intercourse, although there may well be other causes of these symptoms. Radiotherapy, chemotherapy or hormonal therapy may also be used to ensure that all traces of cancer are destroyed. The outlook for women with endometrial cancer is generally good, if it is treated early.

Cervical cancer is most common cancer of the female reproductive system and one of the commonest cancers affecting women. It develops relatively slowly and, if detected at an early stage, has a good chance of being completely cured. Screening programmes for cervical cancer have reduced the death rate from the disease, even though its overall incidence has increased. Before cervical cancer appears, and before a woman notices any symptoms, the cells on the surface of the cervix undergo changes that make them appear increasingly abnormal. There is a risk of cancer developing and the greater the severity of these abnormal changes the greater the risk of developing cancer. Cervical cancer may cause an unusual vaginal discharge or a discharge containing blood in mid- menstrual cycle or after menopause.

The doctor or nurse inserts a spectrum into the vagina, to hold it open so that the cervix can be seen. A small spatula is then used to scrape a few cells from the cervix. This cell sample is smeared on to a microscope slide and sent to a laboratory to be examined under a microscope. If abnormal cells are found on her cervix, a woman will usually be referred for further investigation. Women are now recommended to have their first cervical smear at the age of 20 and continue to have them every three years for the rest of their lives, although some health authorities vary this advice.

A doctor will examine the cervix for abnormalities, using a colposcope. A small sample of tissue may also be taken for investigation in a procedure known as a biopsy. If the biopsy confirms precancerous change, this area of the cervix may be treated by laser, freezing, heating or removal of the tissue with an electric cutting wire (loop excision). If colposcopy indicates that precancerous changes extend into the cervical canal, or the severity is difficult to ascertain, the doctor will perform a cone biopsy. This involves using a laser or scalpel to cut a cone-shaped piece of tissue from the cervix, which can then be examined to see how far the precancerous changes have spread. In 90 per cent of cases, cone biopsy removes all affected tissue.

When cancer of the cervix is diagnosed, treatment will depend on the patient's age and how far the cancer has spread. Some patients are treated with radiotherapy, while in others a total hysterectomy is carried out; in severe cases, a radical hysterectomy may be performed, along with removal of lymph glands. Hysterectomy is the removal of the uterus, performed to treat serious uterine disorders. It is the commonest major operation for women in developed countries. Conditions for which a hysterectomy is usually considered include cancer of the endometrium or cervix, severe and prolonged heavy uterine bleeding (including menorrhagia), severe fibroids, severe uterine prolapse and extensive, painful endometriosis.

Total hysterectomy involves removing the uterus and cervix—and, if necessary, the ovaries and fallopian tubes. Radical hysterectomy—often performed to treat cancer—involves removing the uterus, cervix, surrounding tissues, lymph glands and part of the vagina.

In partial hysterectomy, a surgeon will remove the body of the uterus but leave the cervix. Some women prefer this because they feel it retains fuller sexual sensation.

After a hysterectomy woman will remain in hospital for a few days. Full recovery usually takes up to six weeks; during this time she should avoid over-exertion, but gentle exercise such as walking will help her recover her strength. She can expect light bleeding from her vagina at first and, if her ovaries were removed, she may have hot flushes because of the reduction in oestrogen—if the ovaries have been removed, she is now effectively past menopause. After four to six weeks, she will return to hospital for a check-up. If she and her partner wish, she can then resume sexual activity. In cases where symptoms such as heavy bleeding or pain were debilitating, a hysterectomy can leave a woman revitalised and able to enjoy her sex life more. To some extent, this may be caused by the sudden hormonal changes resulting from removal of the ovaries. However, removing the uterus alone, or uterus plus one ovary, will not cause these changes; and if both ovaries are removed, hormone replacement therapy should help.

Alternatively, depression may be due to anxiety about the effects of hysterectomy. Common worries include:

— fear of ageing rapidly or becoming 'unfeminine'. This is very unlikely if the ovaries are left in place. Again, if the ovaries have to be removed, HRT is generally highly effective;

— fear of losing enjoyment of sex. In fact, after a recovery period, most women should be able to enjoy sex as much as they did before; and

— fear of becoming obese. There is no direct link between hysterectomy and obesity.

Counselling before and after a hysterectomy may help to allay such fears. If the woman and her doctor have fully discussed the extent and possible consequences of the operation beforehand, post-operative problems are likely to be greatly reduced.

3
Family and Sexuality

In common mythology, a typical family consists of mum, dad and two to four children. In reality, however, the family is not a standard-sized and readily quantifiable unit. In fact, the term 'family' describes not only the members of the unit but also the complex interactions that take place between adults and children. True, this interactive unit may consist of two adults—a mum and dad—and their children. But a modern family is just as likely to consist of a single parent with one or more children, or be extended, by virtue of including stepchildren. Despite this range of family structures, it is possible to tease out common factors that affect the way we will behave sexually as adults.

The children of parents who adopt an encouraging, caring and loving attitude, and who have a positive and open view of sex, are more likely to grow up with a well-adjusted attitude to sexual matters. Similarly, if parents nurture and care for each other, their children are more likely to achieve a similar warmth and stability in their own relationships.

The tensions, emotions and interactions that exist between parents, between siblings, and between parents and siblings all serve to shape the family and influence a child's developing sexuality. A further dimension of the family is its dynamism. The family is constantly changing, and parents need to note and cope with these alterations because any change in one part of the family will have an effect on the other part. Such adjustments may be positive and planned—a child starting school, for example, or a new baby. Or they may be devastating and unexpected, divorce or bereavement being the greatest changes that can affect a family. While it is true that divorce rates are increasing, it would be unreasonable to state that all children of divorced parents are unable to forge successful long-term relationships of their own.

FAMILY DYNAMICS

The nature of any relationships within it are of vital importance, both in terms of the happiness and stability of its individual members and as a learning environment, where children can develop an understanding of how people relate to each other. It is important, therefore, that parents (and grandparents) monitor the way they treat their children. Although this may be obvious to most parents, maintaining a positive, affirmative attitude towards their children, especially when they are still young, will go a long way to ensuring the development of a happy, well-balanced young adult.

On the other hand, constantly criticising and denigrating a young child will often have a negative effect, producing a child who is cautious and lacking in confidence. This can all too easily lead to a lack of self-esteem which can have a damaging effect on the development of personality during adolescence and young adulthood, and on future relationships. Family relationships, and the overall shape of the family, do not remain static. From the first moment of interrelationship—be it the first meeting of two lovers, or the birth of a child to a single mother—the family ship begins its long voyage through uncharted waters.

Change and development within the family are ongoing processes. Parents need to monitor the dynamics of their family to ensure that the environment in which their children are growing up is appropriate, and that the family is developing in a positive and not a destructive way.

The relationship between a baby and his or her parents is initiated very soon after birth. Visual, verbal and physical interaction between parent and infant bring the two (or three) closer together, allowing mutual discovery and understanding to take place in a process known as bonding. Although bonding is mostly referred to in the context of a newborn baby and his or her parents, it remains an important aspect of the relationship with both parents throughout childhood and into adolescence.

Quality time can include talking, reading or playing together, or perhaps watching a favourite television programme together. For many parents and children a key bonding time is when a parent reads a bedtime story to the child. Since this can be such a close and warm time, many children still enjoy this long after they are able to read themselves. As children get older, especially during adolescence, the closeness between parents and child may apparently diminish. Talking about worries, stress, boyfriends, girlfriends and all sorts of other problems and interests helps adolescents pass through this challenging part of their life less painfully.

Role of parents

Parents and children spend many years in close proximity to each other within a family making it inevitable that children will be influenced by the way parents relate to each other and to other adults. Generally, if parents have a warm and loving relationship with each other, this influence will rub off on the children. Conversely, if their relationship is not close, and if there are constant arguments, then children may well grow up with a negative model of family relationships. Fathers and sons often form close relationships, and the father is generally the son's main role model.

Similarly, the closeness between most mothers and their daughters means that the girl will be influenced by the way that her mother relates to her partner and to other men. Overall, parents should always be aware of the messages—both overt and hidden—that they send constantly to their children in the matter of relationships, for these will often have a considerable influence over the way that children go on to relate to their partners as adults.

Siblings can be friends, and they can be allies (perhaps against their parents). They can teach, and learn, valuable lessons about sharing—possessions, love and space—and about the importance of loyalty. The better the relationships between siblings, the more confident each child is likely to feel about forming relationships with other people. Same-sex siblings have much to offer each other, whatever the age difference.

Girls can talk to their sisters about any number of subjects that they might find it difficult to discuss with parents. Having a sibling of the opposite sex has its value, too. For one thing, it is useful to develop an awareness from an early age of the differences between the sexes—both physical and emotional. Young people who have grown up, and had a good relationship with an opposite-sex sibling or siblings may find it much easier to relate to the opposite sex during adolescence and adulthood than someone who has grown up either as an only child or with same-sex siblings.

A 'normal' family may contain no children, or five children, so it may contain just one child. While it is true that an only child misses out on some of the benefits that having brothers or sisters can bring, this does not mean that the child will grow up unable to form a close and caring sexual relationship with anyone else. Nor that she or he will become withdrawn and antisocial. The way in which only children develop will depend on their personality, the relationship they have with parents, and the nature of their relationships with other relatives.

One of the advantages of having siblings is that it may make it easier for a child to make friends. Parents can, if they wish, help an only child 'fill in' some of the gaps left by the absence of siblings by encouraging him or her to take part in activities with children of the same age, so that the child builds up a wide social network. Parents should also be aware that because an only child does not have siblings to form a relationship with, he or she may feel excluded by the closeness of the relationship between parents, or alternatively may be inclined to dominate it. While there is no need to smother the child with love or spoil them, parents with an only child may find it beneficial to spend more time bonding separately with the child than they would do with each child in a larger family. There are also undoubtedly some benefits to be gained from being in a sibling-free family. Most only-children get considerably more individual attention from their parents than they would if they had to share them.

Parents often take on stereotypical roles in the way in which they relate to their children. For example, it is common for a mother to take her daughter to do the household shopping, while the father takes his son to watch football. But is there anything wrong with this? Probably not, because it is all part of the bonding process. However, it has been, and still is, traditional in many cultures to view females as the 'weaker' sex and inferior to the males. It is important for parents to make an effort to overcome such stereotyping by treating their children equally and providing them with equality of opportunity regardless of their gender.

A family that spends time and plays together will probably also get on well together. A way to encourage shared leisure activities might be for the family to sometimes go bowling or skating together, to share a hobby, or to go on holiday together. Anything that encourages communication is bound to improve family bonds. Eating together is also an important event within the family. The regularity and constancy of sitting round a table and sharing food is vital in a child's development. As well as being fed, the child learns how to behave when eating, and listens to and participates in the conversations that take place between parents and other family members.

Outside interests and relationships add another stimulus to relationships within the family. They not only provide something else to talk about but also add a new focus of attention, not just for the person concerned but for the whole family. New relationships should never be seen as a threat. Far from replacing the child's attachment to his or her family, they should widen the social circle of acquaintances for both child and parents and, as a result, enrich the existing family attachments.

A parent's relationship with a baby is obviously not the same relationship as the one they have with a toddler, a school-age child or a teenager, and parents must be prepared to adapt according to the changing needs of their growing child. They must accept that their offspring is gradually shedding many of his or her 'childish' characteristics, and they must be prepared, when the time comes, for their child to become independent of her or his family. This gradual letting go may be a painful process but it should also be seen as a natural stage that most families go through.

In particular, it often comes as a shock to parents to realise that a child's sexuality develops at a relatively early age. However, this is just another stage in a child's development, and parents should simply take it in their stride. It is important for parents to discuss their feelings towards their child's development, and any anxieties they may have.

Parents should be careful to present a united front. If a child spots the smallest disagreement between them, he or she is almost bound to capitalise on it and to play one parent off against the other. This is especially true when it comes to discipline. One parent may believe that children should merely have things carefully explained to them when they do something wrong; the other parent may prefer to admonish the child by raising their voice. Whatever they believe, they should agree beforehand on which line they are going to take and adopt a public policy in front of the children.

Sex education

Children need to know and understand about sexual matters, although this need not be a constant topic of conversation. Parents may find it difficult to broach what is traditionally seen as a difficult subject with their children. However, rather than waiting until their children are approaching their teens, it may be wiser for parents to start talking to their children about sex when they are young. At first it will probably be in response to questions such as 'Where do I come from?'

A young person may be able to talk frankly and openly about sex with their parents at a time when it is probably taking on considerable importance in their lives. While most children have some kind of sex education at school, this tends to be fairly anatomical, and not related to the feelings and emotions of sex. Parents can play an important role in their child's future sexuality and relationships by providing them, slowly but surely, with a clear overview of sex, and by giving them the message in a way that shows sex in a positive light—as something enjoyable and pleasurable under the right circumstances. One specific way in which parents can help their children is to prepare them for the physical and emotional changes that will come with puberty.

Hopefully, a girl should, by the age of nine or ten, be aware that she will over the next few years develop pubic hair and breasts, and that her periods will start. Similarly, boys should also know about body hair, penis growth and ejaculation. Sex is not sinful, and ignorance about sexual matters in late childhood can allow a child to grow up with a negative and guilt-ridden attitude towards both sex and relationships. While it is considered important for parents to be positive and open with their children about sexual matters, they may not feel the same about sexual information and images that their children see on television and in other media.

Sex and sexuality portrayed on screen or in books is often dominated by a stereotypical attitude towards sex, and may not match up to the type of sexual message that parents wish to convey to their children. In films men are commonly portrayed as sexual aggressors, and women as passive recipients. Once a couple have adjusted to the inevitable changes to their relationship caused by having a baby, they may be tempted to think that life will soon return to normal. In reality their life will probably never be quite the same as it was before the arrival of a child.

A baby is very demanding and requires attention at any time, day or night. Equally, once children are older—and capable of fending for themselves to a much greater extent—they are none the less bound to make demands on the time, attention and energies of their parents. There will be school commitments, help with homework, and all the inevitable ferrying around to outside activities. There are so many things within a relationship that vie for their attention—job, housework, friends, hobbies—that a couple can end up seeming to have little time for each other. Once a couple have a child, they are likely to have less time for sex. This will be particularly noticeable if they had the kind of relationship before where it was usual for them to have sex as the mood took them. Now this part of their relationship is likely to be relegated to bedtimes and may not be as much fun as before. New parents may also feel differently about sex because, in some subconscious way, having a child has made them identify more closely with their own parents.

The fact that they, too, are now parents may lead them to believe that they should behave like responsible, mature adults, and this may mean that sex plays a less important part in life. There is, of course, no need for this to happen. A couple should try to ensure that their sex life has the same importance in their life as it had earlier in their relationship. But it is very important for a couple to make sure that physical affection remains an integral part of their relationship, particularly at this time, when they are both likely to need the reassurance that they are still loved and that the child hasn't spoiled things between them. It is also important for a couple to talk to one another during this period and tell each other what they are feeling.

This is good for their own happiness and helps them feel secure. It is also good for their emotional wellbeing—and later for their own sexual development—to realise that their parents enjoy a close relationship which involves them showing affection to each other both at home and in public. As children get older they will probably come to realise that an important component of their parents' closeness is their sexual relationship, although this fact should not, of course, be forced on them. Making the link between sex and feelings is almost as important a part of their sex education as conversations with them about sex or their formal sex lessons at school.

Some parents are embarrassed by the thought of their children knowing they have sex, but there is no need for this. Sex is a completely natural activity, and embarrassment or guilt should play no part in it. Anything that helps their children understand the importance of sex in a happy and loving relationship can only be a good thing. Couples who have children often complain that it is difficult to find time to have sex. This is particularly so when there is a baby, because they can demand attention at any time, day or night, but even when the children have grown it can still be a problem.

Many parents find it helpful to teach their children to knock on their bedroom door before coming in; as children get older, a reciprocal arrangement can be established so that parents also knock on the child's door before entering their room. If constant interruption by children, or thin walls between bedrooms, is a problem, it is essential to make time for sex (or at least for uninterrupted intimacy, if the couple are not in the mood for sex at the allotted time). It might be possible for the children to spend the night with a relative or friend or, if they can afford it, for the parents to treat themselves to a hotel for the night while a babysitter stays with the children. This may make sex seem rather too organised. But although spontaneous sex can be wonderful, of course, it is not the only way to make love. Planning it in advance and enjoying the anticipation can be just as exciting.

SEPARATION AND DIVORCE

This is likely to be a dramatic change, not only for them but also for the people around them. Separation can mean great relief or a terrible sense of loss akin to bereavement, or feelings somewhere between these two extremes—it all depends on the nature of the relationship. Separation will also have an effect on the children of a relationship, although these effects may be much more subtle and less obvious. When a relationship ends there is usually one partner who has to move out of the family home that he or she has shared with a partner for, perhaps, many years.

Moving home under any circumstances can be very stressful, but being obliged to leave because of the break-up of a relationship can be even more so. The following may help to alleviate the pain:

— Try to take a positive approach and see finding and moving into a new home as the beginning of the next phase of your life.

— Decorate your new home in a way that reflects your character and feelings.
— If your children are living with your partner, make space for them in a special room that they can play or sleep in when they come to visit you.
— Take your mind off your move by taking up new interests and making new friends.
— Try not to think about your old home and what may be happening to it, in the same way that you should try not to let your old relationship dominate your thoughts.
— Don't see yourself as a loser because you had to move out from the family home.

There are few people who find it an easy transition, although many experience an overwhelming sense of relief that the relationship is over and tensions have been removed. It is important to capitalise on that relief—to enjoy the fact that the house is now, for the time being anyway, yours alone:

— Move your ex-partner's things out of the way, and remove any reminders of them which you find it difficult to have around. This is your (and possibly your children's) home now and it should feel like it.
— Rearrange your furniture as you choose.
— Enjoy your new-found freedom to do what you want, when you want.
— Invite friends round to share your new existence with you.
— Even when you're eating alone, do it properly—cook a nice meal, lay the table, light some candles—and make a fuss of yourself.

Children of separated parents

Stability and continuity are of great importance to a child, and there are few things more worrying than an uncertain future. However, they may, at the same time, experience a considerable feeling of relief when their parents break up, especially if they were aware of tension between them, or if they did not get on particularly well with the parent who is moving out. When parents separate, a child often loses daily contact with the parent who leaves.

A very young child is unlikely to understand exactly what has happened, even when this is carefully explained to them—as it should be. All they know is that the parent has left them and they may feel that it must be their fault. Perhaps they did something wrong, or perhaps they were not lovable enough for the parent to think it was worth staying around. Even an older child, who understands why his or her parents split up, may have similar feelings of guilt or rejection.

Children need a lot of care at this time. They need to know that both their parents love them, that what happened was not their fault, and that their future is not as bleak as they may imagine. This will obviously increase the child's feelings of insecurity and anxiety. Separation may convey the message that love can end unexpectedly and for no apparent reason, and that however strong your feelings for someone, they may still leave.

Feelings such as this can affect a child's lifelong emotional development, so that when that child grows up he or she may find it difficult to trust their partner and sustain a long-term relationship. The more acrimonious the break-up, the more difficult it will be for children to deal with. If children are caught in the middle and are encouraged to take sides, this is even worse for them. Children understand from an early age that they are made up of half Mummy, half Daddy. If they learn to hate one parent, they may begin to hate part of themselves.

Children need to respect both parents in order to develop a healthy self-esteem. And to this end it is very helpful if the parent who has custody of the children refrains, whatever his or her feelings, from denigrating his or her ex-partner in front of the children. Of course it is healthiest for children if the separation can take place quietly and calmly, with ex-partners remaining friends and the children seeing both parents regularly. Both during and after their parents' divorce, children often show their unhappiness in the following characteristic ways.

— Young children in particular may suffer from nightmares, become frightened of the dark or have difficulty in getting to sleep.
— Older children may become withdrawn or depressed and unwilling to communicate.
— Children may become more disobedient or quarrelsome than usual; their unhappiness can also be shown by unexpected aggression to siblings, animals or children at school.
— They may fall behind with schoolwork or make excuses for staying away from school. In any of these situations it is important that the parents don't panic, but try to be understanding and supportive during an unsettling period in their children's lives.

Many people may feel that they will never commit themselves to another relationship. But after a few years—or even months—when the wounds are beginning to heal or they begin to feel lonely, a new relationship may start to seem a more attractive proposition. Although entering a new relationship will initially be exciting and challenging, as with all major changes in life, it may also prove quite stressful.

Someone who has recently escaped from a failed relationship may understandably find it difficult to contemplate the idea of committing himself to another relationship. But unless he chooses to remain single for the rest of his life, there comes a time when he must be prepared to make that new commitment. He may also find that his new sexual relationship is completely different to the one he had with his ex-partner, and that he needs to make adjustments sexually as well.

Stepfamilies

The relationships in stepfamilies are not always easy, be they the one between stepmother and ex-wife, or stepfather and ex-husband, or step-parents and their partner's children. Stepfamilies need a particularly strong relationship between the couple for the simple reason that the parenting bond between them is based not on the fact that they had a child together but on their desire to share their life. For some people, the stepfamily works well from the beginning, and there are few problems. For the great majority of stepfamilies, however, there are bound to be tensions, which need to be resolved.

Children, especially adolescents, may resent the imposition of the authority of a new father or mother, especially if they get on well with the parent who has left the family home. Stepfathers or stepmothers may be angered and upset by the attitude and antipathy of their partner's children—it can be very trying to be with someone you love if their children apparently hate you. As with all family matters, it helps if members of the stepfamily can learn to communicate.

Eventually, in most cases, the stepfamily will work efficiently as a family, and the children of the stepfamily should develop 'normally', perhaps enriched by the change in family structure. If things do not work out, however, it may be worth seeking family therapy so that an outsider can attempt to mediate between 'warring factions' within the stepfamily.

Finding a new partner with whom to start again is seldom easy. Finding a new partner who is also prepared to take on a ready-made family which includes children from a previous relationship can be harder still.

Children often find the new relationship troublesome because they generally find any major change unsettling. They are often reluctant to trust a new partner, and may resent the presence of someone whom they see as usurping their key position in their parent's affections. They are likely to experience a conflict of loyalty between their natural parents—and that includes the absent one—and their new step-parent, a desire to develop a good relationship, and on the other hand a fear of that relationship developing too quickly. The National Stepfamily Association of the UK has predicted that by the turn of the century stepfamilies are likely to be the most common family unit. However, perhaps surprisingly, it is a unit that works well for many thousands of people. If things seem to be difficult at first, it is important not to become despondent and to be patient. Time and commitment are the key factors in making new relationships work.

Following the trauma of separation, a single parent also has to take on the added responsibility of being in sole charge of the child, or children, of the dissolved partnership. However, despite the apparent burdens of this role, many women and men find it not just consoling but also inspiring. As well as company, a child can provide an immediate focus of interest so that the parent can get over the break-up of the relationship by nurturing and encouraging their offspring. Another reason for single parenthood is the choice that an increasing number of women make in favour of single motherhood.

A few women get pregnant with the express intention of raising the baby on their own. Most single women get pregnant by accident and then decide to have the baby rather than have an abortion, even though they are not in a permanent relationship.

When someone first becomes a single parent it is common for her to concentrate all her efforts on her children. But although children need a lot of attention at this time, the parent should not focus every ounce of her worry and attention on the child. She must not forget her own needs or to face her own hurt feelings and anxieties. It is only by facing them that her can resolve them—loneliness, insecurity, uncertainty about the future, money worries, and a sense of panic at having to cope with everything alone. But such people may also feel great relief at no longer being in a possibly unpleasant and bitter relationship; elation at finding new and unfamiliar feelings of freedom; and a positive sense of starting a new beginning, coupled with optimism regarding the future.

The single-parent family

What was a two-parents-plus-child (or children) set-up suddenly becomes one-parent-plus-child. Even if the now-absent parent was not at home much before, he or she was around some of the time, and members of the family were constantly reminded of them. Departure of one parent from the family home is bound to have an effect on the relationship between the remaining parent and children. It is not unusual for the children to express their sadness and anxieties at this time as anger—and the only person who is around to be angry with is the parent with whom they still live.

This can be difficult for newly single parents to cope with, but it is essential that they have the patience and understanding needed to make the effort now in order to avoid damaging their long-term relationship with their children. The lone parent may also be angered—and astounded—by the strong feelings held by a child towards the departed partner, particularly if that partner has behaved badly in the past. This type of behaviour is common in children and should be accepted as such; a single parent should not embark on a propaganda campaign for or against an ex-partner in an attempt to bring a child round to her point of view.

Difficult as things may be, the single parent who lives with their children is comparatively lucky. It is much more difficult for a parent to build a good relationship with children when they don't live with them. His relationship with his children is often overshadowed by feelings of guilt, to try to buy his children's love by showering them with expensive presents. This is unlikely to succeed in the long term, and can only make things worse for the other parent who is living with the child and may not be able to afford to spend money on comparable gifts.

Contact between divorced couples may be difficult, even if they are no longer arguing about money or property. There may still be a residue of bitterness and dislike that is hard to overcome. Children often sense these negative emotions and find them difficult to deal with. It is for this reason that it is so important to try to maintain as civil and smooth a relationship as possible between ex-partners, with as little arguing and sniping as possible.

Although there are far fewer single fathers than there are single mothers, their numbers are increasing and the problems they face are much the same as those confronting single mothers. People are often surprised when a single father makes a good job of parenting, but there is absolutely no reason why a man should not be capable of bringing up a child well and happily without the help or support of a partner.

GAY AND LESBIAN PARENTS

In some families, both parents are of the same sex and having a homosexual relationship. Gay families can attract considerable criticism and prejudice but there is no reason why gay parents of either sex should not have the same close and loving relationship with their children as other parents—as well as the caring, the dedication, the ups and downs, the closeness and the rows found in all families. Some gay parents may have had their children while they were in a heterosexual relationship, and when this relationship finished took their children with them into their new relationship.

Often this happens after a custody battle in which their sexuality may have been raised as a reason why they should not be granted custody. It is more usually lesbian mothers who manage to gain custody of their children, rather than gay fathers. Social disapproval of homosexual men, together with the usual custom of awarding custody to the mother, means that there are very few openly gay fathers who have custody of their children.

Many gay men even have to fight hard for access rights. It may be particularly difficult for a heterosexual partner who was left for the sake of a gay or lesbian relationship to encourage his child to have frequent contact with the homosexual parent, but for the sake of the child he needs to do his best not to allow his own feelings to get in the way. Some lesbian couples start their own families. Alternatively, they might pay for artificial insemination by an agency that provides sperm samples with broad profiles of the males that supplied them.

Children are sure to learn and understand the nature of their parents' relationship from the way they and their friends behave. In this way they should develop an accepting attitude towards both homosexual and heterosexual relationships but not be swayed as to the way their own sexual preferences will turn out. Where a parent has left a heterosexual relationship to embark on a gay relationship the situation may not be so straightforward. It can be still more difficult for a parent to come out and reveal it to their children.

This can be a major hurdle in their relationship with their children, partly because of the social prejudice surrounding gay and lesbian relationships and partly because many people find it difficult to discuss their sexuality with anyone, let alone their own children. However, the more open a parent can be with children, the easier it will be for those children to appreciate and understand the situation, and the less likely it is that their own relationships will be adversely affected in later life.

4

AIDS and Sexuality

In regard to AIDS and sexual behaviour, statistical evidence and the experience of others indicate that the probability and risk of becoming HIV-infected as a result of unprotected sexual intercourse is dramatically high. In reality there is no such thing as safe sex today, outside a monogamous sexual relationship between sexual partners who have not had previous sexual intercourse with others prior to the current monogamous sexual relationship. Popular advice suggests that people discuss with potential sexual partners their prior sexual histories and behaviours, and the probability of their exposure to HIV-infection. Even then, there is no guarantee that the sexual partner who says he or she has never had sexual intercourse prior to the present monogamous sexual relationship is telling the truth. But, sexual intercourse may be made safer through the use of protected sex; using latex condoms during vaginal, oral and anal intercourse.

One significant means of transmitting HIV/AIDS is through the physical intimacy and privacy of sexual intercourse, behaviours and often in the context of insufficient sexual knowledge, experience, and/or a meaningful and caring relationship, people will continue to engage in risk-behaviour.

The use of latex condoms versus animal skin/membrane condoms is extremely important, because HIV can permeate animal membrane condoms whereas it can not permeate latex membranes. Unfortunately, there are no guarantees or absolutes when it comes to human behaviour, or human sexual behaviour. Although one may believe he or she has made a commitment to sexual abstinence and/or safer sex, not all situations are controllable and not all commitments and decisions are final. People do get themselves into difficult situations where they lose control of what is happening to them sexually (e.g., acquaintance rape). And, given the necessary mix of people, relationships, and events (including alcohol and/or other "recreational" drugs), people do change, or are persuaded to change, their priorities and previous commitments. For example, most condom failures are due to the user's lack of motivation and commitment to use condoms, or they are due to the user's inexperience and lack of skill in condom use, not defective condoms.

By definition, life is ambiguous and involves certain elements of uncertainty and risk. At times life is uncomfortable, painful, insecure, difficult, controversial, and unsafe. And, despite our attempts to quantify, measure, and isolate the critical variables that predict and control human behaviour, it remains elusive, unpredictable and in many cases uncontrollable. Accidents happen, mistakes occur, poor decisions are made, and people do what they want to do rather than what they are told to do or warned against.

Some people do seem to learn, however, that even though life is not totally safe, certain, secure, risk-free, or free from pain and controversy, life can be safer, more certain, less risky, more secure, and less painful. Somewhere within this process, most people also learn they are not immortal and that earlier life-risks are no longer worth taking, or that risks can be taken in a safer manner. This process, however, appears to involve the integration of our personal life experiences with what we know (our knowledge base), and with what we do (our behaviour).

In the absence of such experience, young people will experiment to acquire their own life experiences. Not everyone has the same opportunities, however, and the kinds of experiences individual's have may be limited or enhanced by class, ethnicity/race, social level, etc. And the decisions one makes are related to one's personal experiences.

Most decision-making theorists believe that the use of statistics, based on the probability of predicting the specific outcomes of specific decisions, are more effective and reliable in making "good" decisions, while others believe that one's judgment, based on personal experience and sometimes intuition, is more effective in making decisions and predicting the outcomes of those decisions. Experience also provides the opportunity of retrospectively analysing one's prior decisions.

There is also the danger of overgeneralising from one's own experience, denying the experiences one has had, or deleting and distorting selective information from one's experiences. People often assume that what is true in their experience is also true in other's experience. Not everyone, however, has the same experiences, experiments with life's options in the same way, engages in the same level of risks, or experiences the same outcomes as a result of similar decisions. Not everyone experiments with smoking tobacco, using alcohol, taking illicit drugs, having intercourse with same-sex partners, premarital intercourse, or bungee jumping. Similarly, not everyones experiments with or has experiences that involve the same combination of events, people, or situations in the same temporal context.

Some people may experiment with alcohol and/or drug use at the same time that they have sexual intercourse; while others may experiment with alcohol and/or drug use independent of sexual intercourse. And, any of these behaviours may occur with different people in different contexts that involve different antecedent events and consequences. Everyone does not have the same number of sexual partners, everyone does not drink the same number of drinks, and not everyone drives an automobile while drunk or impaired.

There are varying degrees of risk associated with various combinations of experimental behaviours and life experiences. Consequently, the outcomes vary. Some people drink and drive with no negative consequences, while the outcomes for others who drink and drive may be tragic automobile accidents and death.

No amount of statistical evidence or life-experience can ever accurately predict the outcome of such behaviours. There will always be some degree of uncertainty and chance involved in living life. However, the probability of chance of certain outcomes occurring, or the risk involved, can be estimated on the basis of statistical evidence and the experiences of ourselves and others.

In addition to the information attained from statistical evidence and personal experience, there is another variable that requires consideration in the discussion of AIDS and sexual behaviour; emotional awareness and sensitivity to others. As in other human behaviour, emotions and emotional awareness are significant aspects of sexual behaviour. To increase the consistency between what people know and what people do, an understanding of emotions is a necessary addition to the factual knowledge people possess and the personal experiences of ourselves and others.

Because emotions are often difficult to understand and, like personal experiences, are subjective in nature, many people attempt to "get-rid-or" their feelings rather than attempting to understand them. Because emotions are such a significant part of life-decisions, relationships, and behaviours, a lack of awareness about emotions may be as significant an omission as not possessing the required knowledge or having insufficient experience in making important decisions.

It also appears that the emotions most people attempt to avoid, "get-rid-of," or keep from their awareness are negative ones. Pleasant, uplifting feelings typically do not create difficulties in peoples' lives. Unless, of course, we consider people who engage in unprotected sexual intercourse merely for its physical pleasure and satisfaction, in the absence of emotional intimacy and understanding. In the present consideration, pursuing the attainment of positive feelings associated with physical, unprotected sexual satisfaction alone may result in the aftermath of dramatically negative emotions.

The personal accounts and experiences of HIV-infected and AIDS patients reflect common emotional responses to the HIV-disease; fear, hurt, anger, and loneliness. It is extremely frightening to think that we, or someone we love, might become HIV-infected and die of AIDS because of the high-risk behaviours we, or they, may have engaged in prior to becoming aware of, or in spite of, the dangers and risks associated with HIV-disease.

The opportunistic infections involved in AIDS-related death also are dramatically fearful and painful; pneumocystic carinii pneumonia (PCP), meningoencephalitis, retinitis, cytomegalovirus (CMV) infection, esophagitis or enteritis and tuberculosis; neoplasms that involve the skin, mucous membranes, oral cavity, and lungs (e.g., Kaposi's sarcoma); tumours of the lymph nodes and lymphoid tissue (lymphomas); nusologic and psychomotor disorders and deficits in memory, concentration, and attentiveness; emotional instability and apathy; and the extreme loss of body mass and weight through chronic diarrhoea and malnutrition. These are not easy infections with which to cope, emotionally or physically, whether we are the patient who is dying or the person who is watching someone we love, die of such dreadful and painful illnesses.

Since such opportunistic infections can be lingering in their progression, it also is not uncommon for much of the physical and emotional suffering to occur alone. Initially, friends, partners, and family members often do not realise the emotional commitment or time investment involved in the process of AIDS-related death. As the opportunistic illnesses progress, there is typically the realisation that a cure will not be found in time. And prior to the acceptance of death's inevitability and the completion of the loss and grieving process, anger become a dominant theme for the AIDS patient and those close to him or her. In short, the process of losing someone to AIDS can be chronically hurtful because of the hideousness of the opportunistic diseases and the slow wasting of the patient.

Ironically, the negative emotional consequences of becoming HIV-infected also may be the very same emotions, if avoided and blocked from awareness, that put people at-risk of becoming HIV-infected: fear, hurt, and anger.

Earlier discussions of such negative feelings have evolved in an emotional paradigm that, if understood and applied rather than avoided and ignored, may be an important antecedent to engaging in sexual behaviours that place people at-risk of contracting HIV/AIDS.

The paradigm involves a sequence of emotions that describes fear, hurt and anger as the common-core of feelings that are typically ignored, blocked from awareness, or discouraged from expression in our present society. If the three common-core emotions are not expressed and/or blocked from awareness, an individual's emotional responses usually progress through the sequence of boredom, guilt, frustration and confusion, depression, symptomatic self-defeating behaviours (such as sexual promiscuity, "acting-out" behaviour, alcohol and substance abuse, and combinations of these), and in the most severe-case scenario, suicide or homicide.

Popular observations and perceptions among the lay-population are that many people in the United States today are mistrusting of others, disclose very little about themselves, keep to themselves ("co-coon"), are lonely and alienated from others, are somewhat narcissistic, and are fearful of people outside their immediate family, especially strangers and people with whom they are not acquainted. Another popular lay-perception is that many people today do not have a good sense of their self-identity and self-worth.

Although this may be a fairly pessimistic description and view of individuals and relationships in our current society, it also may be worthy of further consideration in regard to AIDS and sexual behaviour If such popular observations are even remotely accurate, in combination with individual's avoidance or lack of awareness of their negative feelings, the importance of becoming aware of, understanding, and expressing such emotions may be a significantly neglected aspect of AIDS and sexual behaviour. That is, if people are aware of the danger and risk involved in having unprotected sexual intercourse, their emotional awareness and response, if consistent with their existing knowledge and experience, should be one of fear and healthy skepticism. And, if fear is understood as the feeling of anticipated and potential loss, most people should realise that emotional pain and hurt are in response to a real and actual loss in one's life.

We do anticipate losses in our lives (fear) and we do experience real as well as anticipated loses in our lives (emotional pain and hurt). Relationships do end, people do get fired and laid-off from their jobs, significant people in our lives do move away from us to new geographic locations, accidents and physical impairments do occur, and ultimately people do die. At some point, and in addition to fear and hurt, most people usually feel angry in response to an anticipated or real loss. Anger is typically part of the emotional process of grieving a significant loss.

If unexpressed, these feelings of fear, hurt, and anger underlie the feelings of boredom, guilt, frustration and confusion, depression, and symptomatic "acting-out" and self-defeating behaviours. Boredom is often used synonymously with apathy. But regardless of the term used, a bored or apathetic person is also an angry, hurt and fearful person. Boredom usually leads to feelings of guilt, or an expression of anger directed at oneself. And self-directed anger (or guilt) typically progresses to frustration and/or confusion about what one is feeling. The next steps in the progression of avoided and unexpressed fear, hurt, and anger are depression and "acting-out," self-defeating behaviour.

In this case, the "acting-out," self-defeating behaviour may be that of a fearful, hurt, angry, and depressed person, unsure of her or his self-identity and with low self-worth, engaging in unprotected sexual intercourse. The high-risk consequences of such emotional avoidance and self-defeating behaviour being that of HIV-infection. Avoided and unexpressed fear, hurt and anger beget further fear, hurt, and anger and the cycle is complete and perpetuated.

If one doubts the legitimacy of the described emotional paradigm, or its significance in becoming HIV-infected as a result of engaging in high-risk sexual behaviours, all one needs do is listen to HIV/AIDS patients recount their personal sexual histories and experiences and describe their current emotional responses of fear, hurt, anger, and loneliness.

Most HIV/AIDS patients are willing to speak candidly and honestly to others about the sexual histories, experiences, and behaviours that resulted in their becoming HIV-infected, as well as to express the feelings associated with their being HIV-infected or living with AIDS. For many HIV/AIDS patients this is a way for them to give to others, to educate others about HIV-disease, to provide some sense of meaning and significance to their lives, to help others learn from their experiences, and to demonstrate their caring for others.

The honesty and caring demonstrated by many HIV/AIDS patients, perhaps motivated by the daily awareness of their own mortality and the feelings associated with that awareness are the honest and caring qualities that could benefit most of us if emulated in our own personal and sexual relationship. Rarely in our society today is honesty the best policy in terms of financial gain and freedom from suffering and pain. But, in terms of AIDS and sexual behaviour honesty is the only policy in terms of freedom from unnecessary suffering and pain.

Unfortunately, many people react to HIV/AIDS patients with responses of fear, anger, disgust, blame, discrimination, and ostracisation—missing the important emotional information and relationship messages being conveyed by HIV/AIDS patients. Rather than using such information to increase their own emotional awareness and sensitivity toward others, too many people respond to HIV-infected people and people living with AIDS by choosing to avoid or to "get-rid-of" their own negative feelings by displacing and projecting them onto the HIV/AIDS patients. Such dishonesty with self and lack of awareness are the antithesis of developing caring attitudes and relationships with HIV/AIDS patients, let alone developing emotionally intimate, honest, and caring relationships with others.

Behavioural assessment is more important than behaviour therapy. Anyone who has struggled with the application of behavioural techniques to complex behavioural problems is aware that the most difficult part of this endeavour is the development of adequate behavioural measures. Once adequate measures are developed, therapy is often a matter of applying the usual and standard techniques of selective, positive reinforcement or modelling, as even a cursory look at the literature.

The notion that assessment will determine the nature of therapy is not limited to the behavioural approach. Bergin and Strupp note that more accurate assessment of various problems comprising any diagnostic category will lead to the construction of specific treatments aimed at specific components of a problem.

Yet the development of the area of behavioural assessment has lagged behind the development of new behaviour therapies. In our headlong rush to develop new treatment in 1960s, assessment efforts by which we judged the adequacy of these treatments were often no better than an answer a patient would give to the question, "How are you feeling now?" In some cases actual behavioural measures were utilised, but more often than not these measures were tangential to the behavioural problems that brought the patient for treatment.

Major issues to be discussed in this chapter include the relationship of self-report to behavioural and physiological response systems in the assessment of sexual behaviour. A second issue involves the use of contrived situations versus naturalistic observation in the assessment of all three components of sexual behaviour. The necessity of assessing early components in the chain of sexual arousal will also be discussed. In addition, the complexity of sexual behaviour, discovered in the last few years, has led to the conclusion that many of our labels for sexual behaviour are inadequate. In sexual deviation, for example, no client is the same. Each has some combination of behavioural excesses and defects, and each requires individual assessment.

The following section discuss the major issue of self-report and its relation to other response systems, as well as contrived versus natural observation in the assessment of sexual behaviour. The three major components of sexual behaviour are sexual arousal, heterosexual social skills (heterosocial skills), and gender identity or gender role deviations.

The importance of assessing all three response systems is one of the more important developments in recent years. The lack of relationship among the verbal, the motoric, and the physiological response systems is well known by now. In the assessment of most behavioural problems, however, differential importance is attributed to these response systems depending on one's general approach or orientation to the problems. Certainly the term behavioural assessment indicates a preference for assessment of the behavioural or motoric response system. Many behavioural clinicians assess self-report only if direct measurements of behaviour are unobtainable.

The tendency to ignore self-report since the development of reliable physiological measures of sexual arousal is not consistent with the discovery of three independent response systems and could even the dangerous. This tendency in behavioural assessment of sexual behaviour or other clinical problems ignores the fact that self-report is behaviour and therefore is just as important as direct observation of physiological arousal or heterosexual social skills, or even direct observation of sexual interactions. This notion is at variance with the approach that categorises self-report measures as indirect measures of behaviour. Since self-report of sexual problems may or may not correlate with the other response systems, it is inaccurate to call these measures indirect.

It is the fact that there are several different types of self-report measures used in the assessment or sexual problems or other clinical problems, some of which may correlate with behavioural or physiological response systems better that others. For example, self-monitoring of sexual behaviour, such as reports of number of orgasms reached during sexual interactions, may correlate highly with directly observed behaviour under certain conditions. Rating scale measures of subjective discomfort during sexual behaviour may correlate poorly with physiological or behavioural measures of sexual behaviour. For example, in a recent study, the sexual responding of six heterosexual and six homosexual males was assessed while they were watching several erotic movies, including a movie depicting homosexual interaction. Penile circumference, subjective reports of sexual arousal, and attitudinal ratings of "pleasantness" were measured. Heterosexual males reported the homo-sexual movie a distinctly unpleasant but demonstrated penile erection averaging 20 per cent of a full erection and also reported being sexually aroused. The point of interest here is the split between two different self-report measures of sexual functioning.

In general, self-report correlates fairly well with objective measures of arousal, at least in nonpatient populations. In the study cited above, a self report measure of arousal correlated 0.64 with measures of erection across all subjects and attitudinal reports of "pleasantness" correlated 0.55. Attitudinal measures and self-reports of arousal correlated 0.82. As Geer points out, this is a higher correlation than is found between self-report and other physiological responding.

In a patient population, however, Hoon, Wincze, and Hoon noted that sexually "normal" women and sexually dysfunctional women subjectively rated their arousal as similar during an erotic movie. But sexually dysfunctional women were not aroused compared to the normal group, suggesting a split between objective and subjective measures in this patient population. A more careful exploration of the different varieties of self-report of sexual behaviour and their relationship to one another as well as to treatment outcome is an important area for future research.

Whenever the results of future research, one can make a strong case that in the assessment of sexual behaviour in the clinic, self-report measures are at present more important than behavioural or physiological measures. This rather unusual statement is true because sexual problems that one confronts in the clinic occur almost entirely in adult populations. These patients are typically voluntary outpatients who report that they have a sexual problem such as a deviant arousal pattern or sexually dysfunctional behaviour. Self-report of these problems, then becomes the only necessary criterion for entry into treatment. This differs markedly form the way in which institutionalised people or other patients in closed settings enter into treatment, a process that usually begins with direct observation of some unacceptable behaviour. Similarly, self-assessment of progress is often the major criterion for terminating the intervention. Accurate depiction of patterns of sexual arousal that are reliably and independently measured and that demonstrate continued existence of a sexual problem will not keep a patient in treatment if he reports that he feels better and has recovered from the problem. When this happens, treatment is over. This fairly common occurrence in the clinic highlights the importance of understanding the relationship of self-report to other response systems and to outcome at follow-up. A further understanding of the variables controlling the reporting of different aspects of self-report is particularly important in cases when self-report diverges from behavioural or physiological measures.

Despite the relatively high correlation between self-report and physiological response in nonpatient populations, experience indicates that it is very common for divergences in the various response systems to occur during the assessment of sexual behaviour in patient populations as in the Hoon *et al.* study. There seem to be at least two reason for this. In our culture sexual behaviour is still a rather sensitive subject, difficult for many people to describe. Second, recent findings from our laboratories indicate that even patients who seem very willing to report their sexual behaviour as accurately as possible produce reports that diverge from objectively measured sexual arousal.

The function of behavioural assessment in an ideal world would be the direct and continuous measurement of the three response systems comprising the behavioural problem in the setting where the behaviour presents a problem. Usually the setting is home, work, school, or social situations, or perhaps all these. Whatever the setting or combination of settings, it has become known as the natural environment. Any procedure other than direct and continuous assessment of behaviour in the natural environment is second and continuous assessment of behaviour in the natural environment is second best. Yet in applied work this principle is constantly compromised for practical or ethical reasons. Thus clinicians cannot or will not measure behaviour in the natural environment if it occurs in settings remote from the therapeutic setting, nor will they measure behaviour such as aggressive behaviour that occurs at very low frequencies. For ethical reasons clinicians also will not observe some behaviours such as sexual interactions in the natural environment beyond the very beginnings of this chain of behaviour. To overcome these problems, contrived situations are devised to observe these behaviours at higher frequencies or in more convenient locations. In some cases the behaviours cannot be conveniently produced even in contrived situations. When this happens, as in the case of sexual behaviour, clinicians move back down the behavioural chain and measure sexual arousal, presumably an earlier component in the chain of sexual behaviour.

These are all necessary and helpful procedures, but it is easy to lose sight of the fact that these measures are only as good as their relationship to the behaviour as it occurs in the natural environment. If these measures predict the occurrence or frequency of behaviour in the natural environment, then they are useful. If not, they are useless. Nevertheless, although one may read journals or listen to presentations on therapeutic intervention in clean experimental designs that demonstrate highly effective therapeutic procedures, one seldom questions the relationship of the analogue measures so commonly used in these clinical trials to behaviour in the natural environment.

We noted that sexual behaviour is more complex that the labels making up our well-known diagnostic categories would indicate. Glibly referring to certain behavioural patterns as "pedophilic" or "dysfunctional" may be useful from a descriptive point of view, but it vastly oversimplifies the components of sexual behaviour elucidated by recent research. First outlined in 1974, these components cut across all sexual problems. It was noted that there are three major components of sexual behaviour-sexual arousal, heterosexual social skills (hereafter referred to as heterosocial skills), and gender role deviations. Sexual problems may be biochemically or genetically based and there are sophisticated procedures for assessing these biochemical and genetic factors. However, it would not be appropriate to consider them in a chapter on behavioural assessment. Nevertheless the behavioural assessment strategies are frequently used as auxiliary measures in the assessment of biochemically and genetically based sexual disorders.

The genital aspects of sexual behaviour have received the most attention over the years in studies of sexual problems, and thus assessment procedures utilising the genitals are the most advanced. The genital component of sexual behaviour involves a chain of events beginning with the early aspects of sexual arousal through sexual contact of some kind and eventually orgasm. If two or more patterns of sexual arousal and/or behaviour are present, they may or may not be related to one another in terms of frequency or strength. For instance, some patients may have frequent heterosexual arousal and behaviour with a spouse and still often engage in alternative forms of sexual behaviour. The "true" bisexual and some fetishistic patients are included in this group. However, deviant sexual arousal is often accompanied by diminished heterosexual arousal. Diminished heterosexual arousal and behaviour do not, of course, necessarily imply the existence of alternative patterns of arousal.

Most cultures have developed elaborate social patterns of behaviour surrounding the genital aspects of sexual behaviour. In our culture many patients may have adequate arousal patterns as well as the necessary behavioural repertoire to engage in the genital aspects of sex. However, these patients may be unable to engage in the type of heterosocial behaviours necessary for meeting, dating, and relating to desired persons. Similarly, many patients have adequate social skills but lack the necessary arousal patterns to engage in sexual behaviour.

A percentage of patients, particularly those with certain patterns of deviant arousal, may have some degree of deviation in gender role. Behaviours appropriate to the opposite sex are present and some preference for the rôle of the opposite sex is verbalised. This is most common in homosexual or transvestite arousal patterns. When opposite sex behaviour is completely adopted and the patient consistently thinks, feels, and behaves in the opposite sex role this mistaken gender identity is called *transsexualism*. Such clients usually request surgery to reassign their sex.

There are three major components of sexual deviation. Each of these components may be assessed in either the natural environment or in contrived situations. Because each component of sexual behaviour can potentially be assessed in each of the three response systems and because these three response systems are relevant to both contrived and naturalistic settings, it is possible to construct a three-by-two grid along these dimensions that results in 18 cells.

Developmental models of human conduct are useful in showing how the numerous elements of a multifactor model interact across the lifespan. They help avoid debates about nature an nurture by clarifying how both biological and environmental factors influence behaviour at each phase of life.

In childrens, the sexual reflexes function from the first days of life: Soon after birth, many boys have penile erections; and some girls, vaginal lubrication and clitoral tumescence. Even before birth, ultrasound studies suggest that erections may occur in male fetuses.

In the first year of life, many babies show the simplest forms of masturbation. Early in infancy, babies explore their environments and their own bodies, touching and looking at many parts of the anatomy with as much interest as they show for the world around them. Out of simple curiosity, they touch their arms, legs, and other parts, and discover their genitals in this process. Touch to the genitals elicits the sexual response, along with pleasurable feelings that reward genital self-stimulation. There are documented cases of babies learning to masturbate to orgasm before one year of age. There is, however, considerable variation among children in early sexual self-stimulation, depending largely on their parent's response to the activity. Some parents punish and suppress early sexual behaviour; whereas others are more accepting. Children who are punished for genital exploration may not learn to touch their genitals. Punishment may in fact condition inhibitions and fears about self-touching.

Sometimes children are inquisitive to learn what other children's bodies look like. Since children's play is not always monitored closely by adults, sexual exploration can lead in many possible directions. Often it leads to nothing more than one child's simply looking at and briefly touching the other child's body, but other outcomes are possible. A 9-year-old brother and his younger sister may innocently engage in mutual sexual exploration and discover that sexual play is pleasurable. In rare cases, after weeks of repeated sex play, they may discover intercourse, without knowing that adults would disapprove. Only later may the children discover that these activities are called "incest" and deemed unacceptable in the larger society.

In culture where people sleep together in a common room or hut, children may see their parents making love and later imitate coital activities during play with other children. There is a great deal of variability among children. There is a great deal of variability among cultures in childhood sexuality; and in societies where parents do not inhibit their children, sexual exploration and play continue throughout childhood: there is no biological determined "latency period" for sexuality.

In homes where early childhood sexual exploration is punished and little sexual information is given to the child, children can grow up with little knowledge and considerable guilt about touching their sexual organs or masturbating. Small degrees of such inhibition may not have long-lasting effects on the person's sexuality; but high levels of guilt and sexual ignorance can make it difficult for a person to develop a happy, uninhibited sexual life in subsequent years. Children who have negative socialisation about sex often develop erotophobia, which is a fear of phobia of sexuality and sexual cues, leading to negative attitudes about sex. In contrast, a positive sexual socialisation tends to lead to erotophilia, positive attitudes about sexuality and sexual cues.

In most societies, including ours, there is a double standard that imposes more sexual inhibitions, guilt, and erotophobia on girls than on boys. Parents are more likely to disapprove of masturbation for girls than boys. Girls are given fewer names for their genitals and are less likely to know the correct names than are boys, and few girls are told they have a clitoris. As a result, girls are less likely to masturbate or talk about their genitals than are boys.

Puberty usually begins between ages 9 and 13 in girls and 10 and 14 in boys. Most girls begin to menstruate between 11 to 14. Boys usually begin to be able to ejaculate at 11 to 12. The hormonal changes of puberty make the genitals more sensitive and more responsive. Adolescents—especially males—begin to experience spontaneous sexual arousal during the daytime and at night—in the form of nocturnal sexual arousal, erections, and orgasms. As a result teenagers typically become increasingly interested in sexuality—unless they have been made to feel very guilty or inhibited about sex.

Boys typically develop sexual interests earlier and more intensely than girls. This is due to both biological and social factors. For biological reasons, boys usually begin to notice sexual arousal—such as spontaneous penile erections—2 or 3 years earlier than girls notice their first sexual arousal. Boys have more penile erections and orgasms—both while awake and sleeping—than girls have noticeable sexual arousal and orgasms. Boys are more likely than girls to be aware of their spontaneous sexual arousal and find it intense. Nocturnal erections occur during dream sleep and boys often wake in the morning with erections, which can help them discover the heightened level of pleasure that comes from masturbation after the onset of puberty. Also, boys have more nocturnal orgasms or wet dreams-than do girls, and these are often coupled with sexual imagery that promote the development of sexual fantasies.

There are exceptions to these generalisation. Erotophobic boys may deny, their emerging sexuality, and erotophilic girls may actively explore their sexuality, even though they experience fewer biological impulses to aid them than boys do. However, most boys feel sexual arousal and interest much more often each day than most girls do.

Boys are much more likely than girls to learn to masturbate to orgasm during the adolescent years. This is due, in parts, to the more frequent occurrences of spontaneous sexual arousal and orgasm in boys and the double standard that imposes less punishment and social inhibitions on boys than girls. In our culture, many boys also experience peer pressure to experiment with sexuality, gain sexual knowledge, and become "sex-experts". Talk in the male peer group often turns to sex, and many boys feel pressure from their peer to lose their virginity and prove their manhood. Success is greeted with social approval, which rewards even more interest in sex.

Girls, in contrast, tend to experience a more cautious socialisation about sex. Yes, there is talk about sex in their peer groups, what it feels like and who is doing it. There is a great deal of variation among girls' peer groups, but these groups are more likely to pass on messages of caution about sex than are boys' peer groups. Girls learn that their more sexually active peers are called "sluts," or worse, and fear of social disparagement can make many girls reluctant to earn that label. Girls' peers may share frightening stories about girls who were taken advantage of by boys, stories of unwanted pregnancies and the subsequent problems, stories showing that STDs create many more complications for females than for males. In addition, girls may continue to hear words of caution from their parents.

Boys tend to want sex more than girls and to push more for it, while girls are more likely to play the gate-keeper role, wanting to know if he really cares about her before proceeding all the way to sexual intercourse. Hence, many girls and boys go through a period of petting or "fooling around" before engaging in sexual relations. Because physical touch to the skin, lips, and other body parts are all pleasurable, it is not surprising that couples enjoy the sensations of touching, fondling, kissing, and hugging. In such close interactions, pressure and touch to the genital areas are quite likely, which can heighten sexual arousal.

Erotic petting may be inhibited in societies that make young people feel guilty about premarital sex; or it can be facilitated in societies that inundate their youth with movies, videos, and stories of people doing sexual activities. Societal messages also influence the next step of sexual exploration: societies with clear messages that premarital sex will be strongly punished may suppress further sexual exploration until marriage; but such prohibitions are not very strong in most Western societies.

Many cultures have strict rules against premarital sex. Since most people throughout history have not had effective means of birth control, premarital sexual activity often led to pregnancy; and young unmarried mothers usually could not find marriage partners. Males often did not want to marry a pregnant woman or a woman with a child—unless it was theirs—because they did not want to devote their child-rearing effort's to raising someone else's children. In such cultures, virginity is very important; and a man may give a woman back to her family if she is found (or suspected) not to be a virgin at marriage. Naturally, there is much variation among cultures, and some societies allow a certain amount of premarital sex, perhaps with a fiance just before marriage.

Since the advent of the sexual revolution, many modern Western nations have experiences significant increases in premarital sexuality, this being due to the development of increasingly effective forms of birth control, the decreasing influence of rigid religious codes, and increased secular culture showing sexy images in videos, TV, and movies. In the United States, increasing premarital sex has led to an increasing amount of teenage pregnancy and teenage abortion, in part because many parents and teachers have been reluctant to provide good birth control information to teenagers. Even though a majority of American parents want sex education in the schools, a vociferous minority tends to block it in many schools. In Western Europe and Canada, where rates of teenage premarital sexual activity are similar to those in the United States, the teen pregnancy and abortion rates are considerably lower. For example, the pregnancy rate among 15 to 19 year olds is 96 per 1000 in the United States, compare to 35 per 1000 in Sweden and 14 per 1000 in the Netherlands. In modern Western European countries, teenagers are given better sexual education and better access to birth control services than in the United States.

While the prevalence of premarital sexual intercourse has gradually increased, the age of onset has gradually declined. For example, Alfred Kinsey, a pioneer sex researcher, found that half of the women he interviewed some 40 years ago had intercourse before marriage; but Morton Hunt found that 81 per cent of 18- to 24-year-old married women had done so in the early 1970s. In 1971, only 46 per cent of unmarried 19-year-old women had engaged in intercourse; but this percentage increased to 55 per cent in 1976 and 69 per cent in 1979. This trend for increasing early sexuality is believed to have levelled off in the 1980s. In 1990, 54 per cent of high school students grades 9 to 12 have had sexual intercourse.

Most parents do not tell their children or adolescents many details about the scripts for sexual intercourse, and many signal a reluctance or unwillingness to talk about premarital sex. As a result, many teens turn to their peers and the media for this information. These multiple and different sources often provide confusing or inaccurate information, with jumbled and often contradictory messages about the events surrounding first sex. Because it can be difficult to tell which of the countless different scripts presented by the media and peers is the best, adolescents often experiment with numerous lines and scripts, combining elements from various ones, not knowing which ones will work best for them until they have tried many. The less accurate information they have, the more likely are to make mistakes. Because many of the scripts used on TV and in movies do not work well in everyday life, adolescence can involve much frustrating experimentation and embarrassment.

Since AIDS has become a serious health problem, considerable efforts has been directed at teaching adolescents safer practices-such as the use of condoms and avoiding anal sex. Although some teens are following this advice, many teens are not using condoms for safer sex. In 1991, 46 per cent of high school students reported using condoms during their last sexual intercourse. Since one-fifth of all people with AIDS contracted the virus as teens, there is room for improvement in education and honest communication with teens about sex.

Gay and lesbian couples use manual and oral stimulation of the genitals, breasts, and anus, along with caressing, kissing, and body rubbing for sexual arousal. Since the advent of AIDS, many gay males have reduced their use of anal sex, since it is one of the activities most likely to transmit HIV (the virus that causes AIDS).

Although females tend to be less interested in sex than males in the teens and 20s, female sexual interest tends to increase in 20s, 30s, and 40s. Many of the inhibitions that girls learned while young are gradually overcome. As women learn how to avoid irresponsible partners, unwanted pregnancies, and STDs, they learn how to avoid some of the problems that had caused them to worry about sex earlier. Also, many learn how to have orgasms more easily, making sex more exciting and fulfilling. Many overcome guilt and other inhibitions as supportive sexual partners, the legitimacy of marriage, and access to more reliable information about sex counteract earlier fears and myths (ignorance). These factors have led many to the generalization that male sex drive peaks at 20 while females peak in their 30s or 40s. This generalisation is somewhat misleading, since (1) many males have very strong sexual interests all through young and middle adulthood, and some even longer, and (2) increasing numbers of young women have fewer sexual inhibitions or are overcoming their sexual inhibitions at an earlier age than their mothers did. Modern books, courses, and workshops on sexuality help them do this.

People in their teens and 20s often explore novel sexual positions and activities, but married couples often settle into a few favourite positions after they have explored a range of possibilities and discovered the ones they like the best. This can eventually lead to boredom with sex. If married couples report that they are losing interest in sex because it has become too routine, sexual therapists and marriage counsellors sometimes give couples books that show multiple sexual positions and encourage them to try novel ones.

5

Sexual Counselling

Many forms of sexual activity are still regarded as 'abnormal' and 'disturbed', and many are still prohibited by law. Some are illegal because they offend against the legislators' sense of morality. Thus in some countries it is illegal for a husband and wife to engage in anal intercourse. But in most Western countries the principle underlying most of the legislation in this field appears to be that the only illegal sexual activities are those that involve some form of victimisation, in that one or more participants do not consent to the sexual activity or cannot fully consent either because they are too young or because they are mentally disturbed. Sexual offences are often extremely damaging to victims, both immediately and in the longer term.

One reason why there are so many victims of these crimes is that many sex offences are 'serial crimes' in that the offender will engage in the same offence repeatedly, often in a compulsive fashion and despite a high risk of prosecution. Most sex crimes are committed by lone offenders, but there are also examples of collusion in sex crimes, of 'gang rape' and 'sex rings' groups of people who conspire to entice children into sexual activities. The term 'sexual harassment' covers many different forms of inappropriate behaviour—actions or words—and is usually applied to behaviour in the work context, or in a school or college setting. The more abusive and offensive types of sexual harassment are easily recognised, but there is often some problem in deciding whether a particular action does or does not constitute sexual harassment. Men often have little idea of how their behaviour affects women and may be surprised when they find that a woman has been distressed and offended by what they had intended to be a compliment, a joke or a mild flirtation. Some men feel that the increasing allegations of sexual harassment reflect an oversensitivity on the part of some women and some suggest that there is now a 'witch hunt' against men in the workplace.

However, many of those who deliberately engage in obscene or intrusive behaviour use the excuse that they were 'only being playful', and men are well advised to avoid any behaviour which might possibly cause offence. Some commentators suggest, as a rule of thumb, that a man should behave towards a female colleague or student only as he would if his boss or his wife were present.

Sexual harassment is all too common, with around one-third of working women having been subjected to serious sexual harassment at work. Women employed in factories and offices and those working within many professions, often report unwelcome touching as well as offensive and sexist remarks. In academic settings, too, many male teachers act in inappropriate ways towards their female students.

Most victims of sexual harassment have a lower status in the workplace than the person who harasses them, and sexual harassment often involves an abuse of power. Harassment frequently includes an element of bribery, with promotion, increased salary, or higher academic grades being implicitly (and sometimes explicitly) on offer in return for sexual favours. Another form of power abuse occurs when a superior persecutes a woman who fails to comply with, or who complains about, harassment. Some forms of harassing behaviour do not involve any attempt to gain sexual favours. Risque comments, or remarks about a woman's physical attributes, for example, are sometimes made in an attempt to put the woman 'in her place'.

Men sometimes use this strategy to assert their superiority over women, or to demonstrate to other men what they can get away with. The display of pornographic posters in an office or at a workbench can be an indirect way of deprecating and humiliating women in the workplace.

Sexual harassment can also be used in an attempt to undermine a woman who is in a powerful position. Some men regard any woman who occupies a senior position as a personal threat or even as an anomaly, and will seek to demean such a woman by making explicitly sexual remarks, using sexual innuendo, or even by attempting to start a sexual relationship with her as a way of attaining control over her. Even male academics, who might be expected to know better, often attempt to use their power to gain sexual favours from students.

On the other hand, some male students sexually harass their female teachers. They may seek to embarrass the teacher by making explicit personal remarks in front of other students, or they may attempt to seduce her as a way of undermining her legitimate power. It should also be recognised that some female students make sexual approaches to their male teachers, perhaps seeking to embarrass them, to compromise their position, or to gain academic favours. In some cases, sexual harassment is homosexual.

Some academic institutions, for example, insist that no male teacher should ever be alone in a closed room with a female student and others stipulate that staff must notify their head of department if they are having an affair with a student. Some companies now make provision for any woman who wishes to make a complaint about sexual harassment to report to a female superior rather than having to complain to a male boss.

United States and in most European countries, the number of cases of sexual harassment reaching courts of law has increased dramatically in recent years. The vast majority involve a woman making a complaint about a man's behaviour. Such cases usually involve a chronic pattern of abusive behaviour, rather than a single dramatic incident, and the man involved will usually have received many clear signals from the woman that his remarks or actions are unwelcome and distressing. A court case may indicate a failure of any disciplinary procedure normally operating within the company or institution. Some types of sexual harassment are illegal because they constitute forms of sexual assault.

Other types (especially verbal harassment) are usually regarded in law as infringing either civil rights or sex discrimination legislation and most cases are dealt with under civil rather than criminal law. Since sexual harassment generally occurs when two people are alone together, there is rarely any hard evidence and most cases involve judgments about which of the two people is telling the truth. Many victims suffer considerable psychological distress as a result of sexual harassment. Such treatment can lead to sharp decreases in self-confidence and work morale.

Some victims become severely depressed or anxious. Victims may attempt to cope with the harassment by trying to ignore it, suffering in silence, or resigning from the job. More assertive strategies include protesting and making a formal complaint, but although these are sometimes effective in putting an end to the harassment, in many cases the victim finds that she receives little support from colleagues and managers.

RAPE

Legal definitions vary across countries and states, but rape always refers to sexual intercourse without the partner's consent. Rape may occur by means of physical force, threat of physical violence, or the use of drugs or intoxicants. Intercourse with a victim who is deemed incapable of giving full consent, because she is intellectually handicapped, mentally ill or below the legal age of consent, is usually classified as 'statutory rape'. The laws differ between countries as to whether rape can only be committed by a male, whether the victim of the rape must be female and whether a man who forces his wife to have intercourse against her will is guilty of the crime of rape.

However, the relevant laws are changing in many countries, so that marital rape is now increasingly specified as an offence, homosexual rape is more widely recognised in law, and women are increasingly recognised as possible perpetrators of rape.

Anthropological studies have found that relatively high rates of rape occur in those societies in which the sexes are sharply segregated, in which women have a particularly low status, and in which male dominance and aggressiveness have a high cultural value. Cases of rape can be classified in a number of different ways. For example, it is useful to distinguish between marital rape, rape which occurs in the context of a dating relationship ('date rape'), and rape by a stranger.

While the majority of rape incidents involve only a single perpetrator, there are many cases in which two or more men are involved in an assault on a woman. Rape can also be classified in terms of the perpetrator's motive, although the principal motive is often assumed to be sexual, anger and hatred appear to be more significant for many rape attacks than any desire for sexual gratification.

A man takes advantage of a situation in which rape is possible and the chances of detection or prosecution are assumed to be very low. In such cases, the motive is usually that of immediate sexual gratification. Many cases of rape fall into this category. The principal motivation behind power rape appears to be a wish to intimidate the victim. Such men often threaten extreme physical harm and their sexual violation of the woman is a deliberate act of degradation. Few of the men who commit power rape have ever had a satisfactory close relationship with a woman. Many lack social skills and feel socially inadequate. Those who engage in vindictive rape appear to be motivated by a desire for revenge.

Many offenders have a profound hatred of all women, or of women of a particular type. Such men seem to derive little or no sexual satisfaction from the assault but use violence and verbal abuse as a way of expressing their resentment. Relatively rare, this type of rape is committed by men who derive sexual gratification principally by imposing extreme suffering on the victim.

Why some men become rapists, none can be said to offer a satisfactory account (probably because there are several types of rape, and several types of rapists). One extreme view is that the majority of men are potential rapists and that if an opportunity presented itself in which a rape would go undetected or unpunished, most would commit the offence. The alternative extreme view is that rapists are 'deviant' and different from other men and so we do not therefore need to offer an explanation of why the minority become rapists.

The trauma following rape is often heightened by other people's reactions to the victim and by the victim's self-blame. There may be some suspicion, even from the victim herself, that she somehow encouraged or stimulated the rapist, that she took too little care, or that she offered too little resistance.

One aspect of help and therapy typically given to victims is to relieve them of any such erroneous and damaging views. The woman needs to accept that she was wholly the victim and in no way the collaborator in the sexual assault. She then needs to develop a view of herself, in the present, not as a rape victim but as a rape survivor. It has been found that many rapists have particularly negative views of women. Regarding women as objects for men's sexual gratification, rapists also tend to subscribe to various myths about rape (for example, the idea that many women enjoy being forced to have intercourse). It is not surprising that many rapists have never been successful in forming a close attachment with a woman.

About one-third of rape victims sustain a physical injury as a result of the rape, but a much higher proportion experience severe psychological distress. Sometimes the trauma takes the form of immediate extreme distress, high levels of fear and anxiety and crying. In other cases the woman shows an initial controlled response before her apparent calm gives way to profound shock and distress. Women who have been raped often remain intensely fearful.

They may experience frequent intrusive thoughts about the rape, flashbacks, and recurrent nightmares, and many strive to avoid any situation which might bring back memories of the rape. The rape victim's judgments about the nature and the causes of the rape will affect her emotional response.

Sometimes victims feel in some way responsible for the rape, and such feelings will often lead to a sense of guilt. Although most victims return to normal functioning some months after the rape, some remain in a chronic state of fearfulness and are unable to recover their trust in other people. Some of those who have been raped become very depressed and some begin to abuse alcohol and other drugs.

Various forms of sexual dysfunction may also arise, and the woman may find it impossible to relax sexually even with a loved partner. Rape victims need help. Immediately after the rape they need medical attention. They may have sustained injuries during the attack, and they need to find out whether they have contracted a sexually transmitted disease or been made pregnant. There is also a need for immediate and sustained emotional support, particularly from close friends and relatives. Initially, they may need to be helped to report the attack. Until relatively recently, rape victims were often treated with a lack of respect and sympathy by the police. Despite substantial improvements in police attitudes and procedures in recent decades, the legal process, involving a medical examination, a full police investigation and a trial, often remains extremely traumatic.

The woman will need to appear in court, to face the rapist once more, and to give a detailed account of the attack. She will also have to submit to cross-questioning by the defence lawyer, who may suggest that rather than being an innocent victim she is a woman who agreed to intercourse and then 'cried rape' after the incident. Until recently, the legal procedures in many countries also allowed the woman's previous sexual history to be examined in detail in court. Following the lengthy, arduous and highly distressing legal procedure, the rapist may then be found not guilty, and such a verdict often constitutes a shattering blow to the victim. Considering the emotional trauma experienced by the victim as a result of the rape and fears about police intervention and possible legal proceedings, it is not difficult to understand why many rape victims fall to notify the authorities of the fact that they have been raped. Many rape survivors benefit from counselling. Talking through the incident with a therapist can often help a victim to identify and express fears, anxieties and anger.

Many women who have been raped also find it particularly helpful to talk with other women who have undergone a similar trauma, and rape survivors' self-help groups are organised in many areas. It is important to recognise that some women manage to cope with rape without becoming traumatised, and that most do recover from the most severe psychological effects within months of the assault.

Relatives, friends and professionals should do what they can to aid the coping and recovery processes, and should avoid obstructing emotional recovery by treating the victim as someone who has become permanently psychologically disabled. Finally, it should not be forgotten that some men are also rape victims.

Men who have been raped by another man are often severely traumatised by the attack, and often feel highly stigmatised, especially if they are homosexual. Overall, the psychological aftermath of male rape appears to be rather similar to that of female rape, except that more male rape victims feel extremely angry with their assailant and engage in fantasies involving retributive violence.

The voyeur (or 'peeping Tom') becomes sexually aroused when he observes people without their permission when they are naked, undressing or engaged in sexual activity. The term 'voyeurism' is not applied to a normal curiosity about sexual activities or sexual responses to pornographic films or strip shows. The invasion of other people's privacy and the forbidden nature of the activity are essential to the voyeur's pleasure. The voyeur seeks out places where he might observe strangers undressing or engaged in sexual activities, and may wait for hours in the hope of witnessing an arousing scene. Most voyeurs are aroused more by their illicit spying activities than by having sexual intercourse with a consenting partner. They gain sexual satisfaction by masturbating while observing a 'forbidden' event or by incorporating scenes from their peeping expeditions into their masturbation fantasies. The vast majority of voyeurs are male, most are relatively young, and most are single. Since they are usually very apprehensive about any direct sexual contact, they rarely make any physical approach to the unwitting victim or commit a serious sexual offence.

Many exhibitionists seek out particular types of victim (women who are alone, for example, or groups of school girls). Some expose themselves whenever an opportunity arises, but others commit the offence only when they are feeling particularly stressed. The majority of offenders are aged between 16 and 30 (although some begin to engage in this kind of behaviour much later in life, often following the onset of senility). Despite the fact that many exhibitionists have poor social skills, are often emotionally immature, and tend to lack assertiveness, most are married. Exposure can take on a somewhat compulsive quality, so that many exhibitionists seem oblivious to what is happening around them. Many do little to reduce the risk of arrest.

A fairly high proportion of offenders are eventually caught, and 'indecent exposure' cases account for around one-third of all prosecutions for sex crimes in most Western societies. Although some exhibitionists masturbate while exposing themselves, very few attempt to touch their victims or incite a victim to touch them. This suggests that the behaviour is generally not to be understood as a 'sexual invitation'. Some exhibitionists hope that the victim will react by showing some sign of pleasure or admiration, but most seem particularly gratified when the victim registers shock, fear or indignation. One explanation for the development of exhibitionism links the behaviour pattern to some chance event which occurred when the person was fairly young.

Some exhibitionists recall with considerable excitement the shock and embarrassment shown by someone who inadvertently disturbed them when they were either masturbating or urinating so that any sign of another person's shock or disgust has become a powerful sexual stimulus. Various methods have been used to treat exhibitionists, although most meet with only partial success. The most effective approach involves training the person to identify particular circumstances which lead to temptation and then helping him to employ strategies to avoid dangerous situations and thus pre-empt the sequence of actions which is likely to result in exposure.

PAEDOPHILIA

Many children are sexually abused, there is a considerable market for child pornography and child prostitution is prevalent in many parts of the world. One study of male students in the United States found that around 20 per cent admitted to having had sexual feelings about young children. For the vast majority of these, however, children were not the principal focus of erotic interest, and they would probably never actually engage in any sexual activity with a child. On the other hand there are some people (mostly men), known as paedophiles, whose sexual interests focus exclusively on prepubertal children. Paedophiles obtain sexual gratification by fantasising about or engaging in sexual contact with children. Although many children fall victim to these men, it needs to be emphasised that the majority of adults who sexually abuse children are not paedophiles.

Many adults abuse children simply because a child is judged to be 'available', 'amenable' or in some other way an easy target for sexual attention. Most paedophiles are sexually attracted to children between the ages of 8 and 12, and while some are principally heterosexual or homosexual in their orientation, many are attracted to both boys and girls. Many paedophiles are law-abiding citizens with no history of psychiatric disorder.

Some are married and many have a good employment record. Many obtain jobs, or positions with voluntary agencies, which bring them into close contact with children, while others make strenuous efforts to become accepted as a friend of a family in which there are children. Other paedophiles 'cruise' for their victims in parks and other places where children may lack adult supervision.

The approach to the child is usually playful and seductive, rather than threatening and most paedophiles 'groom' children in order to gain their trust and acquiescence. The child victims are often given gifts, or may be bribed or tricked into participating in sexual acts. Some paedophiles merely expose themselves or show children pornographic material. Some entice groups of children to join them in sexual activities, and some persuade the children to act together sexually or to pose for pornographic pictures.

Other paedophiles fondle their child victims, or engage in masturbatory acts, but there is rarely any attempt at intercourse. Many are not concerned to reach orgasm while they are with a child, but gain their sexual satisfaction later when they recall their contact with the child in masturbation fantasies.

Few paedophiles behave aggressively towards their victims; most insist that they love children and would never hurt them. They are usually playful or seductive in their manner, partly because this is often effective in gaining the child's compliance, but partly because they often have a genuine affection for the child.

Many paedophiles regard themselves as kind-hearted and 'childlike' and claim that they are attracted by the child's gentle and trusting nature. They generally have no wish to frighten their victims, and also realise that a distressed child is likely to draw attention to the abuse. Nevertheless, following the abuse, the paedophile may threaten the child with a frightening picture of the possible consequences of disclosure. The sexual abuse of children is fiercely condemned, but whereas some people regard paedophiles 'merely' as criminals, others see paedophilia as a psychiatric condition and feel that paedophiles have little control over their sexual preference.

Despite the views of legislators, law enforcement agencies, mental health professionals and the general public, some paedophiles refuse to accept that their actions are either immoral or disturbed. Such men insist that sexual contact between a 'caring adult' and a child is not harmful and argue that such contacts should be permitted within the law.

Some paedophiles appear never to have matured emotionally. They continue to think of themselves as children and claim that they feel at ease only when in the company of other children. A person who initially resorted to sexual contact with a child will eventually come to prefer sex with children. Other instances of paedophilia seem to have developed when a man who has continually fantasised about his own childhood sexual experiences becomes highly aroused when he is alone with children and eventually acts out his fantasies. A relatively high proportion of paedophiles appear to have been victims of sexual abuse during childhood.

CHILD SEXUAL ABUSE

Over the past few decades there has been a growing awareness that child sexual abuse (CSA) is not a rare phenomenon but that a substantial proportion of children are sexually victimised. The alarming rise in known cases probably reflects a growth in the awareness of the problem by professionals, parents and victims themselves, however, and there is little to suggest that the problem itself has been increasing.

'Child sexual abuse' is not a legal term, precisely defined in law in the way that 'incest' and 'rape' are. Although definitions vary (in terms of what kinds of behaviour constitute abuse, the age of the child involved and so on), it is generally agreed that CSA involves a sexual act between a child and someone substantially older.

The act may be intercourse, although this is relatively rare, at least with younger children. More often it is one of fondling, petting or oral-genital contact. Non-contact behaviours, such as masturbating in front of a child, or showing pornographic videos to a child, may also be forms of CSA. An abusive incident may be an isolated event, especially if the perpetrator is a stranger to the child. But many children are abused repeatedly by the same perpetrator, who may be a member of his or her family. Repeated abuse often involves a gradual progression from casual fondling and petting to more serious forms of abuse. Such chronic abuse may end as a result of disclosure by the victim, pregnancy or the diagnosis of a sexually transmitted disease.

However, in the majority of cases it ends when the victim reaches an age when he or she feels powerful enough to resist the abuse. Although few countries have laws which specifically prohibit 'child sexual abuse', all have laws which can be used to prosecute adults who abuse children sexually. Thus prosecutions may be brought under laws relating to rape, intercourse with a minor, or indecent assault. A child's compliance in any sexual activity with an adult is no defence, because it is assumed that a child cannot truly consent to any kind of sexual relationship with an adult.

Relatively few offenders are paedophiles, and most do not have a criminal record for any other type of sexual offence. In many ways child abusers represent a fair cross-section of the male population in terms of their personality, level of education, social class, religious affiliation and so on. Offenders do not engage in sexual abuse because they wish to inflict pain or trauma on children.

In the majority of cases CSA is a selfish act in which the offender uses a child to satisfy some personal hunger. The motive is usually sexual, but some perpetrators use sexual contact with a child to satisfy their craving for tenderness, intimacy or power. Adults are able to gain sexual access to a child because they have power, and abuse is an exploitation of the power, respect and trust that children are encouraged to place in adults.

Some of those who are in a privileged position of power and responsibility betray the trust which others place in them and use their access to a child as a means of gaining sexual pleasure. Although some offenders claim that their victims were 'seductive' in their manner, it is clear that whatever a child's behaviour they had no right to arise the child.

Although the motive of sexual gratification can explain most cases of CSA, some offenders have developed an inappropriate romantic inclination towards the child whom they abuse. In some cases of father-daughter abuse, for example, the father's parental love for his daughter becomes sexualised. While close father-daughter relationships are normal, particularly at certain ages, it is dangerous for a father to think of his daughter more as a girlfriend than as a daughter and fathers should avoid the kind of interactions which blur the generation gap.

A father's romantic feelings towards his daughter, whether or not these feelings ever lead to any sexual overture, may result in extreme sexual jealousy of the daughter's boyfriends. One reason why so much sexual abuse takes place within the family is that relatives may have many opportunities to be alone with the child, behind closed doors. Some adults (relatives or others) deliberately create opportunities in which abuse might occur, but it is likely that most adults who are tempted to behave towards a child in a sexual and inappropriate way find the idea of actually making any sexual overture simply 'unthinkable'.

Inhibitions against approaching a child sexually are sometimes weakened as a result of stress, alcohol or various rationalisation strategies. Thus some sexually abusive fathers convince themselves that sexual contact between fathers and daughters is natural, or they may justify their abuse by claiming that because the abuse does not involve intercourse it is 'not really abuse' or 'not harmful'. Inhibitions may also weaken when an abuser finds that the victims appear to accept the abusive behaviour. Most children are relatively passive when they are sexually abused and this might allow a perpetrator to convince himself that 'she is enjoying it', 'she doesn't mind' or 'she won't be harmed. Despite apparent passivity, many victims experience a complex and diverse assortment of emotions. Many are confused because, as well as feeling guilt, shame, fear, anger and resentment, they may also experience some physical pleasure, a feeling of special closeness with the abuser, and loving feelings towards the offender. Most abusers act as 'careful seducers' rather than as 'attackers', and violence is, rarely used. CSA perpetrators also realise that injuring, marking or traumatising a victim will increase the likelihood that the abuse will be revealed.

A need to prevent disclosure by the victim, however, may lead to threats and warnings following the abuse. Abusers often frighten their victims into silence by warning them about the possible catastrophic consequences of disclosure. Relatively few victims disclose abuse to a relative, teacher or other adult. Various factors contribute to this silence. Young children might not understand that they have been abused, particularly if the offender treated the abuse as a game. Some children are afraid that they will be held to blame, and punished, and many worry about the possible consequences for the offender (especially if he is a relative). Some victims repress memories of the abuse.

The experience of sexual abuse can be severely traumatising, both immediately and in the longer term. No uniform picture can be presented of the typical after-effects of CSA because there is no 'post-sexual abuse syndrome' and the effects are highly varied. They may include anxiety, depression, an abnormal interest in sexual matters, and various forms of behavioural difficulties. In adult life, those who have a history of abuse are more likely than other people to experience anxiety, depression, difficulties in forming and maintaining intimate relationships, and various kinds of sexual dysfunction.

A relatively high proportion of the adults who abuse children were themselves victims of child abuse and it is also true that many women who become prostitutes have a history of sexual abuse during childhood. The psychological damage which results from CSA is not simply a result of the child's experience of the sexual element of the abuse, but may also reflect the child's awareness of powerlessness and the fact that the secrecy imposed by the abuser tends to isolate them from other people, including members of their own family. Some of the trauma experienced by CSA victims may also reflect certain events which may follow disclosure. It would clearly be irresponsible to attempt to understate the adverse effects of abuse, but it must also be recognised that trauma is by no means universal for all abused children, and that, thankfully, many appear relatively unscathed by their victimisation.

Parents, teachers and other professionals must be careful not to undermine children's natural resilience by assuming that a child who has been abused must be traumatised. Any insistence by caring adults that the child is 'different' can communicate unfortunate messages to the child and may constitute unwitting re-victimisation. It must not be assumed that a child who has been abused is somehow destined to fail in relationships, to develop sexual problems in adult life, to abuse other children, or to become a prostitute.

A child who has suffered abuse must not be made to feel that she or he is damaged and will never be the same again. Children should not be made to feel flawed, 'dirty' or freakish because they have been abused. Care should also be taken to avoid any suggestion that the child might have been in some way partly responsible for the abuse, or is at fault in not having disclosed the abuse. Many child victims and adult survivors of CSA continue to feel guilty about the abuse, and such feelings may be exacerbated if other people imply some guilt or misdemeanour.

During childhood or later, because he enjoyed some of the physical and emotional feelings associated with abuse, the child is often confused by a mixture of feelings which are likely to include fear, embarrassment, anger and severe anxiety pornography but which might also involve pleasurable bodily responses and the experience of being wanted. It needs to be emphasised that when ever an adult and a child are involved in any sexual activity, the blame rests entirely with the adult. Similarly, it should not be assumed that because a child has been sexually abused (especially by a member of the family) the child will thereafter hate the abuser and wish to avoid all further contact with him or her. In this, as in all aspects, relatives and professionals need to be sensitive to the child's wishes (while also protecting the child from the risk of any further abuse).

INCEST

Incest refers to sexual relations between people who are closely related to one another. Sexual intercourse between a brother and sister is illegal, as it is between a person and their parent or grandparent. The legal definition of incest varies from country to country. In some cases the incest law prohibits intercourse between cousins or between in-laws. The term 'incest' is somewhat ambiguous, because as well as being applied to cases in which two closely related adults consent to intercourse. It is also used to describe cases in which a child is sexually victimised by an older person within the family (whether or not intercourse is involved).

A strong cultural taboo against incest appears to have been almost universal across societies and throughout history. Among the very few exceptions are the pharaohs of ancient Egypt and the royalty in Hawaii many centuries ago. The extreme stigmatisation associated with incest, and the fact that it occurs within the confines of the family home, means that this offence will come to light only in exceptional circumstances.

PORNOGRAPHY

Pornography may be defined as any depiction of people or acts which is designed to arouse the viewer sexually. However, it is clear that different people respond in quite different ways to the same material. Images which excite some will disgust others, and leave others unaffected. Furthermore, material which was not produced to stimulate any sexual response may prove highly arousing to some people. For example, some paedophiles claim that while explicit child pornography does not arouse them, they are highly stimulated by more commonplace pictures of children (for example, those found in mail-order clothing catalogues).

The impact of pornography also depends to some extent on the cultural context in which it is viewed. Pornography has existed for many centuries and is one of the first ways in which new media are exploited. Thus pornographic images were produced soon after the advent of photography, film and video, and recent technological developments (including the internet) have been similarly exploited. The issue of whether pornography should be available or banned has long been controversial. Some people argue for total freedom of expression and open access to all materials, many favour the prohibition only of certain types of material, and some call for a ban on all sexually explicit publications.

Some couples report that pornography has helped them to reach new levels of sexual excitement, and many men who regularly use pornography claim that its effects are wholly benign. Increasingly, some pornography is being produced specifically for use by women. On the other hand, many of those who oppose pornography claim that it degrades the user and offends against certain moral principles, and many feminists argue that pornography demeans and 'objectifies' women. The large body of research into the effects of pornography, and whether it is harmful, has failed to produce clear answers. But there is little evidence to support the view that people become sex offenders as a result of exposure to pornography. Because pornographic material is generally used during masturbation, and helps the person to achieve an orgasm, it may actually reduce the short-term probability that a sexual offence will be carried out.

In the long term, however, the impact of pornography may be less innocuous. Material which depicts sexual acts involving unwilling partners (who may also end up appearing to enjoy their involvement), for example, may be incorporated into a person's sexual fantasies. Continued exposure to pornography also appears to produce a desensitising effect, so that images which were once arousing eventually lose their power to stimulate; this may explain why those who make regular use of pornography often progress to ever more explicit and 'harder' material.

In ancient Greece and for many centuries in Japan, high-class prostitutes provided sexual and other services for leading citizens and were highly respected. But there have always also been the less respectable prostitutes, the streetwalkers who provide sex for any man who can afford to pay. Men use prostitutes because they do not have a partner, because their wife is unable or unwilling to have intercourse, because they are bored with their usual sex life, or because they wish to engage in sexual practices which their wife disallows.

Many prostitutes offer a range of sexual services which include sadomasochistic practices, oral sex and other specialised activities. Some people regard prostitution as a social evil, while others regard it as a relatively harmless occupation, serving a useful function. Many feminists argue that men who use prostitutes are degrading women, whereas others (including many prostitutes themselves) regard prostitution as a legitimate occupation in which women capitalise on men's 'failings' or simply provide a necessary service. The laws relevant to prostitution differ from country to country.

The laws in some countries permit brothels to operate, and there are frequent calls in other countries for a liberalising change in legislation. Proponents of such changes argue that women would be safer working in such places than walking the streets, and that regular health checks could be enforced to ensure that the women were free from any sexually transmitted disease. Although the practice of child prostitution is universally condemned, many young prostitutes can be found in countries around the world. Boy prostitutes almost always provide a service for gay and bisexual males. Sexual contact with any minor is a serious offence, and older people who encourage children to become prostitutes, or who live off their earnings, are also guilty of a serious crime.

In recent years there have been strenuous efforts to develop treatment programmes which will reduce the likelihood that a person who has been convicted for a sexual offence will offend again, by giving them increased insight into how their behaviour is likely to affect their victims. They are also taught to recognise and avoid situations which may lead to temptation and are shown why beliefs such as 'many women enjoy being raped' and 'no harm comes to children as a result of gentle sexual contact' are untenable.

Some people who have 'merely' been subjected to 'mild' harassment at work, an obscene phone call, or the actions of an exhibitionist will remain highly distressed for a long time, whereas some victims of very serious sexual attacks manage to cope without suffering a breakdown. Any victim of a sexual crime who feels that she or he needs help should make contact with the relevant services available within travelling distance of their home. Voluntary groups (rape crisis centres, child sexual abuse survivors' groups, etc.) operate in many areas, and most are affiliated to national and international organisations. Such agencies may offer telephone contact, counselling, or participation in survivors' groups. Professional help is also available. The first point of contact will often be the physician, although self-referral to community psychological services is now possible in many areas. In addition, numerous counsellors and psychologists work privately and advertise in telephone listings and in the press.

Social services may also be able to provide help, or to recommend a local clinician who specialises in work with victims of sexual crime. Where a child is involved, parents should contact the family practitioner, social services or the school authorities. Various approaches are used to help victims, and there have been major developments in therapy for child victims and adult survivors in recent years. The approach used will depend upon the specific problems presented by the victim and the professional orientation of the therapist. Counselling is likely to be a key element in any work with victims.

Children and adults may be encouraged to give their own account of what happened and how it has affected them. Some forms of counselling rely principally upon such 'talking out' and on the self-healing which may result.

Therapists who operate within a different framework may be more active in giving advice, suggesting alternative ways of looking at events, prescribing 'homework' and so on. In some cases the therapist may suggest that a victim's partner or other members of the family should be included in one or more therapy sessions. Most victims find that they are helped by contact with a therapist or by participation in a group.

6

The Middle Years

The middle years can also be a time of great change. Parents may see their children growing up and leaving home, causing them to redefine their family structure; they may find their relationship with each other is not working, to such an extent that they finally separate and start a new existence; or they may suffer the loss of a parent or find themselves looking after an elderly parent. In the middle years, the physical consequences of ageing have yet to make any real impact. But it is important for individuals to be concerned about their health, however busy they may be. By eating well, exercising regularly and enjoying general good health, men and women in their middle years can be nearly as fit and active as they were in their twenties.

Establishing and maintaining a healthy lifestyle can pay great dividends in old age, by helping to reduce the chances of ill-health. Being fit and healthy will also help a man or woman to look attractive and feel confident, both factors that will enhance their sexuality and help them enjoy a good sex life. Many people feel in their middle years that any sign of ageing will make them less attractive. For most people, especially as they get older, personality and intellect are more important than physical attributes. Couples often find that their satisfaction with and enjoyment of sex increases in their middle years. As they become more experienced and confident in themselves, develop a greater understanding of their partner's needs and desires, and have had the time to explore their sexuality, men and women can feel more sexually fulfilled than when they were younger.

Nevertheless, they may benefit from considering whether their sex lives could be improved if they tried new ways of making love and avoided the same old routines.

PLANNING FOR A LONGER LIFE

The middle years are also a time to plan for the future. Some people already have a healthy lifestyle, with a balanced, varied diet, plenty of exercise, limited alcohol and no recreational drugs. However, anyone in their forties or fifties who has not taken regular exercise before, or who has had any major health problems, should consult their doctor before embarking on an exercise regime, and should take it gently at first, building up gradually.

Smoking is affecting their present health, and is almost certain to shorten their lives. Those who need help to stop should talk to their doctor, who may be able to prescribe a nicotine substitute to help wean them off. Keep trim with regular exercise and a healthy diet. An increasing proportion of men and women in the developed world are overweight, with a smaller proportion of them obese (they have a body weight 20 per cent over the ideal maximum). But by keeping body weight within ideal limits, and by maintaining the proportion of body fat at 15-20 per cent for men or 20-25 per cent for women, the body is under less strain from being overweight, and at much lower risk of disorders such as high blood pressure and joint problems.

Exercise does not need to be a formal session in a gym. A brisk walk through a park, or to work, is a perfectly adequate form of low-impact aerobic exercise. Regular exercise keeps people trim by preventing fat accumulation, and by improving muscle tone so that the body's skeletal muscles perform a better job of supporting the body. It also improves cardiovascular fitness, helping the heart to work more efficiently, and maintains bone mass, counteracting the effect of bone loss which occurs naturally after the mid-thirties. Anaerobic exercise—such as weight training—can also be undertaken to increase muscle bulk, compensating for the loss of muscle tissue which takes place as people get older.

People in the middle years should try to do a range of stretching exercises as part of a daily routine in order to maintain flexibility, improve their posture, prevent aches and pains (including backache), and prevent muscle strains and tears during exercise. A regular programme of stretching will help to avoid postural and joint problems in later life.

A balanced diet keeps the body in a good state of repair; helps to avoid or protect against certain disorders, including cardiovascular disease and cancers; and is essential to keep the body's defence system working effectively.

Regular intake of alcohol can have a beneficial effect on the body. But excessive alcohol—long-term daily consumption of several glasses of wine, beer or spirits—is damaging to health. And because alcohol consists of 'empty' calories (it is not part of a food that contains other nutrients or fibre), it causes weight gain if consumed in excess. If alcohol habit has developed by the middle years, it will probably continue in old age.

Combine this with the tendency of many devoted TV watchers (so-called couch potatoes) to eat and drink while watching the television, and you have an ideal recipe for weight increase and reduced fitness. The solution is to try to ration the amount of TV watched, or, if possible, exercise while watching it by using an exercise bike or ski pad. In the majority of cases, a person's metabolic rate decreases as he or she gets older, as a natural consequence of ageing. But if the same number of calories are consumed as before, there will be a tendency to put on weight.

So it is wise to reduce daily calorie intake as we get older, while not compromising the range and balance of our diet. Also, regular exercise will help to counteract the drop in metabolic rate. As we live in the age of the car, it is only too easy to drive very small distances which we could easily walk. Try walking (or cycling) short distances to do some shopping or buy a newspaper. Given a choice between lift and stairs, take the latter if at all feasible; when taking an escalator or moving walkway, walk rather than stand still.

And there is nothing wrong with people considering during their middle years exactly how mentally stimulated they are. How best to initiate a programme of mental stimulation that will last into old age depends on each individual, but following an academic course, reading, writing stories, keeping a journal or taking up hobbles and games such as cards and crosswords all exercise the mind.

FEELING GOOD AND LOOKING GOOD

Men and women who have been distracted from exercise or good diet by the all-too-absorbing demands of work or childcare may want to alter their lifestyle when they notice the first signs of ageing, in order to improve their fitness so that they look and feel better. Controlling body weight, giving up bad habits (such as smoking, or drinking or eating too much), getting plenty of regular exercise and looking after the skin all help to maintain a positive self-image. Whatever one's past habits, it is not too late to embark on a new regime at this stage.

A good proportion of men and women in the developed world are overweight and, at any one time, many of these people are trying to lose weight. This explains the popularity and financial success of the multinational slimming industries whose interest is in selling slimming products rather than ensuring that their clients' weight loss is permanent. But the following measures may enable a person to attain a body weight within healthy limits, and to keep it within those limits for a lifetime without their weight continually see-sawing up and down.

— Set a target weight by looking at a height-weight chart for your age and sex, or calculate the weight that will give you a BMI of about 24. Do not set a target weight that is too low. It may be difficult to achieve it without losing muscle mass, and may make you look skinny rather than healthy.

— Set a realistic target rate for losing weight—it should be a gradual loss of approximately 1kg (2.2lbs) per week to avoid losing the lean (muscle) tissue you want to keep along with the fat you want to shed.

— Eat small, regular meals each day consisting of a wide range of foods low in animal fats, especially fresh fruit and vegetables; avoid manufactured snacks and junk food. Contrary to popular belief, bread, potatoes and pasta in sensible amounts are not fattening, and provide an excellent energy source. Eat food that you will enjoy continuing to eat once you have reached your target weight.

— Take regular exercise at least three times a week—even a brisk walk. This will increase your metabolic rate, consume fat to release energy, tone up muscles to give the body better shape, and make you feel better and less hungry. By maintaining and perhaps increasing your muscle bulk you will burn more calories each day—muscle tissue consumes more energy than fat.

— Avoid quirky diets, for example, single-item diets (such as grapefruit) or expensive diet products (such as liquid diets that provide unhealthily small amounts of calories each day). Any weight lost this way will be at the expense of lean muscle tissue. These diets also cause the body's metabolic rate to slow down because it 'assumes' it is facing starvation and needs to conserve resources. As soon as the diet stops, the body stores as much food as possible as fat to provide a buffer against future bouts of starvation, so very often the ex-slimmer ends up heavier than before.

— Avoid sugary foods (most processed foods contain 'hidden sugar'), colas and other sugary drinks, and junk food such as burgers, and limit your alcohol intake. Alcohol contains a lot of calories.

— Avoid eating when you are not hungry, even if it is a meal time.

— Use a smaller plate so that there is no temptation to fill the plate with more food than you actually need.

Anyone who keeps to this pattern of diet and exercise can be assured that they should be benefiting on a permanent basis.

Alcohol dependence develops gradually, so that by the middle years someone may not realise how much they are drinking, or how much they need a drink. Apart from liver damage, brain damage and various cancers, long-term alcohol abuse also causes emotional and sexual problems that can put a relationship in jeopardy.

Answer yes or no to these questions to see if you may be damaging your health through drinking too much.

— Do you always look forward to having a drink and plan activities around drinking?

— Do you often drink alone, either at home or in a bar?

— Do you sometimes drink so much that you are unable to remember what happened?

— Do you feel uncomfortable or twitchy if you do not have a drink each day?

— Do you drink as a way of unwinding at the end of a day, to help you sleep, or because it gives you a special 'lift'?

— Do you drink to forget emotional problems, or to overcome depression or anxiety?

— Have you been late for work, taken time off work or missed an appointment because of drinking excessively the night before?

— Do you seem to be able to drink more than other people?

— Do you always look for a refill when your glass becomes empty at parties?

— Do you drink secretively and hide the evidence from relatives or friends?

— Do you set aside money and/or time for your drinking?

Most people with an alcohol problem find this difficult to accept, but it is important to try to deal with alcohol dependence. Seek professional help from a doctor or a counsellor, or contact Alcoholics Anonymous or another alcohol support group—numbers will be in the phone book. Anyone concerned about a relative can contact an Al-Anon Family Group.

Alcohol may have a beneficial effect on health. But what is meant by 'in moderation'? Common advisory limits are around 21 units per week for women, and 28 units per week for men, where one unit is equivalent to a glass of wine, a single measure of spirits, or a half pint (280 ml) of beer. The recommended level for women is lower than for men because of their lower average body volume, and because a lower proportion of their total body weight is in the form of water, so they attain proportionately higher alcohol levels. The alcohol 'allowance' should be spread through the week, not drunk in one session. If you are consuming more than this allowance and you want to moderate your drinking, you could try the following:

— Keep a notebook to record how much you drink every day and how many units you consume each week. Accurate knowledge of how much you are drinking may make you cut down immediately.

— When drinking at home, only drink with a meal. The body absorbs alcohol more slowly with food.

— When you go out for a drink, start with a non-alcoholic drink to quench your thirst.

— Also, instead of drinking one alcoholic drink after another, try alternating alcoholic and non-alcoholic drinks.

— Try alcoholic drinks which are heavily diluted with mixers—such as a spritser (a mixture of wine and soda water).

— Drink slowly and put the glass down between sips.

— Aim to have a number of alcohol-free days each week. Perhaps only drink (in moderation) at the weekend.

Keeping drinking under control makes people feel more in control of life.

Covering the body like a protective overcoat, the skin is constantly exposed to wear and tear. Wrinkles and folds in the skin are one of the first indications that the body is ageing, although, with care, some of these changes can be delayed. The major ageing factor affecting the skin is exposure to sunlight and wind.

Despite the many health warnings—overexposure to sunlight also increases the risk of developing skin cancer—many people still fall to protect themselves against excess sun, especially during the summer months or while on holiday. Ideally, exposing the skin to sunlight, especially at the hottest times of day, should be kept to a minimum and everybody should use a protective suncream or sunblock. Sunhats and loose clothes should be worn whenever possible. Although moisturising cream can never get rid of wrinkles caused by ageing, if applied regularly it can help prevent wrinkles caused by excessive drying of the skin from forming.

Aesthetic plastic surgery, this is not carried out to effect a cure for an illness or deformity but to change, and hopefully 'improve', a person's appearance. Many other middle-aged people do not see cosmetic surgery as necessary because they do not believe that ageing makes them less attractive. Anyone seriously considering cosmetic surgery should realise that it may not necessarily produce the desired alterations to their looks. Nor will surgery automatically remove any negative feelings a person has about their looks or produce a 'new' personality. It is important, however, to consider carefully the reasons for undertaking cosmetic surgery before going ahead with it. It is also important to find a surgeon who has a track record of success in this field. The following are some of the most commonly performed types of cosmetic surgery.

The results of a *facelift* are generally good but it may need to be repeated within a few years, and it can produce a tight-skinned, corpse-like appearance in later life.

Liposuction involves sucking out excess fat from under the skin to alter body shape. Carried out by an expert, the results can be very effective, although with a less proficient surgeon liposuction may leave a lumpy finish. The effects may not last long, however, and it may be more effective to change the diet and take more exercise to tone the body naturally.

Breast enlargement is available for women who feel unattractive because of their small breasts, or would just like larger ones. Similarly, breast reduction can be of great benefit for women who feel weighed down and hampered by over-large breasts.

The amount of collagen present in the skin decreases with age. Collagen injections can therefore be used to give a more youthful appearance to a part of a person's face or the hands, although these injections will need to be repeated when the collagen breaks down, in about two years.

SEXUAL RELATIONSHIPS

Some couples may be quite happy and content with the amount of sex in their lives, whether they make love twice a week or twice a month. In other relationships, one person may feel aggrieved because their partner does not want sex as often as he or she does. But while the quantity of sex may have decreased, many couples who have a happy relationship find that the quality of their sex life has improved over the years.

— As partners get to know each other better, and talk to each other about their feelings, desires and fantasies, they become more in tune with what sexually arouses them.

— Partners are more relaxed about sex, and have become more experienced.

— The nature of most men's interest in sex shifts as they get older. In his teens and twenties, when the physiological response was most rapid and potent, his main focus of sexual pleasure was his orgasm. By the time he reaches his late thirties and forties, a man is less orgasm-driven, and more interested in the sensual pleasures of sex.

— By her thirties and forties, a woman will understand her body better than she did when she was younger, and will be much more capable of sexual arousal and orgasm.

Sexual compatibility and mutual enjoyment is an important factor contributing to the success of most relationships. Providing both partners stay healthy, couples who have a successful, fulfilling and interesting sex life in their middle years are likely to continue to enjoy sex into old age. It may be that their relationship has been allowed to stagnate or that they feel themselves to be no longer sexually attractive; in this situation, the relationship could be enlivened by a few innovations. Alternatively, it may simply mean that the relationship is not working.

If sex becomes a chore it is likely to happen less and less frequently, and a couple's relationship may suffer as a result. But there are ways, given the time and inclination, to liven up flagging sex lives. However, it is important to remember that what may prove exciting for one couple, or for one partner within a couple, may be a complete turn-off for another individual or couple. Here are some of the ways that couples may choose to enliven their sex lives:

— talking to each other about what they enjoy doing sexually, as this can be very arousing;
— complementing each other about how sexy they look, removing fears either partner has about losing their sexual attraction;
— if sex has always been underwear-free, sexy underwear can add another dimension to arousal and lovemaking;
— many men and women enjoy reading, looking at or watching erotica in the form of books, magazines or videos;
— sex manuals can provide some fresh ideas;
— sex toys such as vibrators may help. Women may find that using a vibrator to stimulate the clitoris produces a very intense orgasm;
— meeting 'secretly' at a new location, such as a hotel, to enjoy a sex session;
— sharing sexual fantasies.

Interest in partners can wane as a relationship matures, and a man or woman may seek, and perhaps find, a new sexual partner. There are various reasons why this may happen.

— One or both partners may simply not like the other any more, in which case the relationship is probably doomed.
— One or both partners may be 'lazy' and make no effort to keep the relationship interesting or alive. In this case they may be helped by talking to each other or through support from a counsellor.

— A partner may be feeling 'old' and seek to renew his or her youth by having an affair with a younger partner. If this is the case, the relationship can go either way—it may founder, or the couple may recover.

In general terms it is important to maintain the dynamism of a relationship, keeping it alive by doing different things together, keeping sex exciting, and making a point of not taking each other for granted.

Mid-life crisis may be caused by the realisation that ambitions will never be attained, that old age is getting nearer, that a particular relationship is never likely to work, or by fear of losing one's looks or sexual attractiveness. Not everyone experiences such feelings, and in those who do, they can range from mild discontent to serious depression. In recent years, some experts have gathered such symptoms under the general term 'mid-life crisis'. According to the proponents of the idea of the mid-life crisis, men and women who experience it may feel that they are losing their youthful appearance and sexual vigour.

Women who have spent much of their adult life looking after their children may be faced with a void in their lives when the children leave home. Aware that their 'biological clocks' are ticking away towards the menopause, some women may also experience feelings of disquiet or even panic.

Some men and women may have affairs at this stage if they feel sexually dissatisfied with their partners. They may seek a clandestine relationship with a younger man or woman, believing that this will help to restore their youth. Whether or not a mid-life crisis exists, many men and women in their forties do take stock of what they have achieved and what they want to achieve in the future.

Men especially tend to be worried by the prospect or reality of losing their job, because they have been brought up to see their role as a 'breadwinner'. With more women in high-profile, highly paid jobs, men who are earning less or have been made redundant may feel that they have lost their significance. In this situation, it is often helpful for them to question their role and realise that they are still important as individuals even if unemployed. But if the future does appear worrying, it can be helpful to plan for it—as far as one can—by setting new but attainable goals. Most of all, try if possible to adopt a positive approach—look to the future, not the past.

— If you are not happy with your current career and do not see much future in it, then think about what you would really like to do, and investigate the possibilities of doing it. It is probably not too late! Talk about your thoughts with your partner.

— Consider the advantages of getting older if you have children. When they are in their late teens or twenties, you should find that you can have a more mature, adult relationship with them. And when they have left home you will have more space and time for your partner. If children are younger, think about their education and future; plan all the things that you want to do and share with them.

— Think about parents. As they reach old age, will you be able to provide them with help or care if they need it? A little forward planning now can help you avoid feelings of guilt and pressure later on.

— Plan what you want to do with your partner—places to visit, perhaps where you want to live. Write down when you want to achieve your goals, and tick them off as you do them.

A woman's fertility decreases in her thirties, early forties and, most dramatically, late forties. She and her partner should continue to use contraception until she is certain she has reached menopause. Until then, there is always a risk of pregnancy if a couple have sex without contraception; if a woman embarks on a new relationship without adequate protection she also risks catching a sexually transmitted disease.

The oestrogen in the pills can also offset initial menopausal symptoms. At present, pill-use declines sharply in women over 35 in Britain, perhaps because many women prefer not to continue using a hormonal method for prolonged periods. The POP is also effective in this age group although some women experience irregular periods or loss of periods. The same applies to hormonal implants and injections. Condom effectiveness tends to increase with age, as couples become more proficient in their use and women's fertility decreases. In Britain, 17-20 per cent of couples in their thirties and forties use male condoms. The IUD and IUS are appropriate for women who have had their families. Both are highly effective and can remain in place for years.

Although natural methods are more effective at this age, because of greater experience and diminishing fertility, they are only used by a small proportion of couples. Natural family planning is not recommended once a woman's periods become irregular. Female sterilisation is the most popular form of contraception in the middle years, followed by male sterilisation (in the UK, 26 per cent of women and 22 per cent of men). Although both are effective, and mean that a couple do not have to think about contraception ever again, there may be a tendency to opt for methods which do not involve surgery and are reversible.

PARENTING

Many people face the prospect of their offspring leaving home to go to college, travel, set up on their own, or get married. Some parents react to the departure of children quite happily, relishing the feeling of autonomy and freedom. Others feel grief and loss, which in their most profound form are akin to bereavement and are described as 'empty nest syndrome'. As forward planning, both practical and emotional, can be invaluable, it is worth considering some of these factors:

— Women who have spent their adult life bringing up their family may find children leaving home hard to bear because they have invested all their emotional energy in their children and have defined their life in terms of motherhood. Taking on new interests or work before the children leave home can alleviate feelings of loss.

— Although women are typically seen as the ones who experience 'empty nest syndrome', it can also affect fathers and other members of the family. Open discussion about changes in the family structure can be invaluable in sorting out conflicts and upsets that may occur when children leave.

— The home environment will change, because it is not only the child that departs but also their noise, untidiness, friends and liveliness. This can be the time to reorder the household.

— Younger children who remain at home will probably seek substitutes for the older siblings who have left, resulting in a shift in family dynamics. Parents need to take account of everyone's feelings when a child leaves home: their own, those of the departing child and those of children remaining at home.

— When older children return home for visits, both parents and children need to establish new ground rules so that the parents do not drive their children away by nagging them, while the children should not treat the parental home like a hotel.

Children necessarily require more attention from a lone parent than would be expected from either partner within a two-parent family. This means that the child (or children) often effectively defines the structure of the lone parent's life, a structure which can start to disintegrate rapidly when the child leaves home. While some lone parents, like other parents, may be overjoyed at the prospect of the new freedoms that will come with the release from parenting, many—although wishing their offspring well—experience grief and depression.

Remember that in these circumstances it helps to talk and be open about your worries. Talk over your feelings—and this may be easier for women than men—with friends who are in, or approaching, the same situation, or with any children still at home. You may find support from a lone parents' group. It is also important to remember that the investment a lone parent has put into his or her child does not usually come to an end just because they have left home: he or she will still be much in demand for help and advice.

For increasing numbers of couples, parenthood does not arrive until they are in their late thirties or forties. The first problem for many is that they feel more tired looking after a new baby than younger parents do. Then, as children get older, parents come to recognise the considerable age gap, and may need to adjust their lifestyle to cope with their children's demands. By the time the children are adolescents, parents may be approaching their sixties, and be more in the age bracket of grandparents than parents. But despite these possible problems, being an older parent can be most satisfying.

7

Contraceptive Methods

Contraception or birth control is the prevention of pregnancy. A contraceptive is any device or medication that achieves this. Some contraceptive methods prevent fertilisation, while others permit fertilisation but prevent implantation of a fertilised egg in the lining of the uterus. Abortion, in contrast, is not a form of contraception but the termination of a pregnancy after implantation. There are a number of contraceptive methods available today with varying degree of efficiency and can be chosen from according to individual suitability.

— *Rhythm method*: The rhythm method is keyed to the sequence of fertile and infertile periods of menstrual cycle. If intercourse takes place only in the first week and last week of menstrual cycle, it is unlikely to coincide with ovulation. The method is good in theory but only about 75 per cent reliable in practice, because many women have irregular menstrual cycles and ovulation may occur earlier or (more commonly) later than expected. Moreover it is very difficult to ascertain the exact time/day of ovulation. A convenient and reasonably reliable indicator of the time of ovulation is change, usually a rise in the basal body temperature. Women interested in obtaining an accurate temperature chart should use a thermometer with wide gradations and the temperatures should be recorded in the morning before getting out of the bed. The cause of temperature change at the time of ovulation is not very certain. The ovum lives for approximately 72 hours after it is extruded from the follicle, and sperms apparently survive in the female genital tract for not more than 48 hours. Consequently, the fertile period during a 28-day cycle is actually 120 hours in length

— *Withdrawal method:* (*Coitus interrupts*) In this method the male is supposed to withdraw his penis from the vagina at the moment before ejaculation (semen release). Failures occur because of delay in withdrawal or because the secretion during preliminary skirmishing or before final organism may contain some spermatozoa. Although many partners find it entirely satisfactory a few women fail to achieve orgasm when this method is practised.

— *Douching:* Flushing of vagina with some type of spermicidal solution is not an effective means of contraception. The rationale of the method is to wash the sperm out of vagina. Douching does not work most of the times because immediately after ejaculation thousands of sperms have reached the cervical canal and are beyond the reach of douche.

— *Diaphragm:* The contraceptive diaphragm is a thin rubber cup with a spring in the rim which makes it flexible. The diaphragms are made in various sizes and the correct size must be chosen from for the individual by the physician. When used with spermicidal cream the diaphragm is more than 85 per cent effective in preventing conception. Failures generally result from improper insertion or from neglection of spermicidal cream/lotion.

— *Cervical (or dumas) cap:* This is a small cup-shaped rubber cap which fits over the cervix in the vaginal vault. It is not very effective because it is difficult for the women to put it accurately into position; moreover it is liable to be dislodged during intercourse.

— *Condom:* The condom is a thin rubber sac that fits over the erect penis during sexual intercourse. Semen is trapped within the sealed end of the sac so that sperm cells are never free within the vagina. Condoms are available without prescription and are considered to be free of harmful side effects. They also reduce the risk of transmission of venereal diseases, because contact between the sex organs of male and female is avoided. The latex rubber sheaths (condoms) can also be lubricated with spermicidal jelly for additional contraceptive safety.

One disadvantage of condom is that sexual foreplay is interrupted while the condom is fitted onto the erect penis. Condoms are considered only 90 per cent effective because they sometimes loosen or break, allowing the semen to spill into the vagina. But still they have proven to be the most effective barrier against pregnancy and transmission of infections including HIV/AIDS.

— *Spermicides:* Contraceptive foam and jellies contain condom that kill sperm cells. The appropriate dosage is simply inserted with an applicator into the vagina just prior to intercourse. These preparations are available without prescription. Disadvantages of spermicides are that they are only about 80 per cent effective and that they tend to be costly. Contraceptive jellies are often used in combination with a diaphragm.

— *Intrauterine contraceptive devices (IUDs):* Many different IUDs have been invented, in the form of spiral coils, bows, rings and Ts. They are usually made up of radio-opaque plastic material and can be compressed (or straightened out) so that they can be passed through the cervical canal into the uterus, and so long as it remains there neither the woman nor her partner are required to take any pill or use any appliance.

It is easiest to insert the IUD during menstruation, when the cervix is more open; or it can be inserted in the puerpeperium (the period soon after childbirth). The insertion is almost always possible without anaesthetic substances/chemicals.

Sometimes the device is extruded by the uterus, and if this is not noticed by the patient, pregnancy may occur. Some devices have tail or nylon thread which projects through the cervix, so that continued presence of the device can be proved by digital (with fingers) examination.

The exact mode of action by which the IUD prevents conception is uncertain. One explanation is that the IUD makes the uterus more irritable than normal and that resulting uterine contractions expel the fertilised egg from the body before it can implant itself. Another suggestion is that IUD causes a minor inflammation due to which white blood cells are mobilised and destroy the developing embryo before it can implant. Still a third idea is that the IUD changes the cervical mucus so that it is spermicidal (kills sperm cells). The addition of copper to the IUD (as in copper-T), appears to make the IUD almost as effective as the pill.

In a few women, primarily young, who have not borne children, the IUD is expelled spontaneously. In others, side effects such as discomfort and mild bleeding call for their removal. Occasionally women have become pregnant with the IUD still in place. In these instances the foetus does not appear to be harmed by the presence of the IUD and both are expelled at the time of birth.

The IUD can be easily removed or withdrawn from the uterus by pulling on the tail or thread if it has one; otherwise a small hook or artery forceps must be passed into the uterus to grasp it. An anaesthetic is only occasionally necessary for this.

— *Oral contraception:* Oral contraceptives are the most popular form of birth control in today's world. When used properly oral contraceptives are almost 100 per cent effective in preventing pregnancy. The chief advantage of this method, which was introduced in 1958 by Pincus, is that intercourse can take place at any time without the need for either partner to use any local appliance.

Oral contraceptives consist of hormones that alter the normal sequence of menstrual cycle in such a way as to prevent ovulation. There are many different types and brands of oral contraceptives.

— *Sequential method:* With the sequential pills a woman takes a series of 15 pills containing only estrogen, then a combined oestrogen-progesterone pill for the last five days. The regimen is designed to provide a more normal hormonal pattern. The problem with the sequential pill is that if the woman forgets to take even a single pill, ovulation might occur. Thus there is slightly higher risk of pregnancy with the sequential pills.

— *Combined method:* A tablet containing a synthetic estrogen and synthetic progesterone (called progestogen) is taken everyday from the 5th to the 25th day of the cycle. If a tablet is forgotten the patient must take an extra tablet on the very next day.

— *Continuous method:* Chlormadinone acetate is a synthetic progesterone (6 chloro, 17 acetoxy progesterone) which is given everyday in a dose of 0.5 mg without intermission. No oestrogens are added. Although the pill appears to have fever side effects than the older types, it is only 97 per cent effective.

— *Once-in-a-week pill:* Recently a pill has been developed which is to be taken only once in a week. It is available at select medical stores/outlets in India with a trade name "SAHELI".

CONTRACEPTIVE PILLS: MYTH AND REALITY

According to recent estimates only 1.2 per cent of Indian women are on the pill as compared to say Germany's 59 per cent. The pill otherwise is one of the most effective forms of contraception. Certain myths and misconceptions seem to have outweighed its benefits. Here we have tried to differentiate between myths and reality about contraceptive Pill.

Myth: Pill users are liable to get high blood pressure, blood clots, breast tenderness, cancer and nausea.

Reality: On the contrary long-term use of the pill provides protection against certain cancers, especially those affecting the ovaries and the endometrium (lining of uterus).

Except for the small group affected by the type of breast cancer that is more sensitive to estrogen, there is no positive indication of risk. Women who already have a history of blood clots or "deep vein thrombosis" (VTE) run the risk of these same problems. Nausea and breast tenderness is only a temporary problem, which usually disappear within one to three cycles.

Myth: The pill can lead to a stroke or a heart attack, especially in smokers.

Reality: Smokers are advised to consult the doctor before choosing to go on the pill, especially those above 35 years. Chances of high blood pressure strokes and heart attack are high among the smokers and the pill cannot be considered as causal factor for such complications.

Myth: Prolonged use leads to weight gain.

Reality: The gain or loss, if any is no more than a couple of kilos and that too in the first year only.

Myth: Use of pill may lead to infertility.

Reality: The pill cannot lead to infertility. When women stop taking pill, some conceive immediately, others within a few months. Studies show that even if pill is taken accidentally while pregnancy, the foetus remains unharmed.

Myth: Use of pill affects the libido.

Reality: There is no effect on libido, neither lowers nor raises it. As there is no risk of pregnancy with the pill, it hightens sexual pleasure.

STERILISATION

The only virtually fool proof method of conception control is sterilisation. This procedure is becoming increasing popular, particularly with middle-aged couples who have already produced the desired number of children.

Male sterilisation

The surgical procedure to render male sterile is simple, relatively inexpensive, takes only about 30 minutes, and can be done in a doctor's office. Each vas deferens is severed through tiny incisions made at the top of the scrotum. The out ends of the vas deferentia are cauterised, or tied, so that sperm cannot travel through the vas deferentia to become part of the semen. In a newer and faster procedure each vas deferens is clamped shut with a vanadium clip.

A vasectomy does not interfere in any way with a man's sexual performance. In fact many people (couples) report a positive effect on their life when the fear of pregnancy has been erased. Since most of the semen is produced by the accessory glands, which are still intact and functioning, there is no noticable change in the amount of semen ejaculated. Only the tiny sperm cells are absent. Sperm cells which are produced in the testes, are simply reabsorbed by the body so that no unusual build-up takes place. The male hormone secreted by the cells in testes is transported as usual by the blood, so that there is no effect on the hormonal balance. By surgically reuniting the ends of vas deferentia vasectomies have been reversed and the male have been made fertile again in about 30 per cent of attempts made.

An alternative to reversible vasectomy is the storage of frozen sperm in sperm banks and if the male decides to father another child after he has been sterilised, he can simply withdraw his sperm for use in artificial inseminating his wife, but such banks have not become popular so far.

Female sterilisation

Tubal ligation is the female counterpart of vasectomy. In this procedure the oviducts are severed and the cut ends ligated so that ova can no longer reach the uterus. Like vasectomy operation, tubal ligation does not in any way interfere with sexuality.

Abortion: Abortion is not really a form of contraception, since obviously conception has occurred already.

Spontaneous abortion: Popularly known as miscarriages spontaneous abortions initiated by natural processes.

Therapeutic abortions: These are performed by the physician when the health of the mother is jeopardised by the pregnancy or sometimes when there is good reason to suspect that the embryo will develop in a grossly abnormal manner.

The third type of abortion is performed to terminate an unwanted pregnancy, that is, abortion solely as a means of birth control.

Although the medical risks connected with abortion naturally depend upon the circumstance under which it is performed, an abortion performed by competent physician in a modern hospital or well equipped clinic is among the safest of surgical procedures (approximately 3 deaths per 100,000 abortions). The earlier in pregnancy an abortion is performed, the safer the procedure is. Most abortions are performed using a suction method. The cervix is dilated and a suction aspirator is inserted and used to remove the thickened lining of the uterus. This lining, the same tissue expelled monthly during menstruation, contains the tiny embryo. Abortions performed later in pregnancy involve injection of a salt solution into the uterus. Severe contractions result, and the foetus is expelled. Abortions may also be induced chemically by administration of prostaglandins. This method appears to be extremely safe, non-surgical means for terminating pregnancy.

According to a recently published report, a revolutionary female condom, regarded as having an important role to play in preventing AIDS and other sexually transmitted diseases, should be on sale in India soon. The manufacturers of the product, the American-based Female Health Company, has signed an agreement with the joint United Nations Programme on HIV-AIDS (UNAIDS) to supply it at a favourable "public sector price" to 160 countries.

The condom which will be sold under the name "femidom" is heralded as the only woman-controlled product that provides protection against sexually transmitted diseases, including AIDS, as well as unintended pregnancy.

Earlier also a condom for women was developed by a US based Indian surgeon, Dr. A. V. K. Reddy. The condom developed was like a plastic undergarment (panty) with a built-in slot which, during intercourse could be inserted into the vagina. The disposable device, made of latex, had also been approved by the Food and Drug Administration (FDA) of United States, for marketing in that country.

Most sexually active people have access to a range of different contraceptive methods, which enable them to enjoy sexual intercourse without fear of unwanted pregnancy. The various methods of contraception described in this chapter are:

— barrier methods, e.g., the condom and diaphragm, which form simple obstructions to stop the sperm and egg meeting;

— hormonal methods, such as the pill, which prevent an egg from being released by the woman's ovary or, in some cases, prevent sperm from reaching the egg;

— the intrauterine device or IUD, which sits like a sentry inside the uterus, primarily acting by halting the progress of sperm on their way to the fallopian tubes;

— natural methods, which require couples to abstain from intercourse on the days when the woman is fertile and likely to conceive;

— sterilisation, which offers a permanent surgical means of preventing pregnancy.

Contraception enables us to view lovemaking as an enjoyable activity rather than a purely procreative one. It allows us to have an active sex life as well as controlling whether and when we have children. How risky is sex without contraception? The likelihood of a woman becoming pregnant if she has regular sexual intercourse but no contraception depends on a number of factors, especially her age, because a woman's fertility decreases over time, after peaking in her late teens and early twenties. This means that 85 per cent of women aged 25 are likely to become pregnant within one year if they have regular unprotected sex. For women aged 40 the figure drops to 45 per cent, and by the age of 50 it is down to less than five per cent. Contraception has another important benefit: some contraceptives can help to reduce the risk of contracting a sexually transmitted disease (STD).

Male and female condoms offer effective all-round protection; diaphragms and caps protect against bacterial STDs but not against viruses. Protection against STDs is particularly important for men and women who are not in a long-term relationship and have a number of different partners each year, as they are at higher risk of contracting an STD, including the HIV virus that causes AIDS. With the spread of AIDS, this issue has become even more crucial, and condoms, which had shown signs of fading popularity in the face of more sophisticated contraceptive techniques, are once more playing a vital role. Doctors recommend anyone who is not in a mutually faithful, HIV-free relationship always to use a condom—even if they are also using another method of contraception at the same time. The best protection against infection is consistent, correct use of condoms.

Where to go for contraception depends on the contraceptive method you choose.

— Male condoms are available over the counter at chemists, or from supermarkets, other retail outlets and vending machines, and also from some family planning clinics.

— Female condoms, along with spermicidal creams, foams and pessaries, can be bought from chemists.

— Diaphragms, cervical caps, IUDs and hormonal contraceptives require a consultation at a GP surgery or family planning clinic.

— For sterilisation you need to visit a family planning clinic or hospital, where a trained doctor will carry out the surgical technique.

The right contraceptive will depend on a number of factors: your age, lifestyle, relationship, health and safer sex plan. What might be a suitable contraceptive method for a young, fit, sexually active woman of 24 may not be appropriate for her contemporary who smokes and has a history of high blood pressure, nor for her mother, aged 45, who is in a long-term relationship and has completed her family. Unfortunately, there is no perfect contraceptive method currently available. You and your partner simply have to choose a contraceptive method that provides maximum protection from pregnancy, but also gives you the freedom to enjoy sex without adversely affecting your health.

Some methods are not suitable for a couple and/or a woman if they have never had sexual intercourse. IUDs are not usually prescribed for women who haven't had children, while the rhythm method and withdrawal are generally too unreliable. Most young couples are therefore advised to use condoms, a diaphragm or the pill.

Medical experts recommend that you use condoms early in a relationship to minimise the risk of contracting a sexually transmitted disease (STD), and continue using them until you are sure that neither of you has an STD. It can take up to six months for infection by the HIV virus to show up in a blood test. If you and your partner are mutually monogamous (and neither has an STD), you may want to stop using condoms and find an alternative method of preventing pregnancy that suits you both.

Most physicians advise women to stop taking the pill two to three months before attempting to conceive, to allow their natural cycles to settle down. Fertility should return straight away once an IUD has been removed or when you stop using condoms, caps or spermicides.

Many women are more prone to vaginal infections in the first few months following childbirth, so it may be a good idea to use condoms. During breast-feeding, doctors will probably advise you to avoid the combined pill (which may affect the composition and quantity of milk).

Some couples choose sterilisation as a permanent means of preventing pregnancy. For long-term but reversible contraceptive methods, you could consider hormonal implants, injections or an IUD.

Women with high blood pressure, sickle cell disease or cardiovascular disease, or diabetics with complications or where the diabetic is over 35 years old are advised to avoid the combined pill or any other birth control method containing synthetic oestrogen. If you suffer from side-effects from your present method, or you're tired of interrupting your lovemaking to look for a condom, or you keep forgetting to take the pill, you may want to reconsider your choice of contraception method.

For centuries, however, people have known that pregnancy can be prevented by using some sort of barrier to stop these battalions of sperm from swimming into the uterus and onwards to their goal—the unfertilised egg. Nowadays, such barrier methods are the most universally familiar forms of contraception. The most familiar type is the male condom—also known as a sheath, rubber, protective or French leather—which has been in use for hundreds of years, although the modern version came into being only with the discovery of latex rubber in the nineteenth century. The female condom is a much more recent invention. Many brands of condom are lubricated for ease of use. For additional contraceptive protection, couples are advised also to use spermicidal foam or cream, pessaries or contraceptive film inserted into the vagina. Vaginal spermicides have the additional benefit of killing many of the micro-organisms that cause STDs.

Male and female condoms have just a two-four per cent a year failure rate if used properly, although this figure can increase to between 12 and 15 per cent a year for 'typical use' of male condoms, and current data suggests a similar efficacy for female condoms in typical use. There is evidence that the failure rate for male condoms could be reduced further if they are used consistently and correctly and with a vaginal spermicide. Male and female condoms are readily available in chemists; male condoms can also be bought in many supermarkets and smaller shops, through mail order outlets and from vending machines. Both types of condom may also be available free of charge from family planning clinics and some doctors.

The condom fits snugly over a man's erect penis, so that when he ejaculates inside his partner's vagina the sperms are trapped in the space at the tip of the condom. Male condoms come in many types, including different colours, flavours and shapes. They are generally made in one size, individually wrapped in foil, although some manufacturers make condoms in different sizes—usually called large, magnum or jumbo, but never small. Condoms without this mark are more likely to split or tear.

Using condoms is straightforward, although it may be a little awkward the first few times. It can be helpful for a man to practise on his own, or for both partners to go through the procedure together before they actually have intercourse. A substitute penis, such as a banana, can prove useful when practising.

Male condoms can add to or detract from the pleasures of sex, depending on the attitude of the couple using them. Many couples, for example, incorporate putting on a condom into their foreplay. Also, by reducing the intensity of sensation felt via the penis, condoms can prolong intercourse and enhance pleasure for both women and men. Condoms cut down the mess after ejaculation as well. On the minus side, they can interrupt the spontaneity of sex, and may mean that men feel less intense pleasure during intercourse. Also, some condoms taste unpleasant.

Male condoms are suitable for most men, provided they are prepared to take an active role in contraception and are sufficiently motivated to ensure that condoms are used properly during sex—that is, they put the condom on correctly (without tearing or splitting it) before any sexual contact takes place; they remove it immediately after intercourse, and wash their penis before any further sexual contact; and a new condom is used every time a couple have sex.

Some men and women show an allergic response—indicated by a sore penis or vagina—after using a condom. There are various reasons for this. They may be allergic to nonoxynol-9, the spermicidal lubricant used in many condoms; if this is the case, they could switch to condoms with an alternative lubricant, or brands that don't use a spermicidal lubricant. They may be allergic to the colouring or flavouring used in 'fun' condoms; the solution to this problem is to use a more conventional condom. The female condom is larger than its male counterpart, and is made of a very thin plastic, polyurethane. It works in much the same way as the male condom except that it fits inside the vagina. It is closed at one end and contains a flexible ring to keep it in place. The ring at the open end lies just outside the vulva and holds the condom open. When the man ejaculates, his sperm-carrying semen stays inside the condom, which is then removed and disposed of.

Using the female condom is reasonably easy with some practice. It can be put in the vagina at any time before sexual contact. Some men and women complain that it makes a rustling noise during intercourse (using extra lubrication may reduce this problem), but many other couples are satisfied with it.

While condoms act as barriers to sperm by trapping the semen ejaculated from the penis during intercourse, diaphragms and cervical caps—with the aid of sperm-killing chemicals called spermicides—form barriers by acting as gatekeepers to the uterus, denying access to any sperm. Both diaphragms and cervical caps must be fitted by a medical professional and require a prescription.

The diaphragm is a circular dome made of rubber, kept in shape by a thin piece of rubber-covered metal that forms the rim. It fits over the cervix to stop sperms getting into the uterus. This is not a tight fit, however, and movement may take place during intercourse. For that reason, spermicide cream must be squeezed on to the inside of the diaphragm before it is inserted, to destroy any sperm that manage to get past the rubber barrier. There are three types of diaphragm, which differ from each other in the type of metal spring found in their rim. A doctor (or nurse) will decide which is the best type to fit.

The coil-spring diaphragm is softer and is recommended for women who are sensitive to the pressure exerted by the flat-spring diaphragm. The arcing-spring diaphragm has a firm double metal spring that exerts a strong pressure, making it suitable for women with weak vaginal muscular support. It forms an arc when compressed, and is therefore easier to insert for women who have a retroverted uterus or a long cervix. Used properly, with spermicides, the diaphragm has a failure rate of 4-8 per cent a year, but this rises to between 15 and 18 per cent a year when in 'typical use'.

Diaphragms are like clothes. They have to be the right size to fit. A visit to the doctor or family planning clinic is needed to find out what size diaphragm a woman requires. The doctor or nurse will also describe how to insert it, and how to use it effectively. Women are usually given a diaphragm to practise with at home and asked to return to the clinic a week later with the diaphragm in place, so that the doctor or nurse can check that it has been inserted correctly and is the right size. Following pregnancy or a weight loss or gain of more than 4.5kg (10lbs), women are advised to return to the doctor or clinic to have the fitting of their diaphragm checked, as a different size may now be required.

The diaphragm can be inserted several hours before sex takes place, although couples will need to add extra spermicide if more than three hours elapse between inserting the diaphragm and having intercourse, or if they have intercourse more than once.

The diaphragm must not be removed to do this: simply use some more cream or spermicidal foam or pessaries. Some couples incorporate the addition of more spermicide as part of their lovemaking. After intercourse, the diaphragm must be left in place for at least six hours, to ensure there are no stray sperm left waiting to complete the journey to the fallopian tubes.

The diaphragm should not be left in for more than 24 hours because of the risk of local abrasions or (very rarely) of toxic shock syndrome. After use, the diaphragm is removed by hooking it out with one finger, then washed in warm water with mild soap, rinsed, dried and returned to its storage box.

Avoiding problems

— After inserting a diaphragm, always check that it is covering the cervix properly.
— Take care with sharp fingernails when removing a diaphragm.
— Be sure to have a check-up once a year.

A diaphragm can be inserted a few hours before intercourse, so that it doesn't interfere with sex itself; and it doesn't cause any loss of sensation for either partner. On the other hand, in practice putting in a diaphragm often does mean interrupting sex; spermicide can make sex messy and may interfere with oral sex because of its taste; the woman may be able to feel the diaphragm in certain positions (for example, if she is on top), although this may indicate she has not fitted it properly; and her partner may be able to feel it in the vagina with his fingers or penis.

Diaphragms are recommended for couples who want to use a barrier method—but not condoms—and find other contraceptive methods unsuitable; for women who are committed to using contraception but do not want to take the pill every day; and for women who want to be in control of their contraception and use it only when it is needed. The diaphragm may not be suitable for women who do not feel comfortable touching their genital area; women who have anatomical problems that preclude the insertion and proper positioning of the diaphragm; women with poor muscle tone in the vaginal walls, so that the diaphragm does not stay in place; women who are unable to learn the correct insertion/removal procedure; women who lack the facilities for private and hygienic insertion of the diaphragm, and its cleaning and storage after use; women who are allergic to rubber or the spermicides used with the diaphragm; and women who have never had sexual intercourse, although tampon-users may be able to insert a small diaphragm.

Advantages of the diaphragm

- It has few side-effects.
- It does not affect fertility.
- It reduces the risk of cervical cancer and of catching some STDs.
- Lovemaking is not necessarily interrupted.

Disadvantages of the diaphragm

- Ideally, it requires some anticipation of whether and when sex is going to occur.
- It can be rather messy.

— It has to be fitted initially by a trained doctor or nurse.
— It can increase the chances of urinary infections such as cystitis in some women.
— It does not protect against certain STDs, such as HIV and herpes.

CERVICAL CAP

Like the diaphragm, it must be fitted by a doctor or nurse. The cap fits snugly over the cervix and is held in place by suction. To make it effective, it requires a squirt of spermicidal cream, which should be directed into the cup of the cap (it should be about half-full-2 teaspoons or so) rather than on to the rim, as this might prevent suction.

The cap is inserted by being pushed into the vagina, and upwards on to the cervix, with the fingertips. Once in place, further spermicide is added to the dome of the cap, using an applicator. Instructions for use, removal and cleaning of the cap are the same as for the diaphragm. Fewer women use the cap than use the diaphragm, partly because it appears to be less effective in younger, more fertile and more sexually active women and partly because the shape of the cervix in some women makes it impossible for them to use a cap. The cap is fairly effective, with a failure rate of about 9-11 per cent a year when used properly, increasing to up to 18 per cent a year in 'typical use'.

Caps can be inserted well in advance and left in place for up to 48 hours—for example, to give all-weekend protection—so they do not affect sexual spontaneity. They need only one small application of spermicide before insertion. They cannot be felt during sexual intercourse, so do not affect vaginal sensitivity. They are comfortable to use and there is no smell of spermicide (unlike the diaphragm).

Advantages of the cervical cap

— It has very few side-effects.
— It does not affect fertility.
— It reduces the risk of catching some STDs (but not the HIV virus or herpes) and of developing cervical cancer.
— It does not affect lovemaking.

Disadvantages of the cervical cap

— It requires some anticipation of when and whether sex is going to occur.

— It has to be fitted by a doctor or nurse and requires accurate selection of cap size to ensure it is not displaced during intercourse.

— Women must have a cervix that accommodates a cervical cap—not all do.

— Women with particularly long vaginas find inserting and removing the cap difficult.

— Even well-fitting caps may be dislodged during sex: this may have something to do with intercourse positions or with the changes in vaginal and cervical size and shape during sexual arousal. If it becomes dislodged—you can check after intercourse—postcoital contraception may be advisable.

— Insertion and removal can be more difficult than with a diaphragm.

— An unpleasant odour may develop if the cap is left in place for more than a day or two.

— In some women, using the cervical cap can increase the chances of developing urinary infections such as cystitis, although this is less likely than with the diaphragm.

— It does not protect against certain STDs, such as HIV and herpes.

SPERMICIDAL CREAMS, FOAMS, SUPPOSITORIES, AND FILMS

Spermicides create a chemical, sperm-killing barrier in the vagina. They come in various forms, all of which should be deposited as near to the cervix as possible: foam that is squirted into the vagina; pessaries, creams, and film that are melted by body heat inside the vagina; and creams that can be squeezed into the vagina with a special applicator or used with diaphragms and caps. To be reliable, spermicides must be used in conjunction with some other form of contraception, such as a condom. Always remember to check the expiry date on spermicide packets: after this date the spermicide will be ineffective and should be disposed of.

HORMONAL METHODS

Hormonal methods of family planning alter a woman's menstrual cycle to prevent fertilisation. There are several different types of hormonal contraceptive:

— the combined pill
— the progestogen-only pill or minipill
— injectable contraceptives
— hormonal implants
— the vaginal ring
— IUDs which release progestogen.

How do hormonal contraceptives work?

A regular cycle of changes occurs within a woman's reproductive system. The monthly ovarian and menstrual cycles, experienced by all women between menarche and menopause, prepare the body for possible pregnancy by releasing an egg, ripe for fertilisation, and thickening the lining of the uterus in readiness for receiving the egg should it be fertilised. Both cycles are controlled by chemical messengers called hormones. The hormonal sequence goes like this: the pituitary gland, underneath the brain, releases follicle-stimulating hormone (FSH), which stimulates one of the egg-containing follicles in the ovary to develop. This causes the ovary to release oestrogen, which stimulates the uterine lining to thicken, makes the pituitary gland slow down its release of FSH, and encourages the gland to release luteinising hormone (LH). When LH levels reach a peak, around day 14 of the cycle, the ripe follicle bursts, releasing its egg into the fallopian tube, where it may be fertilised if the woman has had intercourse.

The burst follicle seals itself up, and starts to produce the hormone progesterone, which encourages the uterine lining to thicken further and also begins to thicken the mucus produced by the cervix, making it impenetrable to sperm. If there is no pregnancy, the uterine wall breaks down, a woman has her period, and the cycles repeat themselves. Hormonal contraceptives work by disrupting the normal operation of the reproductive cycles. These trick the body into altering the amounts of natural hormones in the bloodstream. Most commonly prescribed are oral contraceptives, taken in pill form by mouth. When they are swallowed, the hormones inside them are absorbed into the bloodstream. Recently, however, longer-lasting methods of delivering hormones into a woman's body have been introduced. These include the injectable contraceptive, implants and the intrauterine system..

Only a doctor can prescribe hormonal methods of contraception, so a visit to a GP or a family planning clinic is required. Any doctor who is thinking of prescribing hormonal contraceptives must consider his or her patient's medical situation carefully, because particular illnesses or drugs may make such contraceptives unsuitable. Women using hormonal contraceptives are recommended to have regular check-ups to monitor their weight and blood pressure, and to have regular cervical smear tests.

The combined oral contraceptive pill

The combined oral contraceptive pill, better known simply as 'the pill', is the most widely used of all hormonal contraceptive methods. The uterine lining and cervical mucus are also affected. In fact, the pill is in effect making a woman's body believe that she is pregnant. There are various types of combined pill, with varying levels of oestrogen and progestogen.

Some combined pills are taken for 21 days, after which the user has a seven-day break when she experiences withdrawal bleeding—similar to a light period—before she starts the next pack of pills. Others are taken every day, without a break; however, seven of the pills in the pack are hormone-free, so that a woman taking these also experiences withdrawal bleeding. Both 21-day and everyday pills are commonly monophasic: that is, each pill contains the same level of hormone, although with everyday pills seven are hormone-free.

Three different levels of hormones. These are taken in sequence for the first 21 days of the month, producing a variation in the levels of synthetic hormones which apparently reflects more closely the woman's natural hormonal fluctuations. A pack of triphasic pills may also include seven hormone-free pills.

Tests have shown that—provided it is taken correctly—the combined pill is almost 100 per cent effective. With less careful use, the actual failure rate is between two and four per cent a year. Vomiting or severe diarrhoea can stop the combined pill from working. Some women find not having to worry about pregnancy very liberating, enabling them to enjoy sex more. Taking the pill certainly does not interrupt sex. On the down side, some women report a loss of libido, while others find their vaginal secretions decrease and it becomes necessary to use a lubricant such as K-Y jelly to facilitate intercourse. Also, the pill does not protect against STDs, so women who change partners regularly (or who have a partner who changes partners) will need to use condoms or another barrier method in addition to the pill.

Women could carry on taking modern low-dose combined pills into middle age, provided they are fit, not overweight, non-smokers, and do not show any of the accepted contra-indications. However, because a woman's fertility decreases with age so that she does not need such an effective form of contraceptive, and given that she may not want to take hormones for an unduly prolonged period, she may wish to switch to a non-hormonal method by her mid-thirties. The latest IUDs may be a possible alternative if she has had children and is therefore less concerned about the risk of pelvic inflammatory disease (PID), which may sometimes cause infertility.

The following persons should not use the combined pill?

— Heavy smokers (over 40 a day), or smokers who are over 35 and/or overweight.

— Women who have past or present circulatory disease, e.g., thrombosis, ischaemic heart disease or angina, clotting problems, focal migraine, major heart-valve disease.

— Women with high blood pressure, liver disease or breast cancer.

- Women who are or may be pregnant.
- Women who have long-term diseases which require treatment with drugs that interfere with the action of combined pills.
- Women who travel to high altitudes (over 3,000m/ 10,000ft) and are likely to suffer from altitude sickness.
- Women with complicated diabetes or those over 35 years old who have uncomplicated diabetes.

Breastfeeding mothers are generally advised not to use the combined pill. For them, the combination of the minipill and the naturally contraceptive effect of breastfeeding should be sufficient. For mothers who are not breastfeeding, it is advisable to start the combined pill on day 21 after giving birth.

Advantages of the combined pill

- It is highly effective when used properly.
- It does not interrupt sex.
- It makes periods lighter, less painful and more regular, and can alleviate symptoms of pre-menstrual syndrome and anaemia.
- It reduces the risk of PID, ectopic pregnancy, benign breast disease and cancer of the ovary or uterus.
- It has empowered women to have greater control over their sex lives, freed from constant anxiety about unwanted pregnancy.

Disadvantages of the combined pill

- Taking the combined pill means that the normal cycle of the woman's body is interrupted, with the very small possibility that she may develop a fatal complication.
- The pill may increase blood pressure slightly, and with it the risk of developing blood clots, strokes or heart attacks. However, these conditions are rarely caused solely by the pill, and are mainly likely to occur in women who smoke, especially if they are over 35, are overweight and/or have high blood pressure anyway.
- It can have a number of side-effects, including nausea,

headaches, breakthrough bleeding (bleeding between 'periods'), loss of libido (sex drive), breast tenderness, depression or weight gain. If these occur, the doctor may prescribe a pill with a different hormonal dosage, or suggest an alternative form of contraception. Spotting (very light bleeding between 'periods') and nausea are most common in the first few months and get better over time.

— There is some evidence of a link between long-term pill-use and later development of certain cancers such as cancer of the breast, cervix and liver. This has yet to be proved conclusively.

— The pill offers no protection at all against any sexually transmitted diseases (STDs), including HIV.

The progestogen-only pill (POP) or 'minipill'

The works by blocking the cervix with thick mucus to prevent sperms from entering the uterus, as well as making the uterine lining less receptive to fertilised eggs and the fallopian tube less efficient at moving the egg from the ovary to the uterus. In some women, the progestogen-only pill may also stop ovulation.

Used properly, the POP has a failure rate of 0.5-2 per cent a year; in 'typical use' this can rise to about 4 per cent a year. High failure rates have been noted in women under 30 who are not breastfeeding.

Who is the POP suitable for?

— Women who wish to use a reliable form of contraception that does not interrupt sex, but which does not carry the risks associated with the combined pill.

— Women who wish to use a hormonal method of contraception at a minimal dosage.

— Women prepared to commit themselves to daily pill-taking at the same time each day.

— Women over 35 who smoke.

— Women who wish to use oral contraception but have migraines, diabetes, high blood pressure, obesity or a history of circulatory disorders, including higher risk of thrombosis.

— Women who are breastfeeding.
— Women who experience a lot of nausea using the combined pill.

Persons should not use the POP?

— Women who are or may be pregnant.
— Women who require complete protection against the risk of pregnancy.
— Teenage girls, who are highly fertile and require very effective contraception.
— Women with a personal history of severe disease of the circulatory system.
— Women with undiagnosed vaginal bleeding.
— Women who have had an ectopic pregnancy.
— Women who have ovarian cysts, breast cancer or severe liver disorders.

A woman takes the first pill—one marked with the appropriate day of the week—on the first day of her period, to protect her at once, and continues taking a pill a day until she has finished the pack. She starts a new pack next round. If she forgets a pill, she should take it as soon as she remembers and take the next one as normal at the correct time. If the pill is taken more than three hours late, it will give decreased protection, and another form of contraception is needed for the next seven days.

The POP gives a woman freedom from fear of pregnancy, which may enable her to enjoy sex more. Also, it does not generally decrease libido (unlike the combined pill in some women). However, there may be irregular or breakthrough bleeding at odd times of the month.

Advantages of the POP

— It can be taken by older women and those unable to use the combined pill because of side-effects.
— It can be used by breastfeeding mothers.

Disadvantages of the POP

— It is not as effective as the combined pill.
— It may cause irregular bleeding and periods.

Some women have much lighter periods, others none at all. Breakthrough bleeding may also occur. It might help to change to a different brand of POP.

— Like the combined pill, the POP offers no protection against STDs, including HIV.
— It may increase the chances of having an ectopic pregnancy, although recent evidence suggests this is not in fact so.
— Some women gain weight or may feel bloated (but weight gain is less of a problem than for users of the combined pill).
— Some women experience breast tenderness.

Contraceptive injections

The main injectable contraceptive, Depo-Provera (DMPA), is currently available in over 90 countries, including the United States, Britain and many other European countries. The other type most commonly used is Noristerat. Like the progestogen-only pill, the injectable contains progestogen. But its primary action in injectable form is to halt ovulation. It also thickens the cervical mucus and makes the lining of the uterus less likely to receive a fertilised egg. Although not widely used, most users are very satisfied with it. Provided a woman returns on schedule for her injection, injectable contraceptives have a failure rate of less than one per cent a year. Along with hormonal implants, they are the most reliable method of reversible contraception available.

The injection takes seven days to become effective. Women who have recently had a baby should wait until six weeks after the birth before using this method. The injection is given into a muscle, usually into the large muscle of the buttock. In the weeks following the injection, progestogen is released slowly from this site into the bloodstream. How long it lasts depends on the type of injectable used. Of the two types commonly used, Depo-Provera gives protection for 12 weeks and Noristerat lasts for 8 weeks, after which further injections are required if the method is to be continued.

Contraceptive injections do not interrupt sex, and may enhance a woman's sex life by allowing her to relax, free from fear of pregnancy. In most cases contraceptive injections appear not to have any adverse effects on libido, but some women may notice a difference.

Who should not choose contraceptive injections?

— Women who are or suspect they may be pregnant.

— Women who want to conceive in the near future.

— Women with a personal history of severe circulatory system disease such as heart disease.

— Women with undiagnosed vaginal bleeding.

— Women with severe liver disease.

— Women who feel uncomfortable with the menstrual irregularities, including the cessation of periods, that may occur after they have been given the injection.

— Women with high blood pressure (unless it is treated). Women who showed any severe side-effects with the combined pill that cannot be directly linked to its oestrogen component.

Advantages of contraceptive injections

— As with other long-term methods, the injectable can be taken for granted, at least until the next injection is required.

— It is highly effective, with a less than one per cent a year failure rate.

— It can be used by women who are breastfeeding.

— It can be used by some women for whom the combined pill is not suitable.

Disadvantages of contraceptive injections

— It may cause weight gain.

— Once the injection has been given it cannot be reversed, so if a woman does suffer any side-effects she may have to wait for at least 12 weeks—possibly as much as a year—before these subside.

— Periods may become more prolonged or irregular, or even cease.

— Some women suffer mood swings and depression.

- Fertility may take some time to return often several months, and even a year or more should a woman wish to conceive after using the method.
- It does not protect against any sexually transmitted diseases, including HIV.

Hormonal implants provide a revolutionary new system for delivering contraceptive hormones. Inserted under a woman's skin, they release a steady stream of hormones into her bloodstream over a period of five years. Longlasting, usually easily reversible, extremely reliable and with few side-effects, implants have been hailed as the contraceptive of the future. Each implant contains progestogen and acts as a slow-release carrier for the hormone. Once in place, the implants release the progestogen into the bloodstream, which increases the impenetrability of the cervical mucus to sperm as well as reducing the chances of ovulation or of a fertilised egg implanting in the lining of the uterus. Hormonal implants have a failure rate of less than one per cent a year.

The implants are usually inserted on the inside surface of the upper arm, where they will neither migrate under the skin (as they might do at other sites in the body) nor affect the movement of the arm. After giving the patient a local anaesthetic, the doctor makes a small incision in the skin—about 3mm (1/8 in) long—and inserts the six implants in a fan shape just under the skin. The whole process takes about 10 minutes, and no stitches are required. Some women may find bruising and tenderness where the implants have been inserted, but this usually subsides within a few days. Although some women are worried that the outline of the implants will be seen on the skin's surface, this is rarely the case; however, the implants can usually be felt by rubbing a finger gently over the skin's surface. If inserted on the first day of a woman's period, the implants are effective immediately; fitted at any other time they take a week to become effective, and extra contraceptive protection will be needed in the meantime. The implants will provide continuous protection for five years or so. Should a woman wish to become pregnant, however, the implants can be removed by a trained doctor—

this usually takes about 15 minutes. After removal, return to normal fertility is rapid.

Like injectables, implants are reliable and do not interrupt sex. In most women they have negligible effect on libido, but in some cases there is a noticeable difference.

Who should not use hormonal implants?

— Women who are or may be pregnant.

— Women with a history of severe disease of the circulatory system.

— Women with undiagnosed abnormal bleeding from the vagina.

— Women who have breast cancer.

– Women who have severe liver disorders.

Advantages of implants

— Because of their long-term effectiveness, they can be forgotten about until the time comes for them to be renewed.

— They may be suitable for women who cannot use the combined pill.

— They can be used when breastfeeding.

— They have no long-term effect on fertility.

Disadvantages of implants

— They may cause prolonged and irregular bleeding and changes in the menstrual cycle, to the extent that 10-20 per cent of women request removal during the first year of use.

— Other possible side-effects include headaches, nausea and weight gain—like other progestogen-only methods.

— They do not protect against any STDs, including HIV.

— Pain may occur at the site of the implant.

— Removal of implants may be difficult, occasionally requiring two or more visits to the doctor, or even hospitalisation.

Hormonal methods are currently being researched and tested to find those that combine minimal side-effects with maximum effectiveness and ease of use. Two possible future methods are described below.

However, a third type of long-acting hormonal contraception, which can be inserted or removed by the woman herself, may be widely used in the future. This is the vaginal ring. Made of Silastic, the same silicone rubber that is used for implants, it is a ring about 5cm (2m) in diameter and 6mm (¼ m) thick. The inner core of the ring contains the hormone progestogen, while its outer layer consists of Silastic alone.

The woman inserts it by squeezing the sides of the ring together and gently pushing it into her vagina, much as she would a diaphragm. Inside the vagina, where it moves freely, the ring releases a steady stream of progestogen, which is absorbed into the woman's bloodstream through the vaginal wall. Once inserted, the ring can remain in place for three months, although it can be removed should a couple decide they wish to conceive—fertility returns rapidly once the ring is removed. The vaginal ring works in much the same way as the progestogen—only pill: research suggests that it blocks ovulation in around 50 per cent of women's menstrual cycles; increases the thickness of mucus produced by the cervix, making it impenetrable to sperm; and reduces the chances of a fertilised egg implanting in the lining of the uterus.

The failure rate of the vaginal ring is about three per cent a year, which is higher than for other hormonal contraceptives. This rate is likely to be lowered considerably when a combined ring—containing both oestrogen and progestogen, like the combined pill—becomes available. In trials the vaginal ring has proved easy to use. It offers up to three months' contraceptive cover at a time, and can be controlled by the user. The main disadvantage appears to be that some users experience a vaginal discharge. However, like other hormonal methods, it offers no protection at all against sexually transmitted diseases such as the HIV virus or herpes.

In theory, there is no reason why a male pill should not work. In practice, however, most trials of male pills have failed. If a man is given progestogen, his testes will cease sperm production. Unfortunately, progestogen also stops the release of the sex hormone testosterone, causing a loss of sex drive and thereby defeating the object of the exercise. A combined pill containing progestogen and synthetic testosterone would maintain libido but without fully suppressing sperm production, so a high risk of pregnancy remains. However, the results of a worldwide trial of a new type of male hormonal contraceptive, announced in spring 1996, seem more promising.

Trials indicate that it has a failure rate of less than two per cent, and that it does not reduce libido and may increase it. The next step will be three-monthly injections, and the ultimate aim is to administer testosterone as an implant, a patch or a pill. Also, possible side-effects of a testosterone pill may include increased risks of prostate cancer and heart disease.

IUD

IUD (Intra-uterine device) a small piece of plastic, placed inside the uterus, which prevents conception. Two types of IUD are currently in use. The first is T-shaped with a thin strand of copper wire wound around the upright part of the 'T'. The second is T-shaped, but without the copper wire; it is impregnated with the hormone progestogen, which is released slowly and enhances the IUD's activity. Soft nylon threads attached to the IUD pass through the cervix and into the vagina. By inserting a finger into her vagina, a woman can feel the threads and reassure herself that the IUD is still in position. In Britain and the rest of Europe various copper IUDs are available: the Copper-T 380 is favoured because of its effectiveness and lack of side-effects. In the United States the Copper-T 380 is the only type of copper IUD available. The progestogen-releasing IUD is used in some countries: in the United States the only brand available is the Progestasert system, which used to be available in the UK but was withdrawn from use because of the increased risk of ectopic pregnancy.

However, a new form of hormonal IUD, known as the levonorgestrel intrauterine system or LNG IUS, which releases a different type of progestogen (called levonorgestrel) to that released by the earlier hormonal IUDs—and which therefore does not have the same side-effects—has recently become available in Britain and other European countries.

IUDs are very effective, with a failure rate of only 1-2 per cent a year for copper IUDs and up to 0.2 per cent a year for the new IUS. (Progestasert has a failure rate of 1.5-2 per cent a year.) The IUD makes the uterus even more unfriendly so that no sperm—or very few—survive, making fertilisation virtually impossible. Should fertilisation occur, the presence of an IUD also alters the lining of the uterus, preventing implantation of the egg. The copper wire wrapped around IUDs makes them twice as effective as old-fashioned 'inert' plastic IUDs. Because of their greater effectiveness, copper IUDs are smaller and so cause less side-effects than their inert predecessors. In addition to acting in a similar way to other IUDs, hormonal IUDs locally release progestogen, some of which is absorbed into the bloodstream through the uterus.

Local progestogen causes the mucus secreted by the cervix to thicken, preventing penetration by sperm and adding an extra defence against fertilisation. It also causes the lining of the uterus to be very thin and can interfere with ovulation.

The 'Ideal' user is in her late twenties, or thirties or forties, is in a stable relationship and has had some or all of her children.

Following are the Persons should not use the IUD?

- Women who have pelvic inflammatory disease, have had it, and/or are at high risk of getting it (i.e., are not in a mutually faithful relationship). Infection by PID is most common in younger women who have several sexual partners, and who are therefore more likely to contract the STDs that lead to PID. In this age group, PID can lead to sterility if untreated. For that reason, the IUD is not a first-choice contraceptive for young women who have not had children.
- Women who are or may be pregnant.

— Women with uterine fibroids or uterine scars from previous surgery.
— Women who are allergic to copper (copper IUD only).
— Women who have had an ectopic pregnancy (does not apply to IUS).
— Women with very heavy periods or undiagnosed abnormal vaginal bleeding—although progestogen IUDs may be most suitable as a contraceptive for women who have heavy periods, as they decrease menstrual blood loss and the intensity of painful periods.

Inserting and removing an IUD

The more experienced the doctor—and the better his or her track record in trouble-free IUD fittings—the less the chance of unwanted side-effects in the weeks following insertion. IUD must be fitted and removed by a specially trained doctor. Many doctors prefer to fit the IUD near the end of a woman's period or just after it, because it is easier to insert at this time (the cervix is a little softer) and there is little likelihood that she will be pregnant. The IUD will have to be removed when it comes to the end of its natural lifespan (copper IUDs have a lifespan of five to eight years; progestogen IUDs should be replaced after 12 months, and the IUS after five years), or the woman wants it taken out. Removal must be carried out by a trained doctor: never try to remove an IUD yourself. The best time to have it removed is during menstruation. Removal is carried out using a speculum, and the device is gently pulled out by the threads. Any discomfort should be short-lived.

Many women like the IUD because it does not interfere with intercourse, has no effect on libido, and provides reliable protection.

Advantages of the IUD

— It is very effective and requires only that the woman check once a month that she can feel the threads.
— It is immediately reversible.
— It does not interfere with sex.
— In most women there are no side-effects.

Disadvantages of the IUD

— It must be inserted and removed by a doctor.

— Copper IUDs can cause pains and heavy periods.

— It can be expelled without noticing.

— A copper IUD or Progestasert may result in ectopic pregnancy if a woman gets pregnant while she is using it.

— It does not protect against any STDs, including HIV.

— Copper IUDs can lead to increased incidence of pelvic inflammatory disease

— Very rarely, it may perforate the uterine wall. The chances of this are slim (about 1 in 1000), and it is usually the result of faulty insertion. Initially, perforation can go unnoticed, but the woman may soon realise that she cannot feel the IUD threads, and she is likely to experience an unusual amount of pain and bleeding from the vagina. If the hole in the uterine wall is small it will heal itself. The IUD can be removed by laparoscopy.

NATURAL METHODS

Some forms of contraception require neither hormones, specific devices nor surgical procedures. These natural birth control methods are ideal for couples who, for whatever reason, do not wish or are unable to use 'conventional' contraception. The three types of natural method are:

— natural family planning or fertility awareness, which requires a woman to monitor her monthly cycle so that she knows when she is fertile;

— breastfeeding, which is—surprisingly—the most widely used contraceptive method worldwide, as well as being one of the most ancient;

— coitus interrupts or withdrawal, also a very ancient method of contraception.

Natural family planning

A woman is not fertile all the time: she ovulates (releases an egg from her ovary) only once a month, and that egg is

— It does not offer protection against any STDs, including HIV.

Calendar or rhythm method

The calendar or rhythm method looks promising as a natural contraceptive method, but in practice it is relatively crude and inaccurate, and should only be used as a double-check with other natural methods. By keeping a check on her menstrual cycles, a woman will be able to work out on which days she is fertile. Using this method, she keeps a strict record of her menstrual cycles for six consecutive months, taking the day when her period starts as the first day of each cycle. Most women find that their cycles vary in length from month to month.

The timing of the fertile period can then be calculated and applied to the next month. To calculate the earliest fertile day in the cycle, subtract 20 days from the length of the shortest cycle; the figure 20 is made up of 16 days (the maximum between ovulation and menstruation) plus 4 days (the number of days that sperm can survive, plus one for safety). To calculate the last fertile day, subtract 10 from the length of the longest cycle of the previous six months; the figure 10 is made up of 12 days (the shortest time between ovulation and menstruation) minus 2 days (the maximum survival time for the egg after ovulation, plus a day's safety margin).

Unfortunately, because the method is based on evidence from earlier menstrual cycles, it cannot take account of future fluctuations in cycle length. In addition, the time at which a woman ovulates can be changed dramatically by upheavals in her daily life such as illness, stress, bereavement or even jet lag. For those reasons, this method carries quite a high risk of pregnancy. It also means that a couple have to abstain from sex for an unnecessarily long time each month to allow for possible fluctuations in the cycle.

Basal Body Temperature Method

Human body temperature remains relatively constant, usually around 37°C (98.6°F), depending on the individual.

However, everyone's body temperature shows a slight increase and subsequent decrease on a daily basis, reaching a peak between 3.00 and 7.00 p.m. and a minimum in the small hours of the morning between 3.00 and 6.00 a.m. This minimal temperature, attained when the body is at rest, is known as the basal body temperature (or BBT).

Her basal body temperature increases by between 0.2°C and 0.4°C (0.4°F and 0.8°F). The chain of events is as follows: in the ovary the ruptured follicle, from which the egg has been released, seals itself up and starts to release the hormone progesterone, which in turn causes body temperature to rise. By monitoring changes in her basal body temperature, a woman can determine when she has ovulated and when, accordingly, it is safe to have sex. To use this method, a temperature chart—obtainable from family planning clinics or doctors—and a thermometer are required. It is better to use a special fertility thermometer or one of the latest digital thermometers to get an accurate measurement of small temperature changes.

Every morning, at approximately the same time each day, the woman must record her body temperature just after waking—before getting out of bed or having anything to drink or eat. She should leave the thermometer in her mouth for five minutes for the temperature reading to stabilise. Alternatively, she can insert the thermometer into her vagina for three minutes, or, adding a dab of vaseline first, into her rectum for the same length of time.

Digital thermometers give an accurate reading much more rapidly. The temperature should then be recorded by putting a dot in the centre of the appropriate square on the chart; the dots should be joined up by straight lines to form a continuous graph. If, for three days in a row, a woman records a BBT higher than that of all the preceding six consecutive days, this indicates that her fertile time has finished for the current cycle. She and her partner can now have unrestricted sexual intercourse until the end of her next period.

Drinking alcohol the night before, or getting up in the night to breastfeed a baby can also affect BBT. Charts may be hard to interpret, although interpretative skills improve with practice. But probably the greatest drawback is that the method is retrospective: it does not allow a woman to predict when ovulation is due, only when it has happened. This means a longer period of abstinence each month than with other natural methods. Furthermore, if a woman doesn't ovulate in a certain cycle, she will not be able to have intercourse at all that month.

BILLINGS OR CERVICAL MUCUS METHOD

For certain days of the month it virtually disappears; during others it thickens to stop sperm and any bacteria in the vagina from entering the uterus; but during the most fertile time, around ovulation, it becomes thinner and highly sperm-friendly, with hundreds of channels through which sperms can swim into the uterus. So, the quantity and feel of cervical mucus reflects the hormonal fluctuations that precede and follow the ovulatory crescendo.

Most women who use the cervical mucus method do it as a matter of course when they go to the toilet, after urinating. They use soft toilet tissue to blot or wipe their vulva, the area around the opening to the vagina. As moisture is absorbed, the mucus appears as a blob on the tissue. By putting a finger into the mucus and then gently pulling it away, the texture of the mucus can be tested. Mucus texture ranges from scanty and sticky to slippery and very stretchy, depending on the time of the month.

The colour and transparency of the mucus will also change. Both texture and colour of the mucus should be recorded nightly on a chart, either as a written description or by using a colour code. Monthly variations in a 'typical' woman's cervical mucus are as follows.

— 'Dry days' follow her period, when the cervical mucus forms a plug in the cervix, acting as a barrier to sperms; the vagina and vulva feel dry, and there is no visible mucus.

— As oestrogen levels increase, mucus that is white, cloudy and sticky to the touch appears in the vagina.

— 'Wet days' precede ovulation as oestrogen levels peak.

Mucus is clear and slippery, like egg white, and very stretchy, and the vagina and vulva are moist. This is the fertile mucus that nurtures sperm, and allows them to pass through into the cervix. The last day when this fertile mucus can be seen is called the peak day, and it coincides with maximum secretion of oestrogen, which occurs just before ovulation.

— Following ovulation, a woman will find that her mucus becomes more cloudy and sticky (and thus more impenetrable to sperm). This is the result of progesterone production by the ovary, a feature mimicked by the progestogen-only pill.

On the 'dry days' following menstruation it is reckoned to be safe to have intercourse on alternate days—alternate because semen and the lubricants released during sexual arousal can persist overnight and may be mistaken for cervical mucus. As soon as any mucus is evident, the couple should abstain from intercourse until the evening of the fourth day after the peak day. This allows up to three days for ovulation to occur, and for the 24-hour lifespan of the egg.

Bleeding between periods may also make observations very difficult. Women who use this method need good memories, to remember when they last had intercourse, when to abstain, and so on. And mucus production may begin only two or three days before ovulation, making intercourse in the first 'infertile' period that follows menstruation and precedes ovulation relatively unsafe.

The symptothermal method combines several indicators of the possible fertile period—hence the alternative name, the multiple index method—to pinpoint the fertile period accurately. As well as her basal body temperature and the appearance of her cervical mucus, the woman records the following changes on her chart: the position and softness or firmness of her cervix; the pain that may occur mid-cycle when the ovary wall ruptures to release an egg; the show of blood that may occur mid-cycle; and breast tenderness, which can increase after ovulation.

The infertile period (between ovulation and menstruation) begins on the morning of the third consecutive day of high temperature, or the fourth evening after peak mucus, whichever comes last. Infertility is then confirmed by the other indicators. The calendar method can be used at the same time as a double-check to make the method even more effective. The advantages and disadvantages of the symptothermal method reflect those encountered by users of any of the fertility awareness methods.

The main drawbacks are that it requires time and dedication to take readings and maintain the chart, and its failure rate can reach 25 per cent a year, although with careful use—providing intercourse takes place only during the part of the infertile period after ovulation but before menstruation—the failure rate should be as low as two per cent a year. It also means that a couple must avoid unprotected intercourse between the end of the woman's period and the end of her fertile period.

However, they do not have to abstain from all sexual activities during that time: kissing, cuddling, mutual masturbation and oral sex do not involve penetration and so can provide pleasure without risk of pregnancy. The symptothermal method has a number of advantages, despite the frustration of abstinence. It is under a woman's personal control, and it makes both her and her partner aware of her reproductive cycles and fertility.

Several new techniques can enhance fertility awareness methods. Among these are home testing kits that detect levels of luteinising hormone (LH) in urine, using a dipstick that changes colour. LH is the hormone released by the pituitary gland that causes ovulation to occur. By detecting the sudden increase of LH in the bloodstream, the test shows when the fertile phase is about to begin. However, it appears to be more useful for couples who wish to achieve rather than avoid conception.

Breastfeeding

Breastfeeding is the world's 'hidden' contraceptive, preventing more pregnancies each year than all other forms of contraception put together. How does breastfeeding prevent conception? By sucking on its mother's nipple, a baby stimulates the sudden release of a hormone called prolactin from the pituitary gland. In turn, prolactin stimulates the glands in the breast to produce more milk for the next feed. But prolactin also has an effect on the pituitary gland, instructing it to stop the release of the hormones that cause eggs to develop in and be released from, the ovaries. Unfortunately, the situation is not as simple as that.

Prolactin levels surge to 20 times their normal levels when breastfeeding begins, but then subside rapidly when the nipple is no longer being sucked. For women who breastfeed regularly throughout the day and night, sufficient levels of prolactin are maintained to have a contraceptive effect. But in women whose babies suckle six or so times a day, prolactin levels are high only for part of the day, which means that ovulation may well not be suppressed and there is a risk of pregnancy if the couple do not use another form of contraception. Unfortunately, some women have been told—and believe—that breastfeeding will act as an effective contraceptive, and find themselves unwittingly pregnant within months of the birth of their baby.

Withdrawal (Coitus Interrupts)

Coitus interrupts—'interrupted intercourse'—dates from the time, tens of thousands of years ago, when humans first recognised the link between intercourse and conception. How it works is aptly described by its alternative names: 'withdrawal' or 'pulling out'. When a man is reaching the 'point of no return' during intercourse, and knows he is about to ejaculate, he swiftly withdraws his penis from the vagina and ejaculates on or near his partner, rather than inside her. By so doing, he reaches orgasm but stops the sperms reaching the cervix and uterus. Or does he? During intercourse, but without the man being aware of it, a drop of fluid called the pre-ejaculate commonly escapes from the tip of the penis. The other problem with withdrawal is that it requires tremendous willpower and commitment.

Coitus interrupts tends to have a high failure rate, probably up to 19 per cent a year (as against a theoretical rate of four per cent a year), depending on age and experience. Couples who use the method may find that the opportunities for mutual sexual satisfaction are limited, and may be left feeling frustrated (although if a woman has already reached orgasm she is less likely to feel unsatisfied). Certainly, withdrawal remains the most popular method of contraception in countries such as Italy and Turkey, although its popularity in other Western countries has declined sharply over the past 30 years with the advent of the pill and other new and more reliable forms of contraception. Coitus interrupts puts the pressure to make it work on the man, but leaves the possible consequence—pregnancy—to the woman. It puts pressure on the woman, too, as she may want the man to stay inside her longer in some instances.

However, it is free, requires no equipment, and has no side-effects. When no other contraceptive methods are to hand, withdrawal is better than no method at all, especially when the couple are young and fertile.

Increasing numbers of couples are using non-penetrative methods such as oral sex or mutual masturbation as an alternative to intercourse. One benefit is that non-penetrative sex avoids risk of conception, and can be practised, for example, during the fertile period of a woman's cycle. It would be wrong, however, to assume that this offers complete protection against STDs.

Sterilisation

Sterilisation is a surgical technique which blocks the pathway that carries sperm or eggs from where they are made to their regular destination. It is highly effective, but not easily reversible. A woman is most unlikely to bear any more children, or a man to father them. For this reason, careful thought and counselling are required before a couple decide to use sterilisation as their contraceptive method. The technique itself is simple. Minor surgery is used to sever the link between the ovaries or testes and the outside world.

In women, this involves tubal surgery: cutting or blocking the fallopian tubes that carry ova (eggs) from ovary to uterus following ovulation. In men, the procedure is called vasectomy: literally, this means the 'cutting out a portion of the vas' (deferens), the tube along which sperm travel from a testis to the penis prior to ejaculation.

The failure rate for male sterilisation is 0.2 per cent or less. Vasectomy does fail in a small number of cases because the cut ends of the vas rejoin or a new passage forms for the sperm to swim along.

Most couples who choose sterilisation as a means of contraception are older, in their thirties or forties—it is certainly an increasingly popular contraceptive option in this age group—and have completed their families, or are sure that they never want to have children. Doctors are generally reluctant to perform sterilisations on younger, childless women or men in case they change their minds later on. Most couples are advised that if there is any doubt in their minds they should not go ahead with sterilisation lest they come to regret it.

Vasectomy is quicker, simpler and safer. No deaths have been reported following vasectomy; the death rate from female sterilisation is around 3.5 per 100,000 (due to general anaesthesia). Yet more women are sterilised than men. This discrepancy may be a result of motivation—the childbearing partner is more motivated to have the operation—or because, as some men argue, men retain fertility into old age and are therefore more likely to start another family if divorce or death breaks up their present relationship.

The introduction of microsurgical techniques (the same as are used for joining together the broken ends of nerves and blood vessels when re-attaching severed limbs) has increased the success of reversal operations. They are expensive, however, and their reliability cannot be guaranteed.

Tubal surgery is carried out in hospital, normally under general anaesthetic. The most common technique used today is laparoscopy. This technique is minimally invasive, leaving only tiny scars. Once the patient is anaesthetised in the operating theatre, a surgeon makes one or two small incisions in her abdomen and inserts a laparoscope, a pencilsized viewing tube through which she or he can see the reproductive organs. The instruments are then removed and the incisions are stitched up. Most women return home within 24 hours, where they need to rest until the effects of general anaesthesia wear off.

An alternative method, called mini-laparotomy—once the most common method of female sterilisation—involves a larger incision, and tubal ligation (tying off) of the fallopian tubes. This requires a longer stay in hospital and a protracted recovery period at home.

Women are likely to feel some discomfort around the incision for several days, and slight bleeding may also occur—they are generally advised to relax for a week or so. Major complications are rare. Periods should remain the same following sterilisation, because the ovaries, womb and cervix are left intact. Occasionally, however, women experience heavier periods. Some doctors believe this is related to the woman's previous method of contraception—their periods may have been lighter before the operation because they were using the pill, for example (women in their thirties and forties who are not using hormonal contraception often find their periods get heavier); others put it down to the operation—to damaged blood vessels, for instance, which could affect the flow of blood to the ovaries.

A woman can resume sex as soon as she wishes. In general, the only effect that sterilisation will have on a woman's sex life is to enhance it now that she is freed from any fear of pregnancy. The hormones controlling the menstrual cycle are released into the bloodstream by the ovaries, a process that is not affected by the blocking or sealing of the fallopian tubes. Since her hormonal levels remain unaltered, there is no hormonally induced change to her libido.

Most men's experience of vasectomy goes something like this: after the scrotum is shaved, the doctor gently squeezes the skin on one side to locate the vas deferens. He or she then injects a small amount of anaesthetic into the scrotal skin to numb that area, and makes a small incision. The vas deferens is located and either cut or a small piece removed, and then ligated (tied off) or cauterised (sealed by heating). After stitching up the incision in the skin using absorbable sutures, the doctor repeats the technique on the other side of the scrotum. The whole procedure should take no more than 20 minutes.

Most men are advised to take things easy for a day or so, and to avoid lifting anything heavy for 48 hours. Any aches or pains that occur as the anaesthetic wears off can be treated with a mild analgesic such as aspirin; a strategically placed ice pack may also help reduce bruising or inflammation. Most men feel more comfortable if they wear tight-fitting underpants or an athletic support both day and night for a week after the operation. Stitches in the skin of the scrotum will either be absorbed or fall out within a month. A few reports have suggested that there is a link between vasectomy and the incidence of prostate cancer. Further research is needed, but medical opinion currently believes the evidence is inconclusive. There is certainly no causal link to explain why vasectomy should increase the chances of developing prostate cancer However, men who are worried about this should ask their doctor for advice.

During the weeks following the operation, if he and his partner are having penetrative sex, they must use a condom or another form of contraception to avoid the risk of pregnancy. The reason for this is that it usually takes 20 to 30 ejaculations before all sperms are cleared out of the storage areas downstream of the point where each vas deferens is blocked; after this he starts producing sperm-free semen, or 'shooting blanks'. To check whether his ejaculate is sperm-free, he will probably be asked to provide semen samples 12 and 16 weeks after his vasectomy. Provided that both samples are sperm-free, he can have sex without any other form of contraception.

EMERGENCY CONTRACEPTION

Emergency contraception refers to any method employed to prevent pregnancy after, but within a few days of, unprotected intercourse. There are two safe and effective emergency contraception options available for women:

— the postcoital pill

— the IUD

Emergency contraception means just that: it should be used only as an emergency measure and not on a regular basis. However, it does mean that if a woman feels, in the hours and days following intercourse, that she may be at risk of becoming pregnant, she can do something about it. The reasons why couples have unprotected sex are many and varied. They might decide to take a chance; they could get so carried away that contraception is far from their thoughts; they may drink too much alcohol to care; condoms may split, slip off or break if used with an oil-based product which weakens rubber; her diaphragm may not be inserted properly; a woman may forget to take her contraceptive pills correctly; or, tragically, a woman may be raped.

Once known as the 'morning-after pill'—a name no longer used because it gave the erroneous impression that it worked only on the morning following unprotected sex—the postcoital ('after intercourse') or emergency pill must be taken within 72 hours (3 days) of intercourse to be effective. When a woman consults her doctor she will probably be asked to take two postcoital pills immediately, and two more 12 hours later, even if that means getting up in the middle of the night. If lower-dose pills are used then a woman takes four pills immediately, followed by four more pills 12 hours later.

Postcoital pill contain the same types of synthetic sex hormones—progestogen and oestrogen—that are found in a standard contraceptive pill but in higher doses. When absorbed into a woman's bloodstream they either stop ovulation occurring or, if ovulation and fertilisation have already taken place, the hormones prevent a fertilised egg from implanting in the wall of the uterus and developing into a foetus.

Treatment with the postcoital pill within 72 hours of unprotected intercourse reduces the risk of pregnancy by at least 75 per cent. However, couples are advised to use contraceptive protection until her next period in case the woman ovulates later than normal.

A doctor may prescribe an anti-nausea drug (or suggest an over-the-counter preparation). The woman should be made aware that her next period may be delayed, in case she thinks she has missed a period and is pregnant. Whether she has a period or not, a woman should return to her physician three to four weeks after the initial consultation for a checkup. The postcoital pill should not be used by women who show contra-indications to oestrogen—such as a history of blood clots.

The alternative to using hormones to prevent pregnancy after intercourse is to insert a copper-bearing IUD. A doctor may decide to insert an IUD provided that not more than five days have elapsed since the probable date of ovulation. Because of the risk of pelvic inflammatory disease, swabs may be taken (to check for infection) prior to IUD insertion, particularly if the woman is young and is not in a regular relationship. The woman should return for a checkup three to four weeks after the IUD is fitted. If she has had a normal period, the IUD can be removed and an alternative contraceptive method used, if she wishes.

Postcoital IUD insertion is more effective than postcoital pills. RU-486, or mifepristone, is a drug that ends pregnancy in its first few weeks. If a woman's period is overdue, she can take RU-486, followed by another drug (prostaglandin) 36-48 hours later, and this induces an abortion.

The combination is highly reliable; if used alone, RU-486 is less successful. Treatment works by nullifying the effect of progesterone, the hormone released by the woman's ovary which normally enables the early embryo to survive and develop in the uterine wall. RU-486 is also very effective as a postcoital contraceptive, but taken in this way it is expensive and rarely used. The drug is described as postconceptional, rather than contraceptive, because it acts after implantation. This has led to controversy about the use of RU-486, with detractors calling it the 'abortion pill'. Moral arguments about abortion have prevented its introduction in the United States and other countries, although it is available in France, where it was developed, and in Britain. Some doctors suggest that RU-486, or its successor, might be employed as a once- a-month postconceptional pill, producing short-term abortions two or three times a year—the number of times conception and implantation would occur on average in a young, fertile couple having regular unprotected intercourse.

What are condoms called/or known in different parts of the world

1. Australia - Love Clove
2. Brazil - Little Shirt
3. China - Contraceptive Basket (Cantonese)
4. China - Security Cover (Mandarin)
5. Denmark - Rubber Man
6. France - English Raincoat
7. Germany - Nalichty Bac
8. Greek - Overcoat
9. Holland - Small Rubber
10. Hong Kong - Bullet Proof vesa
11. Hungary - Sartey Tool
12. India - Nirudh (It Means Resistance)
13. Indonesia - Penis Gourd
14. Ireland - Jonny
15. Italy - Glove
16. Japan - Bag
17. Lebanon - Coat
18. Nigeria - Penis Hat
19. Panama - Hat
20. Philippines - Little Bag
21. Portugal - Venus Shirt
22. Senegal - Bush Hat

Sex is a subject which is still considered a taboo, even in today's modern Indian society. We have sent satellites in the universe, produced super computers, eradicated smallpox completely, soon malaria and polio will become obsolete, but we simply shy away when its comes to discussing sex, which is one of the major reason for abrupt increase in the sex related diseases, including AIDS. We move hand in hand with Western modes of life or culture, then even we lack in awareness about various aspects of reproductive physiology. This lack of awareness about sex related problems has become a plus point for the road side 'sexologists', they do brisk business by cheating hapless people.

Some times these 'doctors' even give chemotherapic treatment against some of the hormones, natural phenomenons like 'nocturnal emission' and masturbation. Is it not ridiculus that today we call ourselves modern but do not have guts to talk of sex? If we look at our own cultural history, it is found that in ancient times sex was given its rightful place in the human scheme of things. The explicit sexual imagery found in ancient Indian literature (Kamasutra, Kumarasambhava) and sculpture (Khajuraho, Konark) provides sample evidence. The concept of sex and sexuality kept being defined and refined according to the changing times and need of the society. But the importance of sex and sexuality and the influence they can wield have remain unchanged by and large.

Due to improper guidance and lack of scientific awareness our society is full of myths about sex and related processes.

8

Safe Sex among Sex Workers

Educating the masses about the use of condoms is no easy task in the situations surveyed due to a variety of interrelated factors including:

— Lack of education among most sex workers.

— Subordinate position of females vis-a-vis males.

— Presence of language barriers between educators and sex workers.

— Lack of awareness about the nature of HIV and STD among sex workers, including general indifference to health and sanitation.

— The nature of the sex act itself; which usually takes place without conversation, the idea being to have sex as quickly as possible, leaving little opportunity for negotiation.

— The lack of awareness among customers about the nature of HIV and STD, particularly if they are from the ranks of blue-collar workers and other socially underprivileged groups.

— Lack of organisation among sex workers, so that if one refuses to have sex without condoms, the customers will always find another one willing.

— Unwillingness of sex workers to have condoms with them especially in situations where carrying condoms can lead to police arrest or where the sex worker is unwilling to go to a store and buy her own condoms.

— The type of context in which sex takes place; which

may be a dingy room or a public park or a similar place not conducive to either negotiate condom use or even wear one.

— Inability to do close monitoring of safe sex promotion, and

— The disproportional nature of the quantum of NGO intervention in relation to the number of sex workers to be covered in a particular context.

The above conclusions could be arrived at through field observations, and comments of NGO officials surveyed were as follows:

INDIAN HEALTH ORGANISATION (IHO)

IHO managed to ensure free disposal of condoms to nearly 7,000 sex workers in about four large brothels in central Mumbai. This constitutes about four per cent of the estimated population of 175,000 sex workers in the city. Even working among this relatively small number, IHO had to overcome language barriers due to the fact that many sex workers hail from other states or countries, especially Nepal.

In such cases the dangers of HIV and STD was communicated through photo albums focusing on the advantages of condom use; including prevention of STD, cutting down health care costs, prevention of unwanted pregnancies, and saving money to send to dependants. Evidence suggested that the condoms disbursed weekly through the peer educators were in fact being used. Though monitored through regular discussions with peer educators and staff, there is no guarantee of hundred per cent condom use.

Despite these obstacles, safe sex practices are actively promoted by peers educators. Some sex workers however complained about losing business because of condoms, and talking about AIDS: customers think that the sex worker has it. A *saheli* had done role plays in the brothel itself and educated sex workers about how to negotiate with clients. If the customer did not want to put on the condom, the girls put it on for them, making safe sex a feasible proposition.

Sex workers in Mumbai, as in most parts of the world, are not unionised. They cannot demand "No sex without condoms!" Moreover, those who use condoms are small in number, and a customer not willing to use them can always find a willing partner. The crux of the problem is not the sex worker alone; safe sex will simply not be possible on a significant scale without the cooperation of the customers.

GUJARAT AIDS PREVENTION (GAP)

GAP's experience with sex workers is still in the trial stages. With some intervention activity having commenced in Surat's red light area, it sees unionisation as a prerequisite for making safe sex feasible and sustainable. When they say 'we use condoms', it means so once in a while and not for every encounter. If there is hundred per cent use, in one month there should be 150 to 200 condoms used by one person, which means 1,500 to 2,000 condoms per house. In that case there should be a mountain of (used) condoms!

COMMUNITY ACTION NETWORK (CAN)

Furthermore, since CAN disburses Delux Nirodh instead of the ordinary monocoloured variety, it believes that clients and even sex workers will be motivated to buy or use them. One official asserted, "We have Fiesta condoms which are see-through and colourful. It has a fancy element and is attractive, better lubricated and of better quality, and easily available in the market." Whether all this ensures that a client will purchase condoms from either the prostitution network or the open market is open to question.

CAN has a dual monitoring system; one being daily reports from social workers as to how many condoms were distributed among the peer educators, and another independent team which regularly gets report from clients. It is doubtful whether such a monitoring team will have access to either female sex workers or their clients given the secretive nature of prostitution in general.

More particularly is the case of female sex workers who operate entirely in secret. Again, given the large number of sex workers and clients in Madras, and even in the selected intervention sites, such a team could only do spot-checks on a random basis. CAN officials are however optimistic. As one puts it: "The women are responsible and want to take preventive action. The men are at greater fault: they have the money and are, drunk; all they want to do is to have sex".

The women should take the responsibility of always using condoms. They are completely rational and are concerned about their health. In some brothels, women read newspapers while having sex. They can think of other things even when having sex. This observation gives an interesting dimension to the feasibility of safe sex. Merely pushing condom use is thus not going to ensure their use. Negotiation skills have to be placed in the context of sex work, including not only where and how it takes place but also the attitude of the sex worker to clients, and to the work she is doing.

SOUTH INDIA AIDS ACTION PROGRAMME (SIAAP)

SIAAP's director believes that safe sex is feasible, and hundred per cent condom use can be ensured. But a series of obstacles exist and removing them will take time and effort.

The obstacles were identified as:

a) Putting the safe sex message in a broader context than HIV, and in relation to the whole person of WIPs ('women in prostitution' which SIAAP prefers to 'sex worker'). In her words: "We have to approach women with a concern for their care. We don't need to worry about what is happening to the world with HIV, and instead approach the women with a personal concern. In doing so we should be able to explain the situation of AIDS in the context of her reality, and how it is going to affect her lifestyle. Not merely in relation to illness, since she may not even get the virus, but what it will do to the community of which she is a part".

b) Negotiation is done at two levels: negotiating with clients, and accessing the condoms. Elaborating on these SIAAP's director states, "Earlier people were saying that women will not be able to tell a client and

> demand condom use, and many more women never attempted to negotiate. We did not teach them to negotiate. All we did was explain to them the risk. We demonstrated how a condom should be used (using an improvised and less conspicuous penile model than the one conventionally used). Then we asked them how they were going to tell the client, and they came up with six or seven different ways which they started trying. They have more skills than one could dream of".

Psychological empowerment is seen as an indispensable basis for negotiating with condoms. The director's message to the sex worker is: "You are often seen by society either as fallen victims, or at worst, as sinners or criminals. Both are positions of utter powerlessness. You cannot hope to function in a position of powerlessness. We believe you are in a position of power. Why? Because despite everything that has happened to you—rape, being sold, etc.—today you earn a livelihood. You support other people".

"Day after day, despite the brutalisation you have gone through, you stand there, you look good, you have poise. You have so much strength that you are back on the streets. Are you telling me you are not strong? Are you not strong to use a condom? You are strong in the friendships you have. If a lover walks out on you, then you have another. In the real world, you are strong women. Don't let other people tell you that you are weak. Are you not strong enough to stop a man from killing you simply because he is so silly as to have sex without a condom?"

One problem is when clients think the WIP must be having some disease, otherwise why should she ask him to wear a condom? Secondly, the WIP must be convinced about what she is suggesting to the client. If convinced, she believes that negotiation will be hundred per cent effective. Thirdly, the women must be prepared to put on the condom for the man. SIAAP has been able to persuade WIPs to overcome the reluctance to handle a man's penis. It becomes a chore for the man and chances of the condom getting used will be more if the women put it on for the men. Fourthly, some conditions favour condom use particularly when the man has no option but to put on a condom: "In some places, the man has given the money. He has taken off his clothes and is sitting with an erection. The condom is on the table; and she takes it and starts putting it on him. Although he has the option of not putting on one, the situation is such that nine out of ten men will not walk out." One of SIAAP's social workers explains that younger WIP's have a better chance of practising safe sex method than older ones: "Younger women are more willing to participate in the programme. They read some literature and are active and more smart, less fatalistic, and more receptive. Besides, they can always get more clients if one refuses to have sex with a condom."

The second factor is accessing condoms, and here SIAAP's outlook is radically different from that of CAN which believes that sex workers and clients should be asked to pay for condoms. In the director's view such an approach is based on a lack of understanding of the realities of commercial sex, at least in the South Indian context.

The social perception is that if any woman goes to a shop and asks for a condom, she is a prostitute. That itself is a big barrier for condom use even for ordinary people. Besides, the WIP herself has a nagging feeling of guilt that she is doing something wrong, that she is living in sin and has to be hidden every day. The whole world is telling her that, and she lives on the brink of sanity.

The inner world of WIPs is so different from others. The world outside has become more oppressive towards WIPs. Since the advent of HIV police oppression has increased. For the last 10 years, the government has run ad campaigns saying 'Don't go to prostitutes!' The perception is that these women are spreading AIDS. Condoms have been given for family planning for the last 40 years, but now for HIV they cannot.

Unavailability of good quality condoms through government sources is another disadvantage. The director recalls sending them for quality tests which they failed, forcing SIAAP to purchase deluxe Nirodh from the open market, the monthly bill for which is around two lakh rupees. She added with a gesture of despair, "How can we run a programme like that?" Ensuring that good quality condoms are within easy reach of the WIPs has been the central goal of SIAAP.

The first step was to get the cooperation of lodge (hotel) owners and make an appeal to their good senses, "we called them together and said, 'This is a small thing for you (to keep condoms at the lodge); can you imagine saving people's lives? How many have the power to do that?' It touched a chord; to do some good."

Constant persuasion and monitoring through the counsellors and by the director herself is an ongoing process. Daily reports of field staff giving details of how many condoms were given and in what places are followed by checks with lodge owners. The NGO's 18 peer educators and two female field workers are not able to come to the main office regularly but have to be met in the field. Tracking of all WIPs with regard to actual condom use is not practically possible. And the number of condoms disbursed remains the main criteria for monitoring; with nearly 9,000 of the directly distributed by SIAAP in Chennai city alone.

However, SIAAP has been working with three other NGOs in the city, two of which it still funds. Including them the total condoms distributed every month in Chennai comes to about 50,000 pieces. In a sense, SIAAP's activities unwittingly complement those of CAN which does not cover female sex workers in Chennai. The present coverage, however, is limited only to a sixth of the population, and that too without adequate means of delivering safe sex services to them.

TENAGANITA

Although condoms are handed out to sex workers, the NGO does not appear to be conducting any monitoring of their use.

PINK TRIANGLE

A social worker recalls how, "All 30 girls in one hotel decided to use condoms, while earlier it depended on the whim and fancy of the client. Now, if the client refuses, the girl gets her pimp to persuade the client and bring him round to agree." However, as is illustrated, agreement among sex workers is by itself not a sufficient condition.

The cooperation and some impetus from the hierarchy of prostitution is also necessary. Obstacles to safe sex also emanate from two other sources: drug abuse among sex workers, and the nature of the client. As another social worker commented, "Women who take to drugs and are high on it or having withdrawal symptoms, will not think of safe sex." The initiative always comes back to the client even though most girls agree to use condoms. For instance, if the client does not agree, the girl fails to insist otherwise, fearing that the man will beat her. Very often the men do not use condoms because they "would not be getting their money's worth."

On the other hand, if say a woman's husband has been arrested for drugs, and she needs money to support her children, HIV is a remote consideration. Other habits of drug users are a further obstacle. They take a shot and move elsewhere as a result of which they cannot spend time at the drop-in centre. Safe sex education has to be persistent. And such persistent education is not possible given the limited resources of the NGO and lack of staff.

The problems they face daily are talked about and documented; and as needs come up they are addressed. Another necessary condition is self-esteem of the sex worker. The NGO supplies condoms and encourages sex workers to buy them once they have started using them regularly. Of the 1,500 target population in the Chowkit area, it has promoted condom use (not 100 per cent) among 300 sex workers. Negotiating skills have also been imparted, including use of oral sex in place of anal sex among transsexuals.

One social worker's advice to sex worker was, "Tell the client that if he uses a condom, you will feel fine. Tell him you can come even when he uses condoms". Another practical obstacle is the fear of being raided by the police. On how this affects negotiation, the social worker says, "With frequent police raids taking place, sex workers do not want to take much time to negotiate condom use with clients. And without the time they cannot explain things to clients".

THAI RED CROSS SOCIETY

Consequently incidence of HIV and Hepatitis B among them remained low. But when the supply was no longer available this way, condom use dropped. The counsellor recalled how one manager came to his office asking him to bring condoms rather than getting them himself as he (the manager) was too shy. The manager was not even keen enough to send one of the boys to do it.

Given the cultural stigma attached to obtaining condoms, the responsibility for not only promoting safe sex but also supplying condoms falls on the change agent. In this context, the SIAAP director's observations on social marketing are valid for Asian society as a whole, where social taboos regarding condom purchasing hold for males as well. Most female sex workers appear to bargain from a position of social inequality vis-a-vis male clients, and apparently, this determines the outcome of negotiation. As a counsellor at the Red Cross observed: "It is difficult to get men to wear condoms because they are mostly drunk when going to a sex worker. They will have the condom in the pocket but will not use it. They would rather go to the girl who wants money and does not make an issue of condoms".

The policy of each establishment also has a role in promoting safe sex. In Pataya, for instance, if the male sex worker refuses to work without condoms, the bar will compensate him for the time lost. And yet there are others who will say that the customer is always right. What then of the claim that there is hundred per cent condom use in some parts of Thailand? G.C. is extremely sceptical when he says, "The safe sex campaigns conducted by the government are not all that effective. It is typical of Thais to say: 'The campaign is a success; we can stop now.' The campaign was conducted in one or two provinces by supplying condoms to sex workers, giving them condom education, and health officers doing surveillance checks".

"The sex workers were required to go to the clinic for STD and HIV examinations. If they found any incidence of STD, they were given a warning the first time. If they found it again, the bar was closed down for a day, and if yet again, for three days, and then permanently. Overall, condom use registered was about 30 per cent. If the campaign was working as claimed, it would shoot up to 98 per cent. We asked, 'If we have hundred per cent condom use, why do we have so many clients with STD in our clinic?' Also, the information gathered was through interviews. Sex workers are asked: 'Do you use condoms? How often?' The sex worker, knowing that saying 'no' will invite a lecture, says 'yes' all the time. It is a threatening interview process". Differential status among health worker and sex worker is seen as an inhibiting factor. The health workers are way up there and the sex workers are down below in terms of social status.

EMPOWER

The NGO has no condom promotion campaign and lays emphasis on empowerment of sex workers. The logic is that once empowerment takes place safe sex practices would automatically follow along with an increased ability to negotiate condom use with clients. At present, the NGO's activities with regard to condoms include:

- free distribution of condoms to sex workers who attend training programmes, workshops and seminars.
- staging a play with safe sex messages in three locations once a month.
- free distribution of gift-wrapped condoms among customers after the skits on condoms and AIDS are performed.

The coordinator mentioned that there were more men using condoms now than four or five years ago, and that at the moment their primary concern was not AIDS prevention.

AIDS COUNSELLING CENTRES AND COUNSELLING SERVICES (ACCESS)

NGO with safe sex promotion among female sex workers,

although limited in scope, has some useful lessons. When their field staff approached the sex workers in Chiang Mai, they (sex workers) said that so many different organisations had come to them and talked about safe sex that they were willing to use condoms. According to the director, although the local public health office provided them with condoms, "The problem was with the customers. Attempts to educate the customers were not rewarding: We would talk to them before they went in. Some were drunk and could hardly be talked to. Others would harass the female members of our team." The key factor was the push given by the brothel owners who had formed an association and were aware of HIV. What made these brothel owners different? Was it simple concern about protecting the workers from HIV? The scale of the brothel operation and ties with the sex workers based on regional identity and kinship were key co-factors. In northern Thailand, the brothel owners are local people. They are small business people and the relationship between them and the sex workers is quite good.

Community Front for Prevention of AIDS (CFPA)

The NGO began promoting safe sex through condom use by recruiting the first batch of peer educators. Their task was to deliver condoms to peers and/or customers and keep a record of how many condoms were given, and how consistently they were used by those receiving them. Each peer educator was given a handbook containing pictures showing correct use of condoms.

The field staff would visit the peer educators once every two weeks, monitor the progress made, and find out whether more condoms were needed. All monitoring activities were reviewed once every two weeks when the field staff met the programme coordinator. Obstacles to condom promotion came from several sources:

Supply of quality condoms

The first supply of condoms were obtained free of charge through WHO's AIDS Project office in Colombo. Feedback from peer educators revealed that the condoms were definitely better than *preethi,* the cheapest condom brand available in the market, one which was also promoted for family planning. Users of the new condom had found them to be better lubricated and, unlike *preethi,* free of the rubber-like smell. Besides, there was an additional (social) value to the new condom since it was "foreign made" and packed in attractive blue or purple colours.

Unfortunately, as their demand increased, the supply was not sufficient and regular enough due to procedural delays. An adequate stock was made available only in January 1995, five months after the peer educator programme had commenced. As a result monitoring of condom use was hampered from September 1994 to January 1995. To meet the exigency some peer educators had to purchase condoms at their own expense, but given their low income level, it is unlikely that they were able to meet the demand.

Since peer educators kept the condoms in their homes or at some other convenient point, those wishing to use them were spared the embarrassment of going to a shop; a problem common to both men and women in Sri Lanka as in other Asian countries.

When peer educators were asked to keep a record of who used how many condoms and how often, it created a problem. They came from a cultural system in which keeping a close tab on behavioural details was neither the norm nor did it have any value. In the subculture of poverty to which they belonged, maintaining accounts of anything was an irrelevant activity: they lived from day to day, spending all they had earned by the end of the evening. Some were not literate, having only had a primary education. There was no way they could be re-socialised into the middle class values of the change agent. One possible option was to recruit a literate and somewhat educated member.

The demand for condoms was much higher for this sector as opposed to the small numbers required by the street girls. A female sex worker who was the key contact in one brothel had suggested that she be given at least 100 condoms a day. But at that stage in the programme, delivery of large stocks could not be possible without the explicit consent of the management which operated secretly. The next logical step was to obtain their cooperation, but it is not known whether the field staff were successful in doing so.

Some sex workers, particularly females, had complained to the peer educators of vaginal irritation after sex and believed this to be a symptom of STD or a result of using condoms. Once they were free of such infection by getting tested at a clinic, it was found to be a result of not using lubricants. The above fact makes it clear that once people were made sufficiently aware of the health benefits of condom use they were quite willing to adopt them. But this does not end the process of intervention since sustaining it is a shared responsibility involving both change agents as well as the intended beneficiaries.

9

Fighting AIDS Together

Every day, 1,000 children around the world die from AIDS. In 1996 alone, the disease took the lives of 13 million people. About 90 per cent of the 23 million people currently infected with HIV live in developing countries. Experts estimate that 30 million to 40 million people will be HIV-positive by the year 2000, about the same number as the entire population of Argentina or Spain.

In about 30 countries, mostly in sub-Saharan Africa. AIDS is stalling and even reversing the best efforts to improve the health of children and adults, women and men, the poor and the rich. And only 8 per cent (approximately \$1.5 billion) of the \$18 billion a year is being spent on prevention, care and research in the developing countries. Even more ominous is the fact that the majority of newly infected adults are under 25 years old, with all too obvious implications for the future. Women, mostly in their child-bearing years, now account for nearly half of new infections.

And the worst may be yet to come. According to some forecasts, rates of infection will not peak until the year 2010 in 19 of the hardest-hit countries, most of which are in sub-Saharan Africa. While the deaths attributable to AIDS represent a small percentage of total deaths, they are enough to reverse some improvements in life expectancy. Fifteen sub-Saharan African countries may experience a decline of up to 11 years of life expectancy by the year 2000 compared to projections of deaths without AIDS.

Still to face the brunt of the epidemic is Asia, home to over half the world's population. Despite the fact that AIDS has only recently begun to take hold in the region, the number of new infections each day is already comparable to the number in sub-Saharan Africa. Unless major advances are made in preventing and treating the disease, projections are grim for high-population countries like India, where clinic data show that HIV is beginning to work its way into the middle class. And it is not just those who become infected who suffer. AIDS is a disease with strong ripple effects, primarily because it strikes so relentlessly at people in the prime of life. When a mother becomes debilitated by AIDS-related illness, often the first thing to happen is that her children's care suffers. Those children may miss vaccinations, eat fewer and less nutritious meals, suffer more bouts of illness. Then a child (or more than one) is likely to be pulled out of school to work in the market, cultivate the family plot or care for the baby.

When the mother dies, she may follow several other extended family members to the grave, so the likelihood of an aunt or uncle being able to take in her newly orphaned children is slim. In regions that formerly were noted for the unbreakable links of extended family networks, we now have the shocking reality of households headed by aged grandparents or children—12-year-olds responsible for providing food and shelter for a family of even younger siblings.

With this devastation so overwhelmingly affecting the developing world, the effort to fight AIDS is tilted just as overwhelmingly in the other direction, to the industrialised world. The most obvious example of this tilt is the new combination therapies, widely available in industrialised countries. The cost of these drugs—up to $15,000 a year per patient—is inconceivable to most people in the hard-hit nations. For the lucky few who could afford them, these therapies can be found only in middle-income countries like Brazil and Thailand; they are virtually unavailable in Africa. But other examples of the tilt abound. Of the $2.6 billion spent on HIV prevention efforts worldwide each year, only 14 per cent is spent in developing countries. These countries account for an even smaller proportion—6 per cent—of the $11.6 billion spent for care. Research on development of a vaccine, especially crucial in the hard-hit countries, gets less than 5 per cent of the $4.2 billion spent annually on HIV/AIDS research worldwide, according to most recent estimates.

The historical lack of funding for vaccine development is scandalous and irrational, given what is at stake. However, there is encouraging news from the AIDS Research Evaluation Task Force of the US National Institutes of Health (NIH).

The Task Force, overseen and prodded by distinguished independent scientists, has called for a revitalisation of the vaccine quest. NIH is now considerably increasing its vaccine efforts. In addition, a consortium of organisations has founded the International AIDS Vaccine Initiative to stimulate vaccine research. In particular, the initiative will support research targeted at HIV subtypes found in areas of the world where the disease is spreading most rapidly. Governments must also develop incentives to encourage serious investment on the part of drug companies in reaching this goal.

Funding aside, the concentration of research in the industrialised world has other worrying implications. For instance, research on preventing mother-to-child transmission of HIV and on treating HIV-related conditions in children has been very limited, undoubtedly because these are largely problems of the developing world. Developing countries also need to be supported in building their own capacity to make AIDS medications available to their citizens who need them. It is imperative that the resources, the knowledge and the effort in fighting AIDS be spread more evenly around the globe.

At the same time, more must be done to bring comfort to the lives of people sick from HIV-related illnesses. Painkillers, antidiarrhoeals, medicines to treat fungal infections—even these basic medicines are not affordable to people in the poorest countries.

Hanging in the balance are achievements made by the world community over several decades in reducing infant mortality and improving child health and nutrition.

Mortality rates for those under age 5 have been cut in half over the past 30 years. About 8 of every 10 children worldwide are now immunised against six major childhood diseases: measles, polio, diphtheria, pertussis, tetanus and tuberculosis. Polio is on the verge of eradication, and measles and neonatal tetanus are on the same path. Deaths of children from diarrhoea—which, along with pneumonia, is the number one killer of children in poor countries—are also in retreat because of cost-effective treatments like oral rehydration therapy (ORT). Since 1985, 2.5 million young lives have been saved each year through low-cost health programmes.

Worldwide, HIV infection most often results from heterosexual intercourse. Beyond that biological reality, some people are especially vulnerable to HIV infection because of their social, cultural or economic situation. One such cause of vulnerability is the social inequality between women and men. Women, especially young women, have little power to dictate the terms of sexual relationships and are therefore much more vulnerable to infection. The 'sugar daddy' phenomenon is not new, but in the age of AIDS, older men are pursuing ever younger women and girls in the belief that they are less likely to be infected. Thus, a key to stopping the epidemic is action that enhances the ability of women and young people to control their lives, including their sexual relationships.

As real strides are made in the industrialised countries, people are beginning to talk about AIDS as a 'manageable' disease. A magazine article in the US even wondered if we are in 'the twilight of AIDS'. This sort of talk brings the potential of dangerous complacency and of even greater division between the 'have' and the 'have-not' nations. That is a profound mistake on two counts. On an ethical plane, it is immoral to describe as 'manageable' a disease that is only 'manageable' for a fraction of the wealthiest 10 per cent of its victims. On a practical plane, it would be foolhardy for one simple reason: Like all infectious diseases, AIDS will not be defeated anywhere until it is defeated everywhere—miracle, drugs or no.

This is why it is so important that we avoid the temptation to view AIDS as two different diseases, one that is manageable in the wealthier countries and one that is a death sentence in the poorer countries. We are all in this boat together, and if we slip into an 'us vs. them' view of the world, we are sunk.

As former Zambian President Kenneth Kaunda said in a recent speech invoking the memory of his son, dead from AIDS in 1986, "Every one of us ignores AIDS in the house of their neighbour at their own peril." If we can stick together, if governments and NGOs and committed individuals in every community in every country are willing to learn from the painfully earned wisdom of their neighbours around the world, we can slow down and even reverse this epidemic. We do not have to watch these grim numbers continue their march across the world map.

To stop that march, we need accessible, affordable ways to prevent transmission between sexual partners and from mothers to children. This includes access to affordable and high-quality condoms, and increasingly to the recently developed condom for women. In 1994, US trials of a new drug, zidovudine (ZDV), to help HIV-positive mothers give birth to healthy babies had striking results: a two-thirds decrease in HIV transmission. But it is beyond the reach of poor women. UNAIDS, the US Centres for Disease Control and Prevention, and other organisations are now collaborating with researchers in Africa and Asia to find economical ways to make ZDV available where it is most needed. Other low-cost drugs to prevent mother-to-baby transmission during pregnancy and childbirth are under development and look promising.

One of the problems facing families and health workers in developing countries is the potential for HIV infection through breastfeeding. While the factors determining transmission of the virus from mother to baby are not yet fully understood, studies suggest that breastfeeding confers a 1-in-7 risk of infecting the baby with HIV.

An HIV-positive mother now faces a quandary. If she is affluent, she probably lives in a setting that makes the use of breastmilk substitutes a reasonable option. In all likelihood, she has easy access to safe water (or fuel to boil the water) for mixing the formula and cleaning the cups or bottles. She can afford as much formula as her baby needs. Attentive health services are available to treat the additional infant illnesses that may accompany use of breastmilk substitutes. Although in a perfect world breastfeeding is always the best option, for a well-to-do woman infected with HIV, using formula might be a good choice.

But mothers at the bottom of the economic ladder face a cruel dilemma: They can either breastfeed, with the risk of passing along HIV, or they can use breastmilk substitutes, with the risk of exposing their babies to potentially lethal diseases and to malnutrition from formula that is overdiluted.

If we know that some babies are becoming infected through breastmilk, we have a moral obligation to do everything we can to prevent those infections. First, we must make sure that every woman has access to affordable, confidential HIV testing. If she takes the test and it turns out positive, she must be supported in making the agonizing infant-feeding decision. She needs to be informed in a respectful way about the relative risks so that she can make a choice based on accurate facts.

Where safe water is accessible close by, and where breastmilk substitutes are available at reasonable cost, an HIV-infected mother might choose to feed formula to her child. However, she herself is powerless to ensure a reliable water supply or quality health services, nor can she influence the price of formula. These are matters of public health, and that is the responsibility of governments.

A few heroic leaders understand AIDS for the profound development challenge it is, and they have approached it with an unprecedented call to action. When that becomes part of the national consciousness, the worst effects of the epidemic can be avoided.

In South Africa, President Nelson Mandela has called for a national struggle to vanquish AIDS on a scale similar to that mobilised to bring down apartheid. Zimbabwe responded to high HIV prevalence rates with a mandatory weekly lesson in life skills for all students aged 9 to 19. The course, begun in 1993, addresses HIV/AIDS in the context of coping with emotions and expectations, gender roles and plans for the future, and students role-play to develop strategies for responding to peer pressure.

Similar bright spots of leadership are occurring in Asia. Only a few years ago, Thailand was viewed by complacent neighbours as the only country in the region likely to have a significant problem with AIDS. The virus had gained a foothold in 1988, and the availability of commercial sex in the country of 59 million people allowed it to flourish. As a result, about 45,000 Thais died from HIV infection in 1995.

But Anand Panyarachun, who was Prime Minister in 1991 and 1992, instituted a far-reaching AIDS education programme that has put Thailand in much better shape than some of its neighbours. Mr. Anand required every government minister to include a budget line for AIDS. The centrepiece of a public education programme was a series of explicit AIDS prevention messages aired on radio stations at least once every hour. Condoms were widely distributed to brothels. Sex businesses that refused to require condom use were shut down. Calls for abstinence from casual sex were partnered with the condom campaign, promoted tirelessly by the Prime Minister's dynamic AIDS adviser.

As a result, there was an 80 per cent decrease in sexually transmitted diseases in Thailand from 1989 to 1994. The number of new HIV infections in Thailand each year has more than halved since 1990. Success stories like these should be the most powerful argument against complacency. These successes demonstrate that if we focus our efforts on those most vulnerable, if we expand use of the communication tools that work and commit ourselves to developing a vaccine and affordable drugs, we can stop this plague. We already proved we can muster global will and resources with the campaign that raised vaccination rates worldwide from 40 per cent to 80 per cent in just five years. The worst that can happen for our prospects of wiping this virus from the earth is to allow complacency and divisiveness between the haves and have-nots to prevent us from developing responses that work in the countries where they are most needed. We can defeat HIV/AIDS—if we all acknowledge our ownership of it. As the freedom of each nation is interdependent with that of others, so too is the health and wellbeing of their peoples. Nowhere is this more true than in the case of AIDS. The challenge of AIDS can be overcome if we work together as a global community.

No one among us could have imagined the far-reaching devastation of the human immuno-deficiency virus (HIV), but some facts are now clear. Young people—notably women—are the leading victims of this epidemic. More than 7,000 young men and women around the world are infected every day, as are an additional 1,600 children under the age of 15.

Tragically, it is children who shoulder the greatest burden of the epidemic. Worldwide, more than eight million children have had to grow up without their mothers. Over 90 per cent of those orphaned by AIDS live in sub-Saharan Africa. To lose one or both parents to AIDS is to face a childhood of pain and peril. The suffering starts with the grief and horror of watching their parent waste away. Soon they suffer prejudice and neglect at the hands of their guardians and community. Every tenet of the Convention on the Rights of the Child is violated, from their right to education, health and development, to protection from exploitation and harm.

Our experience tells us that orphans have alarmingly higher rates of malnutrition, stunting and illiteracy. Often their community shuns them, presuming that they, too, harbour the fatal virus. Relatives who take them in often seize their paltry inheritance, and local laws offer little recourse to these lonely children.

Worse still, as surveys have shown, children whose parents have died often must shoulder heavier workloads and are treated more harshly than the foster family's own children. They are less likely to go to school and more likely to be depressed. One of our current district development plans reports that "orphan children [are] being defiled, married, neglected and ... subjected to many forms of abuse."

Throughout the continent, young girls are especially vulnerable, and a reported rapid rise in sexual abuse in Zimbabwe, for example, has prompted the Government to set up a special hospital clinic to deal with the victims of this unconscionable behaviour.

Tens of thousands of orphans are simply abandoned to fend for themselves, like the 90,000 in Zambia living on the streets. Tens of thousands more are struggling in households headed by the eldest child. Newspaper reports chronicled the fate of little girls like Kugu Sengane, in Kwazulu Natal (South Africa), who was only 11 years old when she had to nurse both of her parents through the torment of their dying days. As they languished in pain, Kugu was barely able to keep them washed and fed, while having to care for her toddler brother. This is no life for a child.

Nearly half of those caring for orphans in some regions of Africa are elderly grandparents like Ennie Gambushe, who lives up the road front little Kugu Sengane. At age 64, Ennie aches so badly from her chronic arthritis that she has difficulty merely standing up. Yet after both of her daughters died from AIDS, she was left to took after 15 grandchildren, none of them older than 12.

From South Africa up rough central and eastern Africa, such scenes highlight the catastrophic impact AIDS has had on our families and communities, leaving our aging grandparents with an exhausting responsibility. "Young girls—our children, our grandchildren, they are dying before we die," says 79-year-old Elizabeth Chipepa from Zambia, who inherited three small great-grandchildren when her granddaughter succumbed to AIDS. "You can hear others my age saying things like, 'I've lost my three children; the first one has left three children, the second has left six ......"

For a long time it was typical to describe the AIDS epidemic in Africa as 'mysterious' and 'invisible', but that could hardly be further from reality. We have all shared the suffering of dying brothers, sisters and childhood schoolmates. There are empty seats at all of our table, empty desks in our offices. But the loss of a friend or a relative is only the first rupture in the web of family generations that once protected our society.

When AIDS strikes the family breadwinner, his or her income dries up and the rest of the family slips deeper into poverty as they devote their meagre resources to nurse an ailing kill. Our studies show that when a father dies, his widow and eldest children must work two to four hours longer every day. Girls, in particular, may be forced to leave school to help at home and to work in the fields.

Moreover, the deadly virus rarely stops at one family member. Husbands infect their wives; about a third of newborns in turn acquire the infection from their mothers. Again, trapped by the silence and inhibited by the stigma surrounding the disease, women without symptoms of AIDS often discover their infection only after their infant is diagnosed with HIV.

Our continent's human tragedy, caused by HIV/AIDS, is desperately compounded by a social welfare crisis. So many go without treatment for AIDS and it, complications because antiretro-viral drugs—that have kept patients in industrialised nations alive and healthy—cost thousands of dollars a year, making them only a dream for most in Africa. Massive resources are urgently needed to help us treat those infected, look after those orphaned and prevent further spread of this disease.

Prevention efforts need the world's help also, not only to stave off the torrent that has swept southward into Malawi, Zambia, Zimbabwe, Botswana and South Africa, but also to brake its advance into Asia, where seven million people are already infected. India is home to four million people with HIV, and the patterns of transmission indicate that we have no time to lose.

In Chennai (formerly Madras), the HIV-infection rate among truck drivers quadrupled from 1995 to 1996, a haunting echo of the AIDS explosion among the African lorry drivers who travelled the high ways from Nairobi to Lusaka. Also in India, studies of pregnant women in the coastal town of Pondicherry reveal four per cent to be infected with HIV. Roughly a third of their infants will acquire the virus. We have learned that the crucial factor in successful prevention campaigns is the open, unwavering political commitment by each government to confront the epidemic forthrightly, to shatter the silence surrounding the virus and to prohibit discrimination of any kind. Behind the shield of silence, the stigma and shame associated with AIDS only enable this epidemic to further flourish. Nine out of 10 people in Africa with HIV do not know they are infected, and those who do know rarely tell their relatives, let alone their sex partners. Many African newspapers make no mention of AIDS in the bulging death notices.

In Uganda, when President Yoweri Museveni took office in 1986 he recognised the seriousness of this disease and its long-term consequences. He quickly established a national committee for AIDS prevention, which launched an intensive public education campaign based on catchy messages to attract our young people. Among other things, it encouraged condom distribution, voluntary HIV testing, counselling and support services.

With its slogan 'Faithfulness, abstinence, condoms', our AIDS-prevention campaign has made remarkable progress. Many Ugandans are now postponing their first sexual experiences, taking fewer partners and using condoms more often. We have seen the rate of new infections among our people drop dramatically since the dark year of 1987, when we had 239,000 new cases of HIV/AIDS. By 1997, this figure had declined by more than three quarters, to 57,000. We are especially encouraged by the 40 per cent drop in HIV prevalence among pregnant women in urban areas—an important indicator for tracking the spread of the disease.

10

Questions on HIV/AIDS/STD

What is AIDS?

AIDS stands for Acquired (not inborn, passed from person to person, including from mother to baby); Immune (relating to the body's immune system, which provides protection from disease-causing germs); Deficiency (lack of response by the immune system to germs); Syndrome (a number of signs and symptoms indicating a particular disease or condition).

What do we know about HIV?

HIV, like other viruses, is very small, too small to be seen with an ordinary microscope. Viruses cause all sorts of diseases from flu (influenza) to herpes to some kinds of cancer.

What is STD?

STD stands for sexually transmitted disease or diseases. Many different STD have been identified. The most common STD include: gonorrhoea, chlamydia, syphilis, trichomonas, genital warts, chancroid, genital herpes, hepatitis B and HIV infection. In many STD, the early symptoms are often difficult to recognise, and many people ignore them until more severe damage is done. This is especially true for women. This makes early diagnosis and treatment difficult.

What are Antibodies?

The body's defence system (immune system) develops germ fighters, called antibodies to fight off and destroy various viruses and germs that invade the body.

WHAT IS THE "WINDOW" PERIOD?

This is the time that the body takes to produce measurable amounts of antibodies after infection. For HIV, this period is usually 2-12 weeks; in rare instances it may be longer.

WHAT DOES THE ASYMPTOMATIC PERIOD MEAN?

The asymptomatic period is the period of time between infection and the beginning of signs and symptoms related to AIDS.

WHAT ARE THE SYMPTOMS OF AIDS?

This question must be approached with caution in any specific case, since it is often difficult to determine if the symptoms actually mean onset of AIDS or if they are simply symptoms of other conditions. People develop signs and symptoms of their HIV infection before they develop what has been defined as AIDS. AIDS is the final and most severe phase of HIV infection and leads to death.

ARE THERE DRUGS AND VACCINES TO TREAT AIDS?

There are drugs that are effective against many of the infections associated with AIDS. These drugs are not a cure for AIDS but they can postpone symptoms or death.

HOW DO YOU GET HIV?

HIV can be found in body fluids like blood, semen, vaginal fluids, and breast milk.

HOW DO YOU NOT GET HIV?

HIV is not transmitted by touch, coughing and sneezing, cutlery, glasses, cups and food, swimming pools, towels, toilet seats, pets, mosquitoes and other insects, baths or showers.

WHAT DO "SAFE SEX" AND "PROTECTED SEX" MEAN?

Because of the risk of HIV/AIDS, it is necessary to be very clear about the sexual practices which are known to carry a risk of HIV transmission and those which do not.

a) *Safe sex activities* (no risk): Practising the following activities will prevent a partner's blood, semen or vaginal secretions from getting into contact with your blood and thereby prevents transmission of HIV: masturbation, massage, rubbing, hugging, touching genitals.

b) *Low-risk sex activities*: Using a condom correctly and consistently during sexual intercourse, will reduce the risk of infection with HIV and other STD. Latex condoms have been demonstrated to be an effective protection against HIV, STD, as well as pregnancy. Incorrect use of condoms reduces their effectiveness, e.g., they may break. Sexual intercourse with a condom is called "protected sex".

c) Unsafe sexual activities: Practising the following activities is a definite risk: anal sex (penis in rectum) without a condom; vaginal sex (penis in vagina) without a condom; any sex act that makes you bleed; and semen (or blood) taken into the mouth during oral-genital sex.

WHAT IS AFFECTION WITHOUT SEX (NON-PENETRATIVE SEX)?

There are many ways of showing affection and enjoying sexual pleasure like touching, massage, mutual masturbation. In many cultures, penetration is regarded as the only way of having sex. However, alternatives to penetrative sex are often enjoyed by women and men alike.

DO SOME PEOPLE HAVE A HIGH LIKELIHOOD OF GETTING HIV?

Yes. It depends on a person's behaviour Some behaviours/ activities carry a higher risk of getting HIV than others. These include:

— Having many different sexual partners.
— Practising unsafe sexual activities, e.g., have sexual intercourse without a condom.
— Having sex when you have other sexually transmitted diseases.
— Sharing needles and syringes for injecting drug use.

Some situations which are beyond an individual's control can put them at risk. These include:

— Receiving injections with needles that are not cleaned or sterilised properly.
— Receiving blood transfusions with blood that has not been tested.

ARE MEN AND WOMEN EQUALLY VULNERABLE PHYSIOLOGICALLY TO HIV INFECTION?

Women are slightly more vulnerable physiologically to HIV infection than men. The area of mucous membrane exposed during intercourse is much larger in the woman than in the man, and the mucous membrane surface of the vagina (compared to the penis) can more easily be penetrated by virus. Very young women are more vulnerable than women in the 18-45 year age group; their immature cervix and relatively low vaginal mucus production present less of a barrier to HIV. Women are becoming more infected at younger ages than men. This is partly because many young women marry or have sex with men older than themselves, who have already had a number of partners, and partly because of their biological vulnerability.

DO YOU HAVE TO HAVE MANY SEXUAL PARTNERS TO GET INFECTED WITH HIV/STD?

Even one contact with a person infected with HIV is enough to transmit the infection. However, the risk of getting infected with HIV increases with the number of sexual partners and the number of sexual acts. The presence of an STD (e.g., genital ulcers) in a sexual partner increases the risk of transmission of HIV.

QUESTIONS ON TRANSMISSION

a) Is HIV spread by prostitutes and their clients?

Prostitutes and their clients, like any other people with many sexual partners, run the risk of getting infected by their partners. They may then pass the infection to many others. If a prostitute insists on using a condom every time she or he has sex, the risk of infection for her and the partner will be sharply reduced. Many prostitutes have replaced penetrative sex with safer practices, further reducing the risk of infection. Unfortunately clients often refuse to wear condoms and the women are not in a position to insist.

b) If a woman is menstruating is there a greater risk of getting infected with HIV (for her partner and for herself)?

Menstrual blood from HIV-infected women does contain the virus. Infection would be dependent on whether the menstrual blood had contact with the sexual partner's bloodstream. A woman who is menstruating is likely to be at a higher risk for HIV through sexual intercourse.

c) Can you get infected by blood transfusion or by blood products?

Recommended standard practice for all transfusion services is to test and exclude from use all blood and blood products that are "seropositive", i.e., contain antibodies to HIV. In most countries, efforts have been made to test all blood donations for HIV since 1985.

There is a very small chance that an occasional transfusion may contain the virus since an HIV-infected donor might have been in the "window" period (test negative) when giving blood.

You cannot get HIV from donating blood.

d) What happens to a baby born to a woman with HIV infection?

The baby may be born infected with the virus. An infected mother can also pass the infection to her baby during breastfeeding after childbirth.

About 20-40 per cent of babies born to infected mothers will acquire the HIV virus. Some of these will develop AIDS during the first year of life. The majority of HIV-infected babies will not survive to their second birthday. However, some may survive up to seven years or even longer.

It serves little purpose to test babies born to HIV-infected mothers for HIV antibodies at birth. There are likely to be many false positive results because antibodies from the mother are still circulating in the baby's bloodstream. Only at 18 months or older, can an antibody test result be regarded as reliable.

e) Does breastfeeding transmit HIV?

Breast milk of an HIV-infected mother contains HIV which can be transmitted to the baby. However, because of the benefits of breastfeeding, the World Health Organisation recommends that in situations where infectious disease and malnutrition are the main cause of infant deaths, and the infant mortality rate is high, mothers should breastfeed their babies, even if they are known to be infected with HIV, as the risk to the baby is less than the risks involved in artificial feeding.

CAN NEEDLES, KNIVES AND OTHER INSTRUMENTS TRANSMIT HIV?

Yes. Any instruments that cut the skin or puncture the skin can collect small amounts of blood that can be passed on if used again by another person without being sterilised. Avoid tattooing, ear piercing, acupuncture, blood-letting ceremonies or sharing razors unless you are absolutely sure the instruments being used are sterilised or boiled in water.

HOW IS HIV TRANSMITTED WITH INJECTION NEEDLES AND SYRINGES?

Small amounts of blood remain in the needle and syringe after use. If someone else then uses that needle and syringe, any blood left in the syringe or needle will be injected into their bloodstream. If the first user was infected with HIV, then the second person may now also be infected.

Only a very small amount of blood is needed for transmission to occur. Sharing needles and syringes used for anything—medicines or heroin, cocaine, amphetamines (speed) and even water—can spread HIV. It is not what is put into the syringe that transmits HIV, but the blood that remains in the needle and syringe.

Some countries have needle and syringe exchange programmes (used needles and syringes are exchanged for new ones) for injecting drug users. Those who cannot stop injecting drugs can join these programmes to avoid HIV transmission.

If people are not in a position to use a new needle and syringe, the equipment can be boiled or, if boiling is not possible, cleaned in the following way:

— Rinse the syringe out with clean, cold water at least twice (not hot water). Squirt the used water down the drain.

— Rinse the syringe out at least twice with fresh, household bleach, squirting the used bleach down the drain.

— Rinse it out again, at least twice with clean, cold water to get rid of the bleach.

Be extremely careful if you come across a needle or syringe in a park or street. Dispose of it safely without touching it with unprotected fingers.

CAN YOU GET HIV FROM CONTACT SPORTS WHERE BLEEDING MAY OCCUR?

There is no evidence that any person participating in any sports activity has become infected with HIV from, or has transmitted HIV to, other participants.

It is possible that transmission could occur if an HIV-infected athlete had a bleeding wound that came in contact with a cut in the skin or mucous membrane of another person. Even in such an unlikely event, however, the risk of transmission would be very low.

Given this small possibility, it would be wise in contact sports where bleeding might occur to follow these procedures:

1) cleanse any cut with antiseptic and cover it well;
2) if bleeding occurs, stop activity and wait until the bleeding has stopped and then cleanse and treat it with an antiseptic and cover it securely;
3) latex gloves should always be worn when treating injured people.

Do Mosquitoes or other Insects Spread HIV?

The evidence clearly shows that HIV is not spread by mosquitoes and other insects. For example, bedbugs, lice and fleas in the households of people infected with HIV do not spread the virus to the other people living in these households.

If mosquitoes were responsible for spreading HIV, then people of all ages would be infected. In fact, children before puberty are rarely infected, unless they were born to infected mothers or had a transfusion with infected blood.

We know that HIV lives in some cells of the human body but that it does not live in the cells of insects. Therefore, mosquitoes and other insects are not a suitable home for HIV.

HIV is not like the malaria parasite which lives very well in the mosquito and spreads to people when mosquitoes bite, because it is in the fluid that the mosquito injects.

When Should one be Tested for HIV?

There are advantages and disadvantages to being tested for HIV. It is a decision that should not be taken lightly and the implications of positive and negative outcomes should be faced in advance with the assistance of an HIV/AIDS counsellor.

What Happens if You Live Close to Someone With AIDS?

Living near someone who has AIDS or who is infected with HIV will not give you HIV. You can live quite safety in the same room with someone who has AIDS, provided that he or she is not your sexual partner and that you take precautions in handling body fluids (blood in particular).

Appendix-I

Zonal Blood Testing Centres (India)

ANDHRA PRADESH

— Blood Bank, Gandhi Hospital, Hyderabad
— Blood Bank, M.J. Cancer Hospital, Hyderabad
— Blood Bank, Nizam's IMS, Hyderabad
— Blood Bank Instt. of Preventive Medicines, Hyderabad
— Blood Bank, Govt. Headquarters Hospital, Vijayawada
— Blood Bank, Govt. Headquarters Hospital, Karim Nagar
— Blood Bank, Govt. Headquarters Hospital, Cuddapah
— Blood Bank, Govt. Headquarters Hospital, Kammam
— Blood Bank, Govt. Headquarters Hospital, Chittor
— Blood Bank, Medical College, Tirupati
— Blood Bank, Guntur Medical College, Guntur
— Blood Bank, General Hospital, Kurnool

ARUNACHAL PRADESH

— Blood Bank, Government Hospital, Itanagar

ASSAM

— Blood Bank, Guwahati Medical College, Guwahati
— Blood Bank, Medical College, Dibrugarh
— Blood Bank, Medical College, Silchar

BIHAR

— Blood Bank, Medical College, Gaya

— Blood Bank, Patna Medical College, Patna
— Blood Bank, District Hospital, Dhanbad
— Blood Bank, District Hospital, Jamshedpur
— Blood Bank, Jamshedpur
— Blood Bank, Rajendra Medical College, Ranchi
— Blood Bank, Medical College, Bhagalpur.
— Blood Bank, Shri Krishna Medical College, Muzzafarpur
— Blood Bank, Medical College, Dharbanga

GOA

— Blood Bank, Medical College, Panaji
— Blood Bank, Civil Hospital, Panaji

GUJARAT

— Blood Bank, Surat Medical College, Surat
— Blood Bank, Govt. Medical College, Vadodara
— Blood Bank, B.J. Medical College, Ahmedabad.
— Blood Bank, M.P. Shah Hospital, Jamnagar,
— Blood Bank, District Hospital, Junagarh
— Blood Bank, Civil Hospital, Amreli

HARYANA

— Blood Bank, Medical College, Rohtak
— Blood Bank, District Hospital, Hissar
— Blood Bank, General Hospital, Faridabad
— Blood Bank, General Hospital, Karnal

HIMACHAL PRADESH

— Blood Bank, Indira Gandhi Medical College, Shimla
— Blood Bank, District Hospital, Dharamsala

JAMMU & KASHMIR

— Blood Bank, Govt. Hospital, Srinagar
— Blood Bank, Medical College, Jammu

KARNATAKA

— Blood Bank, K.C. General Hospital, Bangalore
— Blood Bank, H.S.I.S. Hospital, Bangalore
— Blood Bank, K.M. Instt. of Ontology, Bangalore
— Blood Bank, K.M.C. Hospital, Hubli
— Blood Bank, Kasturba Medical College, Manipal
— Blood Bank, Medical College, Bellari
— Blood Bank, Kasturba Medical College, Mangalore
— Blood Bank, Medical College, Gulbarga

TAMIL NADU

— Blood Bank, Govt. Hospital, Coimbatore
— Blood Bank, Govt. Hospital, Salem
— Blood Bank, Govt. Hospital, Tiruchirapalli
— Blood Bank Medical College, Tirunelveli

TRIPURA

— Blood Bank, G.B. Hospital, Agartala

UTTAR PRADESH

— Blood Bank, Dist. Hospital, Gorakhpur
— Blood Bank, G.S.V. Medical College, Kanpur
— Blood Bank, Dist. Hospital, Allahabad
— Blood Bank, K.L. Sharma Hospital, Meerut
— Blood Bank, K.G. Medical College, Lucknow
— Blood Bank, S.G.P.G.I., Lucknow
— Blood Bank, Medical College, Agra
— Blood Bank, Dist. Hospital, Dehradun
— Blood Bank, Dist. Hospital, Nainital
— Blood Bank, Dist. Hospital, Shahjahanpur
— Blood Bank, M.L.D. Medical College, Jhansi

WEST BENGAL

— Central Blood Bank, Calcutta

— Blood Bank, C.N.M.C.H., Calcutta
— Blood Bank, N.R.S.M.C.H., Calcutta
— Blood Bank, R.G.K.A.R.M.C.H., Calcutta
— Blood Bank, S.S.K.M., Calcutta
— Blood Bank, Dist. Hospital, West Dinajpur
— Blood Bank, North Bengal Medical College, Darjeeling
— Blood Bank, Dist. Hospital, Jalpaiguri
— Blood Bank, State Hospital, Burdwan

A & N ISLANDS

— Blood Bank, G.B. Pant Hospital, Port Blair

DELHI

— Blood Bank, G.T.B. Hospital, Shahdara Delhi
— Blood Bank, HinduRao Hospital, New Delhi
— Blood Bank LNJP/MAMC Hospital, New Delhi
— Blood Bank, Instt. of Pathology, New Delhi

UNDER INDIAN COUNCIL OF MEDICAL RESEARCH

— Blood Bank, Bhubaneswar

UNDER DIRECTOR GENERAL OF ARMED FORCES

Medical Services

— Blood Bank Command Hospital, Bangalore
— Blood Bank Command Pathology Lab, Eastern Command, Calcutta
— Blood Bank Armed Forces Command Hospital, Delhi Cantt
— Blood Bank Command Pathology Lab, Central Command, Lucknow
— Blood Bank Armed Forces Medical College, Pune
— Blood Bank Command Hospital, Northern Command, Udhampur

In Central Institution

— Blood Bank, Lady Hardinge Medical College, New Delhi

— Blood Bank, Blood Transfusion Services, Safdarjung Hospital, New Delhi

— Blood Bank, Jipmer, Pondicherry

In Autonomous Institution (Other than ICMR)

— Blood Bank, Medical College Banaras Hindu University, Varanasi

— Blood Bank, AIIMS, New Delhi

— Blood Bank, Indian Red Cross Society, New Delhi

— Blood Bank, PGI, Chandigarh

In Private Institutions

— Blood Bank, Christian Medical College, Vellore.

Appendix-II

List of Surveillance Centres

HIV Testing facilities are available in the following centres:

Andhra Pradesh

— Department of Microbiology, Osmania College, Hyderabad

— Department of Microbiology, SV Medical College, Tirupati

— Department of Microbiology, Andhra Medical College, Vishakapatnam

— Instt. of Preventive Medicine, Hyderabad

Arunachal Pradesh

— District Hospital, Itanagar

Assam

— Department of Microbiology, Guwahati Medical College, Guwahati

Goa

— Department of Microbiology, Goa Medical College, Panaji

Gujarat

— Department of Microbiology, BJ Medical College, Ahmedabad

Haryana

— Department of Microbiology, Medical College, Rohtak

HIMACHAL PRADESH

— Department of Microbiology, Indira Gandhi Medical College, Shimla

JAMMU & KASHMIR

— Department of Immunopathology, Sher-e-Kashmir Institute of Medical Sciences, Srinagar
— Department of Microbiology, Government Medical College, Jammu

KARNATAKA

— Department of Microbiology, Bangalore Medical College, Bangalore
— Department of Microbiology, Kasturba Medical College, Manipal

KERALA

— Department of Microbiology, Medical College, Trivandrum

MADHYA PRADESH

— Department of Pathology, Gandhi Medical College, Bhopal
— Choitram Hospital and Research Centre, Indore

MAHARASHTRA

— Department of Microbiology, Seth G.S. Medical College, Mumbai
— Department of Microbiology, JJ Hospital, Mumbai
— Sion Hospital, Mumbai
— B.Y.N. Nair Hospital, Mumbai
— Rajabari Hospital, Ghatkopar, Mumbai
— B.J. Medical College, Pune
— Department of Microbiology, Govt. Medical College, Nagpur
— Civil Hospital, Kolhapur
— District Hospital, Chandrapur
— Governmental Medical College, Miraj

MANIPUR

— J.N. Hospital, Imphal

MEGHALAYA

— Civil Hospital, Shillong

MIZORAM

— Civil Hospital, Aizawl

NAGALAND

— Naga Hospital, Kohima
— District Hospital, Dimapur

ORISSA

— Department of Microbiology, SCB Medical College, Cuttack

PUNJAB

— Government Medical College, Amritsar

RAJASTHAN

— Department of Microbiology, SMS Medical College, Jaipur

SIKKIM

— S.T.N.M. Hospital, Gangtok

TAMIL NADU

— Department of Microbiology, Instt. of Child Health and Hospital for Children, Chennai
— Department of Microbiology, Madurai Medical College, Madurai

TRIPURA

— District Hospital, Agartala

UTTAR PRADESH

— Department of Microbiology, K.G. Medical College, Lucknow

WEST BENGAL AND A & N ISLANDS

— G. B. Hospital, Port Blair

DELHI

— Department of Microbiology, University College of Medical Sciences, Shahdara, Delhi
— Deptt. of Microbiology, Maulana Azad Medical College, New Delhi

LAKSHADWEEP

— Govt. Hospital, Kavaratti

PONDICHERRY

— Government General Hospital, Pondicherry

UNDER INDIAN COUNCIL OF MEDICAL RESEARCH

— Central JALMA Instt. for Leprosy, Agra
— Regional Medical Research Centre, Bhubneshwar
— Regional Medical Research Centre for Tribal Health, Jabalpur
— Tuberculosis Research Centre, Chennai
— Rajendra Memorial Research Institute, Patna

UNDER DIRECTOR GENERAL OF ARMED FORCES MEDICAL SERVICES

— Indian Naval Ship Hospital, Ashwani, Mumbai
— Indian Naval Ship Hospital, Cochin
— Armed Forces Command Hospital, Delhi Cantt
— Department of Microbiology, Armed Forces Medical College, Pune
— Indian Naval Ship Hospital, Kalyani, Vishakapatnam

IN CENTRAL INSTITUTIONS

— All India Institute of Hygiene and Public Health, Calcutta
— Department of Microbiology, JIPMER, Pondicherry

IN AUTONOMOUS INSTITUTIONS

— Department of Microbiology, Instt. of Medical Sciences, Varanasi

— Jawahar Lal Nehru Medical College, Aligarh
— Department of Immunopathology, PGI, Chandigarh
— National Institute of Mental and Neurosurgery

IN PRIVATE INSTITUTIONS

— Kamla Nehru Memorial Hospital, Allahabad.

Glossary

AIDS: An acronym made of the first letter of the words Acquired Immune Deficiency Syndrome. AIDS, strictly speaking, is not a disease but more accurately a "syndrome"—a collection of various symptoms infections and conditions.

AIDS Test: There are a number of tests to detect the HIV. Blood tests are done to look for specific antibodies produced by the HIV.

Ano-genital Wart: Raised skin in anal or genital region occurring as a response to infection with papilloma virus.

Antibiotic: A substance or a drug that kills, inhibits or retards the growth of micro-organisms.

Antibodies: Specific substances produced in the blood in response to an antigen or a foreign body.

Antigen: Any substance that the body regards as foreign and against which it produces an antibody.

Antiretroviral: A substance or drug active against retroviruses, usually HIV. Antiretrovirals used in humans include ZDV, ddl and ddc.

ARC: AIDS-Related Condition/Complex. A term for possible combination of conditions experienced by people with symptomatic HIV infection.

AZT: An abbreviation for Azidothymidine.

Abortion: Means spontaneous or induced termination of pregnancy before the foetus is independently viable.

Androgens: Hormones secreted by the testes and adrenal cortex.

Androgyna: A pseudofemale hermaphrodite, i.e., one in whom the female characteristics are predominant.

Amnion: The innermost membrane enclosing the foetus and containing amniotic fluid.

Amenorrhoea: Absence of menses.

Amastia: Congenital absence of the breasts.

B-cell: A lymphocyte which matures in the bone marrow, and produces antibodies to pathogens.

Bacteria: A group of micro-organisms, also called 'schizomycetes'.

Bacterial Vaginosis: It is a most common disease among women of child-bearing age. However, the organisms responsible for BV have also been found in young women who are not sexually active.

Blood Count: Calculation of the number of red or white cells per cubic millimeter of blood, using a hemocytometer.

Blood Transfusion: The intravenous replacement of lost or destroyed blood by compatible citrated human blood.

Bisexual: Having the characteristic of both sexes.

Carrier: A person who appears well but is capable of transmitting an infection to another person.

CD4 Cell: A type of lymphocyte crucial to the normal function of the immune system.

Chancroid: An STD transmitted through sexual contact. The disease is common among men who have contact with prostitutes.

Chemotherapy: A treatment of disease by any drug or a specific chemical agent.

Chlamydia Infection: Chlamydia is yet another STD prevalent among both men and women. This disease is caused by bacterium called chlamydia-trachomatis.

Cervix: The check of the uterus.

Cervicitis: Inflammation of cervix uteri.

Contact Tracing: Finding and talking to people or the partners who have been diagnosed as having a sexually transmissible disease.

Clitoriditis: Inflammation of the clitoris.

Colpohysterectomy: Removal of uterus through the vagine.

Colpocentesis: Withdrawal of fluid from the vagina as in hematocolpos.

Cytome Galovirus: CMV is a member of herpes virus family. The virus has been found in various body fluids including urine, saliva, semen and cervical secretions.

Cyesis: Pregnancy or conception.

Cyesis (Pseudo): Signs and symptoms simulating those of early pregnancy occurring in a childless person with an overwhelming desire to how a child.

Dementia: Irreversible organic deterioration of mental faculties.

Disorientation: The loss of normal relationship to one's surroundings, particularly the ability to comprehend time, place and people.

DNA: Deoxyribonucleic acid, the nucleoprotein of chromosomes. The virus also contains DNA as its genetic material.

Drug Trial: The clinical trial or experiment through which researchers deliverers the effectiveness of different forms of treatment.

Durabolin: An agent with testosterone-like activity.

Dysmenorrhoea: Painful menstruation.

Elisa: Enzyme linked immunosorbent assay—the most commonly followed procedures to look for specific antibodies produced by the HIV. It is a type of blood test.

Ectopic Pregnancy: Extriuterine gestation, the fallopian tube being the most common site.

Ellipto Cytosis: Anaemea in which the red blood cells are oval.

Endocervicitis: Inflammation of the mucous membrane lining the cervix uteri.

Endometrium: The lining mucosa of the uterus.

Epidemiology: The scientific study of the distribution of disease.

Fidelity: Refers to being faithful to one's chosen sexual partner(s) and having sexual intercourse only with that/those partner(s).

Factor IX: At protein essential for normal blood coagulation, it is deficient in patients with haemophilia type B.

FIT: A needle as a syringe used to inject drug intravenously. This is the term used by users themselves.

Factor VIII: That factor in the blood which is essential for clotting. People with haemophilia type A have a factor VIII deficiency and people with severe haemophilia require factor VIII replacement with specially prepared blood products.

Foetus (Fetus): An unborn child.

Fissure (anal): Linear ulcer on the margin of the anus.

Foreskin: The prepuce, a skin covering the glans penis.

Frigidity: Lack of normal sexual desire used mainly in relation to the female.

Fungi: On cells organism in the plant kingdom.

Genital Warts: Caused by certain types of HPV (Human Papillomavirus). Genital warts are contagious and spread by sexual contact. The warts usually occur within three months of exposure.

Gonorrhoea: An infectious disease of venereal origin in adults.

Granuloma Inguinale: Granuloma inguinale is an STD which frequently occurs in tropical areas. It affects both men and women. The common symptom of this disease is more painless, beefy red open sores that slowly enlarge usually appearing within a week of the exposure.

Group B Streptocci Infections (GBS).: Group B streptococci are infections commonly found in the genital tracts of both men and women. It is one of the leading causes of infection-related death among newborns.

Gud: Genital ulcer disease.

Gynaecology: The science dealing with diseases which are peculiar to women.

Gestation: Pregnancy.

Gynaecomastia: Enlargement of male mammary gland.

Gynaecography: Radiological visualisation of internal female genitalies after precumoperitoneum.

Gyrectomy: Surgical removal of a gyrus, a convoluted partori of cerebral cortex.

Hydrocele: A swelling due to accumulation of serus fluid in the tunics vaginalis of the testis, as in the spermatic cord.

Haemophilia: Disease in which patient is subject to prolonged bleeding following minor injuries.

Hepatitis: Hepatitis is basically an inflammation of the liver. The cause of the inflammation can be in many cases due to certain viruses. There an several types of viral hepatitis.

Herpes: There are two major types of herpes simplex viruses (Type I and Type II) in humans. Some herpes viruses cause cold sores and some cause genital herpes. Genital herpes is common opportunistic infection in people with AIDS.

Herpes Zoaster: Painful ivaicular enceptions on the skin and mucous membranes caused by the varicelle zoaster virus.

HIV: Human immunodeficiency virus. The virus which cause AIDS and renders the humane immuno system deficient and unable to resist opportunistic infections.

HIV-1: HIV-1 was find discovered in 1983 in France and appears to be more prevalent in Europe and the Americas.

HIV-2: HIV-2 was first discovered in 1986 and is more prevalent in Africa. Both HIV-1 and HIV-2 have been detected in India and both lead to AIDS.

Homosexual: Often used to describe a person who indulges in sexual relationship with a member of the same sex.'

Human Papillomiavirus: One of the most common STDs that affects men and women. It is reported that there are over 60 types of HPV.

Hormonotherapy: Treatment of hormones.

Immunodeficient: When a person's immune system cannot satisfactorily protect body, resulting in an increased susceptibility to various infections.

Immune-Supression: Occurs when the ability of an individual to resist or overcome some factors has been severely reduced due to dry treatment, disease or frequent infections.

Immune System: The body's defence system against attack by bacteria, virus, harmful food substances and some proteins, etc.

Immunity: The condition of a living organism whereby it resists and overcomes infection and disease.

Incidence Rate: The number of new cases of a disease that occur per population of risk, often reported per year and per 100,000 people.

Infectious: A person is infectious when he/she has been infected with a pathogen, like HIV, and is capable of transmitting that pathogen to another person. In all categories of HIV infection a person is considered infectious for life.

Infection: The invasion of a host by organisms such a viruses, fungi, protozoa, a bacteria with consequent disease.

Incubation Period: The time between infection with a disease causing organism and the onset of the visible signs and symptoms of the disease.

Intra Venous (IV): Inject or delivered through a needle into a vein.

IV Needles: Needles used to inject drugs directly into the bloodstream. They are inserted with veins.

IVDU: Intravenous drug user.

Jaundice: A condition characterised by a raised bilirubin level in the blood.

Kaposi's Sarcoma: A rare cancer—a tumour of the walls of blood vessels. It also affects the living of interval orgasm.

Klinefelter's Syndrome: A person with UV autosomes and XXY sex chromosomes, making a total complement of 47. Individual appears to be male but he has large breasts, small genitalia atrophied testes and is sterile. Genetic female but pragmatic male.

Lymphadenopathy: Swollen, firm and possibly tender lymph nodes commonly found in the grain, armpits and neck. The cause may range from an acute infection (like flu) to lymphoma (cancer of lymph nodes) a HIV infection.

Lymph Glands: These are small nodes, which usually contain large numbers of white bodied cells. Agents of infection may be gathered around these areas so they become battlegrounds. Infections can therefore cause swelling of these glands.

Lymphocytes: A class of white blood cells responsible for regulation of the immune system. Divided into B-cells (which produce antibodies) and T-cells.

Lentivirus: A sub family of retrovirus. Also called slow viruses because they how a long incubation period. It seems that HIV is such a virus, if so, it is the only lentivirus so far known to infect humans.

Labia Majora: Two large lip-like fields extending from mons veneris to encircle the vagina.

Labia Minora: Two smaller folds lying within the labea majors.

Labour: The act of giving birth to a child partivition.

Leucorrhoea: A sticky, whitish vaginal discharge.

Leukaemia: A malignant proliferation of the leucopoietic

tissues usually producing an abnormal increase in leucocytes in the blood with immature cells among them.

Leukoplakia: White thickened patch occurring on mucous membranes. Occurs on lips, inside mouth of a genitalia. Sometimes due to syphilis.

Monogamous: Sexual relationship with only one person partner.

Macromatia: Abnormally large breasts.

Mammography: X-ray examination of the breast after injection of an opaque agent.

Mastectomy: Surgical removal of the breast.

Menopause: The cessation of menstruation occurring normally between the ages of 45 and 50.

Menorrhagia: An excessive regular menstrual flow.

Menstruation: The flow of blood and other dead cells from the uterus once a month in the female. It commences about the age of 13 and ceases about 45.

Mastalgia: Pain in breasts.

Neurological Disorders: Some people who have been infected with HIV symptoms develop symptoms indicating deterioration of mental faculties, e.g., denentis, memory loss, ematic emotional state, neurological damage can also cause deterioration in physical coordinator.

Neurosyphilis: Infection of brain and spinal cord by Treporeme pallidum.

Neuropharmacology: The branch of pharmacology dealing with drugs that affect the nervous system.

Neuropsychiatry: The combination of neurology and psychiatry.

Opportunistic Infections: Organisms which cause infection in individuals with an impaired immune system.

Obstretics: The science dealing with the care of the pregnant women during the stenatal parturient and puerperal stages, midwifery.

Occulogenital: Pertaining to the eye and genital region, as the virus Tric. It is found with male and female genital canals and in the conjunctional sacs of the newborn.

Pandemic: An epidemic over a large or wide geographic area, usually worldwide.

Pap Smear: A simple test which is recommended for women on a regular basis, usually once a year. This test is also known as "Smear test" and "Papanicolou Smear" and detects pre-cancerous changes in the cells of the cervix.

Pathogen: A living micro-organism or virus capable of producing a disease.

PGL: Persistently enlarged lymph glands.

Panhysterectomy: An old term for the removal of the uterus and adnexis: more accurately described as a total hysterectomy.

Pneumonia: A type of inflammation of the lungs with production of alveolar exudate. Common behaviour or characteristic placing them at risks for HIV infection that is higher than general public.

RN: Ribonucleic acid, genetic material inside a cell.

Rh: Rhesus factor.

Rape: Forcible or fraudulent sexual intercourse especially imposed on women.

Safer Use: Those IV needle/syringe drug administration techniques which reduce the risk of transmitting HIV.

Sero Conversion: When an individual who is HIV antibody negative becomes HIV antibody position after exposure to the virus, i.e., blood serum has converted from negative to positive.

Sero Positivity: Synonymous with antibody positivity.

Sero Negativity: The absence of antibodies directed against HIV and indications of no infection, synonymous with antibody negativity.

Serum: The cell free fluid of the blood stress such that appearing in a test tube after blood clot.

STEI: Sexually transmitted euteric infections.

SAIDS: Similar immunodeficiency syndrome.

STD: Sexually transmissible disease.

Prenatal: Existing or occurring before birth.

Prevalence: A measure of how common or widespread a disease is in the community or population group.

PTSWS: Professionally trained social workers.

Pubic Lice: Pubic lice or parasites which often spread by sexual contacts. One must be extremely careful to avoid handling and touching the clothing and bedding of an infected person.

Paralysis: Complete or incomplete loss of nervous function to a part of the body.

Prolapse of Uterus: The uterus descends into the vagina and may be visible at the vaginal orifice.

Puberty: The age at which the reproductive organs become functionally active.

Quarantine: Any limitation of movement a isolation on an individual to prevent infection or the spread of contagious disease.

Retrovirus: One a class of viruses characterised by their ability to convert RNA and DNA during replication in the host cell. HIV belongs to this group of virus.

Risk Group: A group of individuals sharing.

Syndrome: A set of symptoms and signs resulting from a single cause, or so commonly occurring together that a definite pattern is apparent.

Syphilis: Syphilis is an STD caused by bacterium called Trephoneus Pallidum.

Scrotum: The pouch in the cude which contains the testicles.

Sperm: Abbreviation for spermatozoa. Spermatozoa is a natural reproductive cell.

Spermicide: An agent that kills spermatozoa.

Spermatogenesis: The formation and development of sperms.

Spermatorrhoea: Involuntary discharge of semen without orgasm.

T-Helper Cells: Also called T-4 cells. This is one type of white blood cells or lymphocyte that help in defending against the disease by initiating antibody production.

T-cell Ratio: The proportion of T-Helper to T-supressor cells detectable. In a healthy person, this proportion is approximately 2:1. In AIDS it drops below 0.5:1 (i.e., invert).

Thalassemia: A hereditary disease, widespread in the Mediterranean countries, Asia, Africa, in which there is abnormality in the protein part of haemoglobin molecule.

Thymus: The gland responsible for the development of lymphocytes (hence T-cells).

Toxoplasmois: An infection caused by a protozoan parasite. Transmission may occur from women to child across the placenta by ingestion of raw or uncooled meat, or by exposure to animal faeces, most notably by cats. For people with AIDS it is an opportunistic disease which can cause severe illness including brain abscones.

Transmission: The spread of infectious pathogens from one person to another. The most common methods of HIV transmission is by allowing infected blood, semen and vaginal fluid with the body during sex and by allowing infected blood with the body by sharing IVDU equipment.

Virus: An extremely small organism visible only through electron microscope. Viruses cause a wide variety of disease in humans. They do not respond to treatment with antibodies.

Trichomoniasis: Another STD that often develops without any symptoms. If symptoms occur, they usually appear within 4-20 days of exposure. In some cases symptoms may occur years after infection.

Tonography: Continuous measurement of blood or intraocular pressure.

Vaccine: A substance which contains antigens of an organism. In vaccinated person it stimulates active immunity and future protection against infection of that organism.

Vulvovaginal Candidacies: Vulvovaginal candidacies is a common cause for vaginal irritation. There are several factors associated with the occurence of VVC such as pregnancy, uncontrolled diabetes Mellitus use of oral contraceptives, use of douches, use of perfumed feminine hygiene sprays, use of tropical anti-microbial agents and the use of poorly ventilated clothing and under garments.

Ureterovaginal: Pertaining to the urater and bladder.

Urinogenital (*Urogenital*): Pertaining to the urinary and genital orgasms.

Western Blot: A test to diagnose HIV infection through detection of antibodies against the virus.

Window Period: The period of time during which a person may be infected with HIV, but before antibodies have been forced. This period is usually two to three weeks and is rarely longer than three months. The virus is in the blood and may be detected by antigen test but an antibody test will be negative.

Bibliography

Balaskas, J. and Y. Gordon, 1992. The *Encyclopedia of Pregnancy and Birth.*

Bromwich, P. and T. Parsons, 1990. *Contraception—the Facts,* 2nd ed.

Carroll, S., 1995. *The Which Gudie to Mens Health.*

Clubb, E, and J. Knight, 1992. *Fertility—A Comprehensive Guide to Natural Family Planning.*

Coopre, J., 1993. *The Menopause—Coping with the Change.*

Delvin, D., 1991. *The Complete Guide to Sex and Loving.*

Einon, D., 1988. *Parenthood: The Whole Story.*

Fenwick, E. and T. Smith, 1993. *Adolescence.*

______________, 1994. *How Sex Works.*

Gilada, I.S. 1994. *Aids Indian Scenario Grim. AIDS ASIA.*

Greyanus, D.E. (ed.), 1991. *Caring for Your Adolescent.*

Guillebaud, J., 1993. *Contraception—Your Question Answered,* 2nd ed.

Hass, K, and A. Hass, 1993. *Understanding Sexuality,* 3rd ed.

Harkness, C., 1992. *The Infertility Book—A Comprehensive Medical and Emotional Guide,* 2nd ed.

Hatcher, R.A. (1994). et al, *Contraceptive Technology,* 16th ed.

Johnson, M.A. and B.J. Everitt, 1995. *Essential Reproduction,* 4th ed.

Jolly, H., 1986. *Jolly Book of Child Care.*

Khan, M.E., Barge, S. and Patel, B. 1991. *Asia—The Smouldering Volcano Aids and Society.*

Kitzinger, S., 1989. *The New Pregnancy and Childbirth.*

Lansdown, R. and M. Walker, 1991. *Your Child's Development from Birth to Adolescence.*

Llewellyn-Jones, D., 1993. *Everywoman.*

______________ , and S. Abraham, 1992. *Everygirl*, 2nd ed.

Loudon, N., 1991. *Handbook of Family Planning*, 2nd ed.

Madaras, L., 1989. *What's Happening to My Body—a Growing-up Guide for Parents and Daughters.*

______________ *What's Happening to My Body—A Growing-up Guide for Parents and Sons* 1989.

Masters, W.H. 1994. et al, *Heterosexuality.*

McCoy, K. and C. Wibbelsman, 1992. *The New Teenage Body Book.*

Michael, R.T. et al, 1994. *Sex in America—A Definitive Survey.*

Mosse, J. and J. Heaton, 1990. *The Fertility and Contraception Book.*

Phillips, A. and J. Rakuse (eds), 1989. *The New Our Bodies Ourselves.*

Reinisch, J.M. with R. Beasley, 1991. *The Kinsey Institute New Report on Sex.*

Rix, J., 1995. *Is There Sex After Childbirth?*

Stoppard, M., 1994. *Menopause.*

______________ , *Complete Baby and Child Care* 1995.

Tucker, G. (ed.), 1995. *The National Childbirth Trust Book of Pregnancy, Birth and Parenthood.*

Wellings, K. 1994. et.al, *Sexual Behaviour in Britain—National Survey of Sexual Attitudes and Lifestyles.*

Winston, R., 1994. *Infertility—A Sympathetic Approach.*

Weeramunda, J. 1990. "Prostitution and Aids in Sri Lanka". *Aids and Society.*

Index

Abortion pill, 203
Acquaintance rape, 100
Aggressiveness, 125
AIDS Counselling Centres and Counselling Services (ACCESS), 215
Alexander technique, 66
Amenorrhoea, 68
Amphetamines, 235
Anaerobic exercise, 143
Anaesthesia, 199
Androgens, 2
Angina, 177
Anorexia nervosa, 69
Antibiotics, 55
Antibodies, 230
Antidiarrhoeals, 221
Antifungal drug, 48
Anti-inflammatory drugs, 33
Anti-nausea drug, 203
Antipathy, 94
Antiretro-viral drugs, 228
Apathy, 103
Aphrodisiacs, 17
Aromatherapy, 66
Aspirin, 66
Assertiveness, 129
Asymptomatic period, 231
Attackers, 135
Attentiveness, 103

Bacterial vaginosis, 47
Balanitis, 40
Behaviour therapy, 106
Benign prostate hypertrophy, 43
Billings, 194
Biological clocks, 152
Biopsy, 72
Bisexuality, 16
Blue-collar workers, 206
Bread-winner, 152
Brisk walk, 146
Bungee jumping, 101

Candida albicans, 48
Candidiasis, 53
Cannabis, 62
Cardiovascular fitness, 143
Cardiovascular system, 60
Careful seducers, 135
Catastrophic consequences, 135
Cervical canal, 158
Cervix, 55
Chancroid, 230
Chemotherapic treatment, 205
Chemotherapy, 78
Child sexual abuse, 132
Chlamydia, 64
Chlormadinone acetate, 161
Cleanliness, 39
Coil-spring diaphragm, 170
Coitus interrupts, 158
Colposcope, 79

Combination therapy, 54
Community Action Network (CAN), 208
Community Front for Prevention of AIDS (CFPA), 216
Cone biopsy, 79
Contraceptive methods, 157
  rhythm method, 157
  withdrawal method, 158
  douching, 158
  diaphragm, 158
  cervicalcap, 158
  condom, 158
  spermicides, 159
  Intrauterine Contraceptive Devices (IUDs), 159
  oral contraception, 160
  sequential method, 161
  combined method, 161
  continuous method, 161
  barrier methods, 165
  hormonal methods, 165
  natural methods, 165
  sterilisation, 165
Contraceptive pills, 161
Copper-T 380, 186
Cystitis, 47
Cytomegalovirus, 103

Defence system, 230
Depo-Provera, 181
Diabetes mellitus, 33
Diphtheria, 222
Displacement behaviour, 13
Diuretic drugs, 66
Dizziness, 41
Dual monitoring system, 208
Dumas, 158
Dysmenorrhoea, 66
Dyspareunia, 58

Ectopic pregnancy, 180
Embarrassment, 89
Emergency contraception, 201
Emotional instability, 103
Empty nest syndrome, 154
Endometriosis, 25
Endorphins, 39
Enteritis, 103
Epileptics, 33
Erotophobia, 115
Esophagitis, 103
Exhibitionism, 129

Fallopian tubes, 198
Family dynamics, 83
Female sterilisation, 163
Femidom, 164
Feminine hygiene, 49
Fertility awareness methods, 195
Fertility, window of, 190
Fetishism, 17
Fibroids, 77
Flat-spring diaphragm, 170
Focal migraine, 177
Follicle-Stimulating Hormone (FSH), 175
Food and Drug Administration (FDA), 165

Genital herpes, 55
Genital warts, 56
Genito-urinary medicine, 46
Gonorrhoea, 57
Gujarat AIDS Prevention (GAP), 208

Halt ovulation, 181
Heterosocial skills, 108
Hidden sugar, 146
Hormonal implants, 184
Hormonal therapy, 78
Human Immunodeficiency Virus (HIV), 50
Human Papilloma Virus (HPV), 57
Hydrocele, 44
Hypothalamus, 7

Hysterectomy, 34

Immune system, 230
Indian Health Organisation (IHO), 207
Infertile period, 195
Influenza, 230
Initial acute infection, 52
Insomnia, 41
Intrauterine device, 67
Intrauterine system, 176

Kaposi's sarcoma, 103

Lactobacillus acidophilus, 49
Laparoscope, 200
Laparoscopy, 75, 199
Laparotomy, 76
Latency period, 114
Lesbian parents, 97
Lesbian, 16
Levonorgestrel, 187
Life expectancy, 219
Limbic system, 7
Liposuction, 149
Loop excision, 79
Luteinising Hormone (LH), 175
Lymph nodes, 103
Lymphadenopathy, 52
Lymphomas, 103

Macrophages, 52
Male sterilisation, 163
Mammography, 71
Mammoplasty, 73
Mastectomy, 35
Meningoencephalitis, 103
Menopause, 3
Menorrhagia, 67
Menstrual cycle, 3
Metabolic rate, 144
Mid-life crisis, 152
'Minipill', 179
Monogamous sexual relationship, 99
Mucopurulent cervicitis, 54
Multiple sclerosis, 34

National Institutes of Health (NIH), 221
Natural family planning, 189
  basal body temperature method, 190
  rhythm method, 190
  cervical mucus method, 190
  symptothermal method, 190
  multiple index method, 195
Nausea, 161
Negative effect, 83
Neisseria gonorrhoea, 57
Neoplasms, 103
Nocturnal emission, 205
Non-gonococcal urethritis, 54
Non-penetrative sex, 232

Obesity, 81
Oestrogen, 65
Oral cavity, 103
Oral Rehydration Therapy (ORT), 222
Oral sex, 9
Orange peel skin, 71
Orchiclectomy, 42
Orchitis, 44
Ostracisation, 106
Ovarian cancer, 75
Ovulation, 3

Paedophilia, 130
Parenting, 154
Pelvic Inflammatory Disease (PID), 59, 177
Penicillin, 60
Personal hygiene, 39
Pertussis, 222
Pigeon-holes, 15
Pink triangle, 212

Pituitary gland, 197
Pleasantness, 109
Pneumocystic carinii pneumonia, 53, 103
Podophyllin, 57
Polycystic Ovarian Syndrome (PCOS), 75
Population explosion, 47
Pornographic pictures, 131
Pornography, 137
Priapism, 27
Progesterone, 65
Progestogen-Only Pill (POP), 179
Prolactin, 197
Prosta-glandins, 66
Prostatectomy, 35
Prostate-specific antigen, 44
Protected sex, 232
Psychomotor disorders, 103
Puerpeperium, 159

Quandary, 223

Radiotherapy, 78
Recreational drugs, 100
Recurrent nightmares, 127
Red Cross, 214
Resectoscope, 44
Retinitis, 103

Sado-masochism, 17
Safer sex, 51
Sebaceous glands, 40
Seropositive, 234
Sexologists, 18
Sexual fantasy, 17
Sexual promiscuity, 104
Sexually Transmitted Disease (STD), 50, 166
Shooting blanks, 201
Single-parent family, 95
Skirmishing, 158
South India AIDS Action Programme (SIAAP), 209
Spermatozoa, 158
Spermicidal cream, 158
Spermicides, 167
Spontaneous abortion, 163
Spritser, 148
Statutory rape, 124
Stepfamilies, 93
Stereotypical roles, 86
Stigmatisation, 137
Strenuous efforts, 139
Syphilis, 60

Tenaganita, 212
Testosterone, 2
Tetanus, 222
Therapeutic abortion, 164
Thrombosis, 177
Toxic shock syndrome, 171
Transurethral resectoscopy, 44
Transvestism, 17
Treponema pallidum, 60
Trichomoniasis, 49
Tubal surgery, 198
Tuberculosis, 103, 222

Uganda, 229

Vaccinations, 220
Vanadium clip, 163
Vas deferens, 163
Vasectomy, 163
Vein thrombosis, 162
Voyeurism, 128

Warring factions, 94
Window period, 231
World Health Organisation (WHO), 51
X-rays, 71

Yoweri Museveni, 229

Zidovudine, 223